SWIMMING
with **CROCODILES**

SWIMMING
with CROCODILES

A True Story of Adventure and Survival

WILL CHAFFEY

ARCADE PUBLISHING • NEW YORK

FIRST NORTH AMERICAN EDITION 2009

The author has changed some names for reasons of privacy.

Cataloging-in-Publication Data

Chaffey, Will.
  Swimming with crocodiles : a true story of adventure and survival /
Will Chaffey. —1st North American ed.
      p. cm.
  First published: Sydney : Pan Macmillan, 2008.
  Includes bibliographical references.
  ISBN 978-1-55970-902-6 (alk. paper)
  1. Prince Regent River (W.A.)—Description and travel. 2. Prince Regent River Region (W.A.)—Description and Travel. 3. Chaffey, Will—Travel—Australia—Prince Regent River Region (W.A.) 4. Adventure and adventurers—Australia—Prince Regent River Region (W.A.) 5. Wilderness survival—Australia—Prince Regent River Region (W.A.) 6. Crocodiles—Australia—Prince Regent River Region (W.A.) 7. Chaffey, Will—Travel—Australia—Western Australia. 8. Americans—Travel—Australia—Western Australia. 9. Western Australia—Description and travel. I. Title.

  DU380.P75C47 2008
  919.41'4—dc22
  [B]   2008054516

Published in the United States by Arcade Publishing, Inc., New York
Distributed by Hachette Book Group

Visit our Web site at www.arcadepub.com
Visit the author's Web site at www.swimmingwithcrocodiles.com

10 9 8 7 6 5 4 3 2 1

EB

PRINTED IN THE UNITED STATES OF AMERICA

To every person who picked me up beside the road

CONTENTS

SWIMMING
with **CROCODILES**

CHAPTER 1

THIRST

Let him live under the open sky, and dangerously.

Horace

The four-wheel-drive track to Port Warrender on the northwest coast of Australia was not frequently traveled. The thin wheel ruts cut past narrow canyons and across palm-studded plateaus of orange sandstone. Termite mounds sat solid as concrete in the middle of the track. As we turned up a hill of yellow grass, a faded sign warned of abundant crocodiles and mosquitoes near the coast. The radio in our jeep picked up nothing but static from one end of the dial to the other.

We had crossed a desert continent to arrive here – rattled west from the rain forests hugging the eastern seaboard across the dry flat interior with its roadhouses and isolated towns, through Queensland, the Northern Territory, Western Australia, the Tanami, Gibson, and Great Sandy Deserts, the Durack and Leopold Ranges, and over the rugged basalt, shale, and sandstone plateaus of the Kimberley in a tiny Daihatsu jeep averaging no more than twenty miles per hour.

In the back of the jeep I had a loaf of hard bread, tomatoes, cheese, some spicy sausage, a few cans of sardines, rice, a knapsack with a few spare clothes, a camera, boots, a manual typewriter, and not much else. My traveling partner, Jeff, had brought ten gallons of water and ten gallons of extra fuel in jerry cans. There would be no one to help us here should the jeep break down.

The engine growled in compound low down a final ridge, and the road, such as it was, ended. Jeff and I stepped out into the quiet heat.

North of us, huge inlets of gray mud spread away from the coast. Outcroppings of maroon sandstone rose above the tides, interspersed with green pockets of vegetation. Through all pervaded an intense heat and the vast eternal silence on the edge of outer space.

It was early in the month of May and the beginning of the dry season in the far north. The dry begins with the end of the rains in April or May, and already Crystal Creek was no more than a trickle. In a few more weeks water would evaporate from all but the deepest pools between the rocks. By November the wild dogs and cockatoos would linger by their dwindling waterholes, waiting for rain.

The creek trickled through a fissure in the fractured sandstone a hundred yards away. Jeff stood beside the jeep cutting slices of sausage and cheese onto bread for breakfast.

I walked to the edge of the creek, studying the intersection of blue sky and orange coast under the sun. These rocks may have been the first to emerge from an ocean that covered the entire planet 2,000 million years ago. A white finger of beach jutted into the azure waters of the Timor Sea in the distance.

Having crossed the continent, I wanted to touch the sea.

Pockets of green behind the beach meant mangrove swamps, home of the estuarine or saltwater crocodile, *Crocodylus porosus*, a creature virtually unchanged since the days of *Tyrannosaurus rex* and its ilk. In retrospect, I brought with me a great deal of inexperience. The sun shot like a kite into the sky.

2

"Hate to come all this way and not reach the beach."

"Not me," Jeff said, chomping on the sandwich under his beard. "Watch out for crocs."

My first enduring image of the crocodile was a picture in black and white of a foot and the lower half of a leg rising out of a cardboard box: the remains of a Peace Corps worker attacked near Lake Turkana, Africa, in 1962. He had been twenty-six years old and all that remained of him was a foot and a few pieces of flesh. In the Top End, often all that remains are a few buttons, some fingernails, or a rifle propped against a tree near an innocent-looking billabong, or water hole.

Judging the land from this height, the journey to the beach looked to be no more than two hours walk.

"I'll stay here," Jeff said, declining my invitation to walk to the coast, "but you go ahead."

Standing beside the jeep, I held my compass at arm's length and sighted down the needle to the spit of beach in the distance: a bearing of 300 degrees.

"See you in a couple hours," I said and set off, trying to follow the compass heading in a straight line over the broken terrain.

Jeff called after me, "Drink plenty of water before you go." At the thin fissure of Crystal Creek I filled my stomach and my canteen with water.

The jeep, a white speck in an immensity of orange stone, disappeared behind me. My eyes moved often from the compass needle to the fractured landscape of boulders and spinifex grass.

Captain Phillip Parker King was the first to systematically chart parts of this thirsty coast back in 1818. He had written of the landscape: "The surface of the ground was covered by spinifex, which rendered our walking both difficult and painful; this plant diffuses a strong aromatic odour." The sharp spines poked into my ankles above my boots, but King was right, the fragrance was delightful.

The needle of the compass did not deviate from the symbol N on the face of the dial: magnetic north. I walked carefully, not wanting to tread on a snake, or twist an ankle. Jeff had reminded me how far we were from civilization before I set out: 1,300 miles from Perth, and more than 1,800 miles from Brisbane, Sydney, or Melbourne.

As the sun neared its zenith I crossed a ridge and again viewed the coast. My shirt was soaked with sweat. The beach beckoned in the distance.

When my boots stopped, an immense silence rushed in like the tide. I had never before experienced such utter quiet, never felt so small. I walked across the afternoon, farther from home than I had ever been before, a stranger to planet Earth.

The Kimberley region of northwest Australia is an impossibly ancient landscape. One of the world's longest wilderness coasts, it contains some of the oldest rocks in the world and the earliest celled life forms. The rocks of the Pilbara and southern Kimberley region, at close to 3.6 billion years old, are among the most ancient on Earth. Farther south on the coast at Shark Bay, rare communities of single-celled organisms called stromatolites, one of the first forms of life to arise some 3,500 to 3,700 million years ago, still lived in warm shallow waters as they had since long before the explosion of life forms in the Cambrian.

The tide was out. Near the coast I encountered an inlet of gray silt fringed by knobby-rooted mangroves. Should I skirt the inlet, or press on in a straight line? I took a sip from my canteen. Almost empty. Should I turn back?

I hung my boots over my shoulder and sank up to my knees in the sucking mud, studying the shade under the mangroves. How fast do big reptiles move, exactly?

Small fish with bulging eyes walked upon the slick mud with their fins: the first signs of animal life on this distant, quiet planet. The fish had large eyes and square heads. They moved atop the mud, occasionally hopping onto rocks and turning their heads to stare at me. What were fish doing on land up here?

From this place, the oldest terrestrial wilderness on Earth, the bog between land and water, it was not hard to imagine the beginning and endpoints of human history. Man's ancestor, an amphibian, a gilled salamander with the ability to breathe air and water, crawled out of a swamp perhaps like this one on the Euramerican continent at the end of the Devonian period, the age of fishes, some 370 million years ago, giving rise to amphibians, reptiles, and mammals.

One of the fish studied me. Cousin? Had I crossed these swamps before? Had, somewhere, a little heart been beating every few seconds for all this eternity? Fossil evidence indicates man's amphibian ancestor evolved from one of three groups of lobe-finned fishes: the lungfish or dipnoans, which still live in rivers on the eastern side of the Australian continent and in Africa; the coelacanths or actinistians, long thought extinct before being discovered still swimming in the deep waters off Madagascar in 1938; or the rhipidistians, now extinct.

Judging from the intelligent movement of the creatures from rock to rock, these cavorting fish were kin, separated from me by a mere 370 million years. Would their progeny one day evolve into an intelligent being, able to walk some remote coast and speculate on the passage of time? Perhaps in another 370 million years. How strange it was, sentience.

Reaching the far edge of the mud flat, I stopped and took a swig from my canteen. So thirsty. Must not drink too much. It was all I could do to stop swallowing and leave a little water in the bottom for later.

"The true peace of God," Joseph Conrad wrote, "begins at any spot a thousand miles from the nearest land." Perhaps in this modern world the same could be said about our proximity to man-made things. I had never been this far from a gas station, a telephone, or a hospital.

Water began spilling back against the coast, trickling in a narrow gray stream into the inlet. The tide had turned. I clambered over the mangrove roots to the edge of the sea.

What had appeared from the jeep as white sand was in fact bleached coral. My boots scattered shells as I walked out on a narrow peninsula. White, green, orange, blue. Beach, mangroves, sandstone, ocean. The smell of mud and salt, the sun on my skin, the line of sight before me, jolting up and down with each step. Thirst impinged on my hallucination of reality. I was utterly, utterly alone.

There were no other sounds, no breeze in the air. I had reached this distal point after walking five hours over ridges, boulders, and mangrove thickets. I celebrated with a final gulp from my canteen.

Turquoise water lapped quietly against the shore. Islands of red stone loomed in the distance. Somewhere beyond the horizon lay the islands of the Indonesian archipelago: Java, Sumatra, Bali, Timor.

What was real? I shook the canteen. Empty.

I waded up to my knees in the warm Timor Sea, keeping an eye out for crocodiles.

Captain King, in his journeys to the northwest coast, wrote of the reptiles:

> The appearance of these animals in the water is very deceptious; they lie quite motionless, and resemble a branch of a tree floating with the tide; the snout, the eye, and some of the ridges of the back and tail, being the only parts that are seen . . . The animal that we fired at was noticed for some time, but considered to be only a dead branch, although we were looking out for crocodiles, and approached within six yards of it before we found out our mistake; the length of this animal was from twelve to fifteen feet; I do not think that we have ever seen one more than twenty feet.

Not more than twenty feet? Nothing to worry about then.

I took a picture of myself with the self-timer on my little camera: a thin figure sitting uneasily on a rock near the water's edge, my face shaded by the brim of my hat.

So thirsty. I tried drinking a handful of the sea, and spat it out. Too salty. Time to head back.

Behind the beach, a ridge rose above the jagged coast. I could see nothing of the landscape behind it, nor the white jeep that lay somewhere a good distance beyond. No water for the journey.

I looked at my compass, orienting myself 180 degrees from the bearing I had followed from the jeep. Better get a move on. I clambered over mangrove roots, over hard curved elbows and stunted sharp ends. With a start I found myself staring at a pool of gray water.

The tide had come in.

Wait a minute. I had crossed mangrove thickets to get here, mangroves that were now flooded with the rising tide. What was I thinking when I did that? I couldn't walk in a straight line back to the jeep – I would be wading up to my neck in briny water.

Jeff and I had studied the tracks in the mud days before: a wide swathe with star shaped claw prints at intervals on either side, disappearing into the water. Crocodile tracks. I must find some other way around. To wade across these partially submerged inlets now would be madness. This was dinosaur country.

I climbed over the roots and leapt from rock to rock. The tide had filled in the low area behind the beach, and always when it seemed I was about to break through the swamp and begin my ascent away from the coast, the way was blocked by a stretch of gray water.

Should I take a chance and swim for it? The other side was so close, only fifty feet.

I walked the length of the beach, growing desperate. How had I been so stupid?

If there was a way over, it had to be through here . . . My God, this was supposed to be just a little hike and already I was in serious trouble.

At the end of the beach I climbed through the mangroves to find a broken line of boulders stretching across the water, their tops jutting just above the rushing tide. There was no time, I had to go now. I leapt across the boulders and quit the coast with profound relief.

Two hours later, climbing steadily, I stopped. No water. Thank God for my hat. Hold on, had the sun been over my left shoulder or my right before? Where was I?

Silence receded to the jumbled orange boulders and escarpments from one side of the horizon to the other. It all seemed wildly desolate. Was I headed the right way? I was returning on my initial bearing, wasn't I? The beach now lay below the ridge.

Damn it. Why hadn't I turned around earlier and taken a back bearing?

Something was wrong. There was no bay there before. The orange peninsula seemed more to the east than I remembered it on the few times I had looked back. It wasn't supposed to be there.

The landscape had changed. The Kimberley tides, with a variation of forty feet I later discovered, are the second-highest in the world, and the highest of any tropical coast. What had been land was now water. My compass was telling me to move in a direction utterly contrary to my sense. I should head that way, I thought. Or maybe that way? The landscape, a pile of giant boulders, said nothing. I felt the first surge of panic. The ocean had been over there, I told myself, now look where it is!

My only interest now was finding a white speck among this orange stone: the jeep.

Jesus, it was hot. I had walked for seven hours just twelve degrees of latitude from the Equator. Without water, I could die in a day. Jeff had reminded me of that when I set out.

"*Would* die in two days," he said. "Definitely."

Trust your compass, I thought, not reassured. The needle pointed to magnetic north no matter what direction I turned, as it should. The jeep should be somewhere in that direction, almost sixty degrees off my compass heading. Was my compass wrong? Don't panic.

I had been in Australia for four months. The stories of people becoming lost, disoriented, and dying in the bush were all too common. If there was ever a place to disappear in, it was here.

The explorer Leichhardt and his party had perished without a trace in a trackless interior, swallowed up by a monotony of space and time. In 1967, Prime Minister Harold Holt had disappeared while swimming off the Victorian coast. The prime minister! I couldn't imagine the president of the United States ever just disappearing, never to be seen again. But that was Australia.

More recently, two boys from Halls Creek had gone missing with their truck, three hundred miles to the south. They were sixteen and seventeen years old, the eldest only a year younger than me. I had heard the story on the radio upon first arriving in the country. Now, I did not want to be among the disappeared. There was so much space to get lost in, so many cracks in the rocks.

I stumbled over the boulders, fighting the urge to change direction, keeping a lid on panic. I had read that pilots sometimes rejected the artificial horizon that told them they were flying upside down. Believing they were right side up, they crashed when they tried to land.

My father had told me once to trust the compass.

"A compass will almost always be more accurate than your own sense of direction." He had added as an afterthought, "Unless there are large deposits of iron about. Then your compass might point to them."

Deposits of metal or ore affect the bearing of compasses. Were there such deposits here? The sandstone was laid out in great terraces, like reefs marooned by a receding sea. It was an unsettling thought.

A rock wallaby bounded away silently and disappeared among the boulders. This was home to someone.

I followed the compass, looking from its face to the rock-strewn country before me, gaining altitude as I moved away from the coast.

A rock pigeon sputtered out of the spinifex, pffft! its white quills suffused with bronze disappearing in waves of heat.

This could not be right. I had been walking for hours, over one ridge and down another. No sign of the jeep. Soon I would be among the eucalypt savannah, the endless tall grass, the scattered trees. How would I find the jeep then? I would be totally lost.

I looked toward the coast at the mangrove swamps now submerged by the tide, forlorn and lonely under the sky. Please, God . . . God, I am begging you, please . . .

The rocks were silent.

Coming up on three and a half hours without water.

I could walk for weeks, months even, without finding a road – except that I would not last that long. I could wait until nightfall, hiding from the sun by day, perhaps finding my way back to the track at night.

Over boulders the size of houses I jumped and squeezed between cracks, as alone as I had ever been.

Late in the afternoon I collapsed in the only shade I could find, cast by an overhanging rock. The sun lingered outside like a wild dog.

As my eyes adjusted to the light I saw a picture rendered in white ochre on the rock above my head. A tree frog. It looked toward the coast with wide, white eyes. A cave painting. I was not alone in this remoteness. There was magic here, a presence.

I looked at the coast. These waters Aboriginal man and woman had crossed in simple rafts with their fire and stone tools, perhaps as many as sixty thousand years ago. Their journey may have required the longest ocean voyage undertaken by *Homo sapiens* up to that time. Except for fluctuations of sea level that had turned inland hills into offshore islands, the terrain before me had changed little from that day.

I wondered at the artist's hands that had conjured this likeness of a frog in white ochre upon the stone, of his thoughts among these endless horizons. Someone else had spent the better part of an afternoon here, somewhere in eternity on this quiet coast, in the shade of a rock.

With a start I realized that had it not been for the sudden intercession of my own race, this continent would still be the sole domain of the Aboriginal people. What I thought of as civilization might have occurred at any time in the past 60,000 years. It just so happened, it was happening now.

With no Greenwich meridian, no calendars, no clocks, no roads, no degrees-minutes-seconds of longitude and latitude, with only the observed motion of the sun, moon, planets, and stars for reckoning, where was *here*? Silence stretched for eternity in all directions. My God, I had woken up in the middle of outer space. Where was anywhere?

Before the histories, myths, biases, orthodoxies, traditions, faiths, and paradigms had been created by an intelligent animal trying to make sense of its world, someone had gathered white stones and ground them together, forging this symbol on stone. What did it mean? I sat quietly in the shade. Ripples transfixed in the sandstone told of past oceans.

My whole life I had grown up thinking I had been born in the twentieth century. With a shock I realized there was no such thing as the twentieth century. It was all a comfortable fabrication, a complete artifice. There was no single point to hang duration on. The wind blew, the sun arced across the sky. Stars burned for a time and went out.

Long before Buddha, Confucius, Zoroaster, Moses, Christ, and Mohammed, before the great books, the apostles, disciples, and the minor prophets, before the pyramids, the first cities, the rise of nation states, or man's attempts to fix his position temporally with the Julian calendar, the Gregorian calendar, railway, and atomic time, this frog reposed on stone. And long after. This was the Dreamtime, All Time: past, present, future.

It was all too real.

Sometime before me a sentient spirit moved through here, a human being with profound powers of perception and under–standing, who wondered at the lightning and the dry silence, who lived and died.

I moved out of the cave and kept walking against the sun. I might die out here, but I would not be the first being to do so or the last. This was not a lonely place to die; it was just a place.

At the top of a ridge, I stopped. My shirt was crusted with dried sweat. I had no spit. My face was on fire. No sign of the jeep. I needed to make some decisions fast, or I wouldn't make it out of here. I was obviously lost.

Then I heard it – the trickle of water through stone. No sound had ever given me such joy. Exultant, I climbed down into Crystal Creek, not bothering to take off my boots. I gulped mouthfuls of water. Submerged, I listened to the current rush past my ears, drinking it in. Hallelujah! Cool, cool, holy water. The sun had fallen to the west. I was in a shallow pool, breathing in deep.

After all this time, I knew where I was: here! In a rocky creek near a coast, on a continent called by its present inhabitants Australia. And I was alive!

The jeep would be just behind that ridge. A true spaceship. A symbol of the twentieth century.

Coming over the line of boulders, I caught sight of a tiny white object amid the stone. The jeep! Jeff sat in the shade next to the back tire looking at the map as I walked up.

"There you are," he said. "Thought I might have to come looking for you soon. I was wondering where to start."

"I was wondering myself."

I looked back at the coast, quiet under a lowering sun. I had lived one day in eternity. One day stumbling over the Precambrian geology. One day on the Devonian coast. One day in the age of dinosaurs. One day before God and the twentieth century.

It was no time at all.

Had I known then in what dire straits I would later find myself, I would have taken the first plane home.

CHAPTER 2

DEPARTURES AND ARRIVALS

It's a long way from a New England prep school to the outback. But in a sense, that's where it all started.

Looking out the train window on the way to New York out of Boston, I had no idea what I would be doing in the months to come. I had graduated from Milton Academy that previous spring and in the fall had helped move several friends into their dorms at colleges like Columbia, Brown, and Harvard. I watched them go off to classes with regret and some envy. Though the graduate of a prestigious New England preparatory school, I had not been accepted into college. Instead, I was taking what the college counselors grimly called time off. At times, I thought I was a failure.

The train pulled out of South Station and past the Gillette factory, World Shaving Headquarters. I had a duffel bag and a small backpack on the seat beside me, a six-month visa, a ticket to Australia, and a thousand dollars in traveler's checks. I wondered if I would have the energy to sustain myself for what I assumed would be six months away from home. It had been a tough year.

I thought about what my parents and I hadn't said to each other before I left Boston. They were worried about me, and now

14

I was going halfway around the world with no real plan. I had been surprised not to have been accepted anywhere, and reapplied to colleges before leaving Boston. True, my grades had not been great in my senior year, but I had a lot of extracurriculars; I was in the student government and had been literary editor of the school magazine. What was wrong with me – why had I not been accepted at college?

It has been reliably said that few people reach the age of eighteen in New England without wanting to kill themselves. My father once told me in a reflective moment that if he found himself seriously contemplating suicide he would go to live on an island in the South Pacific to fish and hunt wild pigs and eat coconuts. If, surrounded by nature in a tropical paradise, he still wanted to kill himself, then he would do it – but he doubted he would still feel that way.

It was too bad that my father and I didn't have time for each other. He was busy with his career, and I was groping around trying to figure out what to do with my life following a disastrous final year of high school. With winter coming on, I realized I had to get out of the cold and dark.

There were interim programs for people like me who hadn't been accepted into college. I was interested in one that involved sailing a tall ship down to Australia. The program fell through, but by that point I felt like I'd been with "the program" long enough. I held on to the idea of Australia, working the summer on a farm in my hometown and in the fall as a driver's assistant for United Parcel Service, saving money for a ticket.

It was a few days after Christmas and the bare trees beside the tracks poked out of the ground like gray skeletons. Why was I leaving Boston now? I had a steady job and a steady girlfriend, Christine. I had pulled myself from the depths of suicidal de–pression to mere clinical depression. If I could just work the next eight months and then go back to school . . . I remembered back to Milton Academy. All those things that had seemed so important, I just couldn't hang on to them anymore.

The morning of my departure for Australia I woke up in an apartment on Madison Avenue in New York. I walked the man-made canyons of Manhattan down Broadway, the former Lenape Indian trail to the Hudson Valley, and stood in the middle of Times Square. A man with a map approached me.

"Excuse me, can you tell me where I am?" he asked.

We stood outside a peep show adorned with neon breasts, surrounded by a million watts of blinking lights and the big Sony billboard above the Armed Forces recruiting station. The day before I had thought hard about joining the navy.

"You're in Times Square," I said.

He looked confused.

"Times Square, New York City."

No sign of recognition.

"Times Square, New York City, *Planet Earth*."

He moved closer, proffering the map. "Can you show me?"

In the map of Manhattan, folded between Lexington and Third, was a green bud of marijuana.

"That's an ingenious subterfuge," I said.

"Great Thai stick, thirty bucks an eighth," he whispered.

"No thanks – I'm going to the airport."

"Twenty bucks?"

"Not today."

"Well, you have a good day."

I walked up Broadway. It was time to head for JFK airport.

The plane lifted out of New York and turned west. Most of the other passengers closed their window blinds and watched the in-flight movie. How could they fail to be astounded at the Earth from this height? This was once the New World. Now it just seemed very complicated. I watched as down below thousands of square miles rolled passed, literally, square miles, with a neat farmhouse on each corner. It was all bought, paid for, borrowed against. Where was the room for adventure in that space? It is safe to say I left the United States and arrived in Australia at the lowest point in my life.

After a brief stop in San Francisco followed by an eternity of ocean, the northeastern coast of Australia burst out of the blue Pacific in greens, yellows, whites, and dark blues down below. Reefs of purple and turquoise outlined in blue water lapped against rain-forest mountains and black granite. Paradise.

The plane touched down in Cairns, at the time a town of about forty thousand people in the heart of the tropics. The engines stopped, and two flight attendants walked down the aisle spraying either some type of air freshener (we had all been on the plane for almost fourteen hours and probably didn't smell too good) or pesticide. I had already fallen in love with the women's Australian accents.

We disembarked onto a strip of hot tarmac laid over a mangrove swamp and walked to the terminal. Vegetation rioted right up to the edge of the runway. A man in white shorts, shirt, and knee socks examined my passport and visa.

"Purpose of your visit?"

I didn't know what to say. Most of the people on the flight with me had been Japanese. I wasn't one of the tourists. What *was* the purpose of my visit?

"Just traveling."

"Where will you be staying?"

"Uh . . . around Cairns."

I knew no one on the entire continent.

"How long will you be in Australia?"

I didn't know. I had a visa for six months.

"A few months, I guess."

Once past customs I faced a crucial question: what now?

I hadn't thought of anything beyond my arrival. Somehow I figured when I got to Australia it would all be made clear. I hadn't even bothered to look at a map of the continent.

I did have a great-great uncle, George Chaffey, who with his brother, William, had pioneered irrigation on the Murray River and established the town of Mildura in Victoria. In fact, there was even a statue in the town dedicated to William Chaffey, my namesake. I figured at the least I could get to Mildura and be accepted joyfully as a long-lost cousin by members of the Chaffey clan. I'd just show them my Massachusetts driver's licence and be given the keys to the town.

In my luggage I had brought with me two aerobies – a type of super-frisbee designed by a Palo Alto rocket scientist – and the farthest-thrown object by man. My conception of Australia was such that I expected to give the aerobies away to the first tribe of Aboriginal people I encountered upon stepping off the plane. The inventors of the boomerang were sure to be impressed with the aerodynamics of the thing.

There was no tribe camped beside the tarmac. The other passengers quickly boarded shuttle buses or taxis for their hotels. The airport had only two international flights a day and was soon deserted. I sat on my duffel bag in the grass in front of the terminal for a time, watching ants.

The taxi driver, clad in shorts and knee-high socks, seemed surprised when I took the back seat. I was struck at once by a different attitude. Australians were much more egalitarian than Americans. The driver dropped me off in town by the bus station, which was closed. I couldn't imagine the Greyhound bus station in Boston ever being closed.

"She'll be right, mate. They've just gone for smoko," the driver said. I paid him and he drove off. I felt suddenly adrift. The jet lag was wearing off and I realized I was as far away from home as I had ever been.

It was market day in Cairns. I wandered around for several hours. In the tropical town, people took their lunch on park benches under blue-blossomed jacaranda trees. Under canvas awnings, custard apple, pawpaw, taro root, star fruit, raw sugar cane, guavas, passion fruit, mangoes, bananas, oranges, grapefruit, and lemons tempted me. I bought a stick of sugarcane for twenty cents and sucked on it as I walked down the street, a free man. Retired fishing boats sat up on stilts in tropical front yards.

It was January, the height of the wet season and the southern hemisphere's summer. Inside the Hides Hotel, men in faded T-shirts nursed "pots" of beer. At three stories, the Hides Hotel was among the tallest buildings in Cairns. I passed an Aboriginal woman in white lace pushing a baby carriage. So this was Australia: the antipodes of all prior experience. It occurred to me that I had no idea where I would sleep tonight.

The bus dropped me off at Edmonton. I walked the railroad tracks out of town past fields of sugar cane. Stacks of cut cane occasionally rode by on little trolleys, sap glistening at the roots. Cairns relied on sugar, bananas, the railway, fishing, and more recently tourism to keep money in people's pockets. Tin, gold, and marble came from the west and places like Croydon and Chillagoe.

A strong back and quick hands could always find me a job. At the very least, I could pick bananas. So what if I wasn't using my mind to do something more refined, to *get ahead*. This was authentic experience, the ore of knowledge. I would learn from the people I met. And there was no law against reading books.

A friend of a friend had given me a number to call, suggesting

I might find work on a dairy farm in a town with the unlikely name of Millaa Millaa. What was up with these names?

The phone number had only six digits. The farmer's two teenage boys were at boarding school in Brisbane, and he said he could use a hand in exchange for room and board.

"Do you have transport?"

I did not, but assured the farmer I'd make my way to the town of Millaa Millaa. I had never actually hitchhiked before. For an hour the occasional car drove by. Once outside town, I was amazed by the stillness. You could hear a single car coming from a long way off. I had spent too much of my life within earshot of highways. My worry and loneliness changed to exhilaration as I walked the miles from town. I was free. Nobody but me knew where I was. I could sleep in a grove of trees over there if I had to.

An old man picked me up beside the road.

"Thanks for stopping," I said and climbed into a dilapidated VW beetle. Clive was in his late sixties. We drove beside fields of sugar cane before taking the winding road up the coastal ranges. I noticed with growing alarm that Clive's hands shook, and his wallet and glasses were connected to his car keys by a string.

"Otherwise I forget them," he said. "I'm recovering from my third heart attack, and I had a mole removed this morning. But don't worry, I'm taking strong medication for the pain."

While Clive recited English poetry with vigor, I wondered if my journey would end at the bottom of the steep cliffs on either side of the road. The land, already strange, grew stranger as we ascended the face of the Gillies Range to the Atherton Tableland. Trees and plants I had never encountered before dotted the landscape. Cycads and smooth-barked eucalyptus trees gave way to dense forests of Queensland ash, maple, walnut, and strangler fig. Before arriving I had been under the impression that the continent was one vast desert. No one mentioned that Australia had rain forest.

Looking out the window, I wondered vaguely where I was

heading. I wondered about my family, and about my friends finishing their freshman year of college back in the northeastern United States. I had hoped to travel with a friend, but everyone I knew was too busy moving forward in their lives.

It's the curse of prep school, the need to be productive, to achieve, to have a curriculum vitae filled with achievements, rewards, and accomplishments. Unaccounted-for time, like blank sections in a resume, like solitude, was not really encouraged. I wondered what I would put down on a college application to account for this year.

"You're not a tourist are you?" Clive asked. He rolled the "r" in such a way that the word sounded like "terrorist."

"No."

"Have you seen what they've done to Port Douglas?" he asked. I shook my head. "It was a beautiful place, sleepy fishing town. Real character. Now there's a real estate agent on every corner."

In between Clive's poetic ejaculations, we had an honest conversation. He was writing a book on his life and experiences in the war. We talked about Nevil Shute's book *On the Beach* and Australia's literary place in a post-fallout world. I asked Clive about his life, and he talked about his experience.

"After the fall of Singapore, it felt like Australia was next. Most of our boys were over in North Africa fighting for the Crown. I don't suppose you've heard of the Rats of Tobruk?"

I shook my head.

"Australia was facing extinction, man! Extinction! We were going to leave the north and try to hold the Japs at the Brisbane line. But General MacArthur changed all that. The battle for Australia would be fought in New Guinea. And it was.

"I used to look out through holes in the clouds and wonder about our boys down below, fighting the Japs," Clive said softly. "Those Australian boys were the best fighters of the war."

He studied the trees beside the road. "I stayed on in New Guinea after it was all over."

Two of his boys still lived in New Guinea, where he had worked as an administrator before Australia gave New Guinea its independence.

"It was too early. They're carving up New Guinea now for copper, gold, and timber. Where are you from?"

"Boston."

"Boston? What brings you here?"

"Having a look around," I said, not wanting to go into the particulars of my exile.

"How old are you?"

"Eighteen."

"I was a waist gunner in a B-24 when I was your age. It was just yesterday."

Clive studied me for a moment. "I was just going to go and feed the geese at Lake Barrine, but since you're new in the country, I'll take you all the way to Millaa. I'm not doing much this afternoon."

As the miles went by, Clive told me, "Australians are a bit funny about Yanks. Your soldiers got more pay than the average digger, and usually more girls." He smiled at the recollection of it. Then he said matter-of-factly, "In the end, the Japs didn't invade Australia – the Americans did."

He dropped me off beside the dairy farm at the end of a dirt road. We both studied the farmhouse for a moment from the car.

"If you need a place to stay, I have a spare room." He wrote his telephone number on a piece of paper. "In this country, you make your luck."

I took my pack out of the back, thanked him, and waved goodbye.

CHAPTER 3

MITCHELL PLATEAU

His is one of those cases which are more numerous than those suppose who have never lived anywhere but in their own homes, and never walked but in one line from their cradle to their graves. We must come down from our heights, and leave our straight paths for the byways and low places of life, if we would learn truth by strong contrasts; and in hovels, in forecastles, and among our own outcasts in foreign lands, see what has been wrought among our fellow creatures by accident, hardship, or vice.

Richard Henry Dana Jr.

A languid flock of red-tailed black cockatoos flew above the scattered trees in the pink light as Jeff turned the jeep south from Crystal Creek, down a track to the Mitchell Falls and the abandoned mining camp. Eucalyptus trees called ghost gums persisted in the undulating, hot space, growing up on smooth white trunks out of the ochre soil. Livistona palms bore the mark of a sweeping fire.

The oldest part of the oldest continent, the Kimberley consists of five rugged basalt plateaus, the core of Australia's so-called Ancient

Plateau, eroded over the eons by torrential rivers into gorges, escarpments, and grottoes. Subject to intense monsoonal storms and terrible heat, it is a land that has little use for modern man.

The Kimberley covers an area of over 130,000 square miles, and is home to only 24,000 people, mostly Aboriginal peoples scattered in small towns and stations to the south. Boab trees, called bottle trees because they are round and filled with water, grow out of the dry grassland and rocks, a relative of baobabs in Africa – relics from a time when the southern continents were joined together in the supercontinent Gondwanaland.

The wet season cuts off access to the outside world for months as rivers rise and inundate dirt roads, rendering them impassable. The land contains few roads and only one paved road at its southern extreme. The Great Northern Highway, a single lane wide enough for a car, was the last part of Australia's perimeter highway to be paved the year before. Jeff had said it was the last frontier of Australia. That meant it was the last frontier in the world.

All that remained of the mining camp were several bare concrete slabs, an old well, and sheets of tin scattered among the trees. Termite mounds by the thousands watched over this lonely terrain. Through the windshield the landscape arrived and departed slowly, our jeep averaging no more than fifteen miles per hour on the dirt road.

"We're here," Jeff said as we pulled up to the middle of no-where. "We'll spend the night and head out to the falls tomorrow."

Camp Creek, a thread of water fringed by spiky-crowned pandanus plants, trickled over the rocks. I strung my hammock up between two cocky-apple trees. In the last daylight I swayed back and forth, listening to a tape a friend had made me before I left New York. The "Down But Not Out Mix" included such tracks as "The Wind" by Cat Stevens, "Feelin' Alright" by Joe Cocker and Traffic, "Sitting in Limbo" by Jimmy Cliff, and "Stuck in Lodi Again" by Creedence Clearwater Revival. If there was a Lodi, the mining camp felt like it. If only I had known then that the only wasted days are the unremembered days, that, as Emerson wrote, "the scholar loses no hour which the man lives."

Jeff walked off into the bush to collect water from the creek. When he returned he started his camping stove, pumping the fuel bottle, waiting until just enough gas covered the coils before flicking the sparker. He pumped the bottle a few more times as the liquid burst into flame and settled into a blue jet. The sputtering hiss of the stove was the only sound. When the water began to boil, he poured in a cup of rice.

"It'll burn six kinds of fuel, including diesel, kerosene, and whiskey," he said. "Very useful in New Guinea."

"I bet by the time you're out of regular fuel, the whiskey's long gone," I said.

"It is."

"When did you come over here from New Guinea?"

"Around eighty-two, or maybe it was eighty-three. Can't remember."

"How did you get a visa to stay in Australia this long?"

"I'm Canadian, remember?" He wanted to drop the matter.

I had only known him for three months, but within a few days of meeting him, I realized that Jeff had had another life. That life was over, and it was important not to ask too many questions.

He once showed me a picture of a woman to whom he had been engaged: a young woman holding on to the roll bar of a jeep in the Anza-Borrego desert. Things had ended abruptly, and instead of getting married, Jeff had left for New Guinea and Australia. In all our travels together, I never learned exactly why.

Jeff wasn't Canadian, he just didn't like being identified as an American. Jeff wasn't even his real name, though I didn't find that out until much later. Every month someone wired a small amount of money into his bank account.

Despite being well-read and smart, Jeff had trouble spelling and doing basic addition, though he was a master chess player. Sometimes he repeated himself. Although he never told me ex-plicitly, I suspected that Jeff had suffered some trauma that had changed the course of his life forever.

With the sun down, the air was warm and pleasant.

The headlights came first, two prongs of light stabbing up the track in the distance. The sound of an engine carried across the valley.

Jeff turned off the stove quickly.

"What's up?" I said.

"Shhh."

A four-wheel drive pulled up and stopped beside the concrete well fifty yards from us. A blond man with a mustache turned on a flashlight as he stepped out of his Toyota Land Cruiser. He caught us in the beam as he swept the abandoned camp.

"Jesus! You startled me," he said. "Didn't expect to find anyone up here."

The man didn't ask, but he must have wondered why we were sitting in the dark. I was wondering myself.

"We've just come down from the coast," I offered.

"What's it like up there?"

"Hot."

"My wife and I are going to do some fishing," the man said. They didn't have a boat. *Good luck*, I thought, remembering the mud.

"Hello," she said, stepping out of the Land Cruiser. She spoke with a German accent. They lit a propane lamp and busied themselves with making camp. Jeff and I finished our sardines and rice by the light of a candle.

"Let's go," Jeff said when we had eaten.

"What do you mean?"

"I don't like to camp near other people."

I thought Jeff was being a little paranoid, but I took down my hammock. We drove a half mile down the track and pulled out of sight among the scattered trees.

"Why didn't we stay at the camp?" I asked.

"The first rule of traveling in the outback: If they can't see you, they can't kill you."

I tied my hammock between two stunted trees. The sky glowed white with stars between the dark branches. Jeff put his sleeping mat and bag on the hood of his jeep. He slept there to be above the snakes and ants.

"That doesn't look very comfortable," I said.

"Better than getting bitten in the face by a taipan."

"Are you worried about that?"

"Not really, even though there're probably six poisonous snakes per acre out here."

I began to drift off to sleep.

"Red rum. Red rum," croaked a voice from the darkness. Jeff was making fun of the fact that I wasn't entirely sure he wasn't a serial killer. We'd only known each other a short time, and if ever there was a good place to kill someone and get away with it, it was here. His favorite movie was *The Shining*, after all.

"Cut it out, man, you *are* starting to scare me."

"Good movie, though . . . when he comes through the door with the axe: 'Heere's Johnny!'"

"The book was better."

I tried unsuccessfully to fall asleep before Jeff began to snore.

In the outback the night sky is actually white, with enough starlight on a moonless night to throw shadows. Only one area of the sky, called the Coalsack, is dark. It is an area where interstellar gas obscures more distant stars. I drifted off to sleep amid the Magellanic clouds.

The next day we hid the jeep among some bushes and shouldered our packs before setting out into the chest-high speargrass. A compass heading took us to Merten's Creek.

After several hours hard slogging we emerged onto the edge of a chasm at Merten's Falls. The waterfall was no more than a trickle, spilling four hundred feet into a deep red gorge.

"Mitchell Falls are just around the corner," Jeff said. We crossed the creek and soon heard the roar of water.

The Mitchell River flowed through a gorge of red sandstone two hundred yards across, picking up speed as it thundered over three gigantic falls cut in the escarpment. We climbed out to the rim of a massive waterfall and looked over the edge. The sandstone was as smooth as polished mahogany. Each fall spilled hundreds of feet into large clear pools before rejoining the river six hundred feet down. Boulders the size of houses shimmered in the emerald water below.

Loose rocks had scoured deep holes in the bedrock over time. I climbed into one of the holes. It was smooth, with concentric ridges – like the inside of a clay vase. Perfectly round boulders lay trapped at the bottom.

"This is incredible!" I shouted to Jeff.

"I told you it was worth the drive. You should see it in the wet."

I thought to myself that if this were the United States, there would be park rangers, fences, and even an interpretive center. Not here. It would be hard to connect with the infinite after paying an entry fee.

Jumping from boulder to boulder, we hiked down below the massive falls and rejoined the river. The canyon walls rose hundreds of feet. At the base of the cliff wall was a gallery of cave paintings. Amid red ochre figures of kangaroos, several simple drawings depicted what appeared to be propeller-driven aircraft, with wings and a cockpit.

"The Aboriginals didn't leave this area until the 1950s and '60s," Jeff said. "This airplane, if that's what it is, probably marks their first interaction with the outside world."

Farther up the gallery I found a life-sized outline of a human on the cliff wall. The entire body was drawn in necrotic purple, and at the foot, sinewy lines depicted a striking snake.

"Snake bite," Jeff said. "Looks like it was fatal."

The continent is home to eighty-one described species of the poisonous snake family Elapidae, the family that includes the Indian cobra and the African mamba. Common Australian species such as the taipan and king brown are more poisonous than either cobras or mambas.

"Wouldn't life be boring if the only thing left that could kill you was another human?" Jeff liked to say.

Of the world's twenty most poisonous snakes, eighteen inhabit Australia, including the inland taipan or "fierce snake" of central Queensland, the most poisonous snake in the world. A single bite from the fierce snake is seventy-five times more powerful than that of a diamond-backed rattlesnake.

"The Aboriginals were scared to death of poisonous snakes," Jeff said. "But for them, walking was the same as hunting. Most snakes didn't move away at their approach."

All snakes lack external ears, but they are able to perceive some low-frequency airborne sounds, and they can sense vibrations conducted via the ground. Jeff and I moved about this environment knowing that most snakes would disappear at the first strike of our boots. Nonetheless, I measured each step carefully. The charmingly named death adder would not move, relying on its camouflage to keep it safe.

Other images on the wall were stencils of hands, created when an Aboriginal man filled his mouth with crushed ochre and water, put his hand on the cliff wall and sprayed the paint onto the stone. Several of the impressions seemed to be missing fingers.

"Could be that these are hunting signals, or maybe the finger just wasn't there – not unusual, given that these tribes did a lot of fighting with clubs," Jeff said.

We stepped out of the shadow of the canyon.

"I know a good camp farther up," he said, "We'd better get going."

We hiked back above the falls and for another hour while we followed a compass heading of 220 degrees. The river was broad and smooth here, flowing lazily between the red walls of the gorge. The cliffs rose thirty feet above the water now, but it was clear that during the wet season the water climbed above the level of the gorge and scoured the rock in a floodplain a half mile wide. The landscape looked like pictures I had seen of Africa.

"There it is," Jeff said, pointing. Ten feet from the top of the cliff wall and twenty feet above the water, a rock ledge leaned out over the river. We climbed up to it using natural steps in the sandstone. The ledge was smooth, with enough room for two sleeping bags. Jeff put his pack down.

I walked out to the edge and looked down into the green water. "You're not afraid this thing is going to break off in the middle of the night, are you?" I asked.

"Could happen," he said.

We spread out our sleeping mats and bags. The ledge looked out over the water below and a broad floodplain of burgundy sandstone on the opposite bank. The rock was worn smooth.

I pulled a handline out of my pack. "Wonder if there's any fish down there." Jeff was not a fisherman.

I lowered a piece of macaroni into the water and within moments had hooked a large fish. I pulled it wriggling up to the ledge.

"Holy shit," I said. In short order two more fish joined the first on the ledge. I built a fire and after gutting them we roasted the fish whole on the coals.

We picked white flesh from the bones in the firelight. At our feet the Southern Cross revolved in the heavens.

"Man, you could live out here."

"I'd like to," Jeff said. "Every time I leave, I want to come back."

I carried a small journal. In it I wrote that all a young man needs is a backpack and fishing line, good boots, some flour, rice, and tea, and plenty of wild space to move around in.

After dinner we put on our headlamps and walked the edge of the gorge until we neared a small waterfall. Half a dozen red eyes floated eerily in our spotlights.

"Dinosaur! Dinosaur!" Jeff shouted, and took off running. He splashed across a shallow pool. "There he is! There he is!" Jeff grabbed the creature by the neck and tail, holding it up. It made a croaking call, "Mumma, Mumma."

"I wonder where Mumma is?" We looked over our shoulders into the darkness.

Two types of crocodiles inhabit the Top End. The freshwater crocodile or *Crocodylus johnstoni*, like the one we had just caught, is not considered a threat to humans, though it has a mouth full of sharp teeth and can grow to a length of ten feet. It preys on fish, goannas, insects, and small mammals. Its much larger cousin, the estuarine, or saltwater crocodile, *Crocodylus porosus*, can grow to twenty-five feet and weigh two tons. *Porosus* is a confirmed man eater.

As its name implies, the saltwater crocodile prefers salt water or tidal areas, though specialized glands enable it to live in fresh water as well, and it will sometimes swim as much as fifty miles upriver in search of food. Being in or close to the water anywhere in saltwater crocodile habitat is extremely foolish. While I was in Australia, five people were killed by crocodiles. Fortunately, the Mitchell Falls would be an impassible barrier to any roving "saltie," so we were safe on this part of the river.

We let the crocodile go after marveling at its sharp teeth and fine leathery skin. It skittered over the rocks and into the water with amazing speed, a miniature dinosaur.

Jeff lay down in his shorts in the shallow pool to cool off before sleep and I did the same, my head resting on a rock. I turned my headlamp off and for a moment lay spread-eagled among the stars of the southern hemisphere.

We hiked back downriver and sprawled out on our ledge above the water. I dangled a line into the river.

"This is the first time I've ever fished from my bed," I said to Jeff. A small fish took the hook. I reeled him in and then left him on the line as bait, tying the line to a log. I wondered if a larger fish would come along.

The next morning the log and my fishing line were gone.

"What monster pulled *that* off the ledge?"

I walked down the gorge. The handline and log floated ominously among some lily pads in the middle of the river. Whatever it was might still be attached. Did I really need that fishing line?

I reasoned that no estuarine crocodiles had made it up over the falls, so I stripped down to shorts and dived in. Fifty feet from the bank, swimming briskly, I was absolutely certain that a crocodilian from the Mesozoic was still lurking on this forgotten edge of the planet – having lived above the falls for seventy million years. The water was primordially deep here. Pushing into the lilies atop a submerged boulder, I grabbed the handline and began streaking for shore as I spooled out the line, expecting at any moment to be pulled under by an armor-plated cousin of Godzilla.

Panting on the rocks at the water's edge, I congratulated myself on being alive. I pulled the line in. The hook was gone.

Jeff studied the track as we drove south from the Mitchell Plateau. He would not let me drive, probably because the jeep was one of his few possessions and he did not want to be left homeless if I rolled it. We followed a thin line back to the twentieth century.

Big gray kangaroos bounded out of the bush suddenly. Free-range cattle stood in the road, stared dumbfounded at our approach, and had to be shooed away.

We stopped abruptly in a wave of dust, and Jeff leaped out of the jeep.

"There he is! There he is!" He ran in the direction where we had last seen a goanna fleeing ridiculously on hind legs.

"I think it was a Gould's goanna, *Varanus gouldii*!" he said, returning empty-handed. "Pretty common. In the Tanami we should find some Perenties, *Varanus giganteus*, largest goanna in Australia – the second-largest lizard in the world after the Komodo dragon." Jeff's passion was reptiles.

We turned the jeep down the track toward the Drysdale River Station. After a week in the bush, we looked forward to buying a cold drink at the station's small store and fueling up. It was early in the dry season, and the cattle muster had not yet begun. A gate, a concrete bunkhouse, and a tin hangar announced our return to civilization.

A single caretaker, an older man, walked toward us as we drove up in the jeep. We were almost out of fuel. I could not imagine walking out of this area if the jeep broke down or if we ran out of fuel. It was too hot, too remote.

The caretaker eyed us suspiciously. "You camp up by the mine?"

"Yes," Jeff said, "four days ago."

"You see anybody else up there?"

"Yeah, we ran into some people, a couple in a Land Cruiser."

The caretaker nodded. "What'd they look like?"

"He had sandy hair, a mustache," I said. "His wife was blond. I think she was German." Jeff nodded.

"You need fuel, huh?" He walked around our jeep. Jeff tossed the empty jerry cans out of the back.

"Do any camping up at the falls?" the man asked.

"Yeah, we were there too," Jeff said.

The caretaker looked at us warily. "Funny thing," he said, "that guy with the mustache . . . somebody siphoned sixty liters of petrol out of his tank during the night. That was four days ago, the same day you were there. I have to say, I was a bit suspicious of you – he was too – but I see now you're out of fuel. You see anybody else up there?"

"No." We hadn't.

"Fancy stealing petrol from someone in a place like this." He shook his head. "Took him three days before he could get a lift out to here. Had to leave his wife up there alone, hiding in the bushes." He looked at us. "Stealing petrol out here could be a death sentence. Who would do that to a man?"

Back in the jeep, I asked Jeff what he thought.

"Rock punctured his fuel tank. Slow leak. Happens all the time," he said. "Bushies know how to fix it with a bar of soap."

Sixty miles away, smoke from a burned-out jeep was already spiraling into the sky. It was not a leaky fuel tank, and we would find out soon enough who would do that to a man. I had been right in thinking that if ever there was a good place to kill someone, it was here.

CHAPTER 4

MILLAA MILLAA

Before landing in North Queensland the pilot tells you to set your watch back twenty years. In the small towns of *Far* North Queensland you might set it back eighty.

Not far from Cairns, the town of Millaa Millaa lies in a region of rolling volcanic hills at the top of the Gillies Range. Originally a logging town, Millaa Millaa is a place of perpetual mist and quiet, surrounded by pockets of rain forest and cut pasture. On rare clear days Mount Bartle Frere, the highest mountain in Queensland, rises to the east, its flanks covered in unbroken shades of green.

Just outside the center of town, a circular blade, tall as a man and rusting under a tin roof, bears witness to an earlier time. The sawmill stands silent. The great trees have been cut and have not yet returned.

Millaa now relies on dairy farming, and the town's prosperity is reflected in the shiny chrome of the milk tanker that every afternoon travels the side roads and gravel byways to the milking sheds. The driver checks for iodine in the milk and, finding none, collects the milk through a long hose before heading off to the next farm.

Along the main street of Millaa Millaa stands a butcher, a baker, the pub, the newsstand, the grocer (where you can still buy kerosene, top hats, *and* ballroom dance floor dust), a fish and chip shop, the Eacham Historical Society Museum, the defunct cheese factory, and the old timber-frame movie theater. Pictures of Humphrey Bogart and Bette Davis adorn the theater entrance, remnants of the last double feature.

Up the street lies the post office, the primary school, the town's only policeman, and the ambulance service, which, with the Royal Flying Doctor Service, is a mainstay of healthcare in the isolated Far North – the idea being that, even though you're hundreds of miles from the nearest hospital, the ambulance will get you there as fast as it can, and please, sir, try not to bleed so much.

The tablelands were once covered with rain forest and inhabited by Aboriginal people the size of pygmies. Millaa is an Aboriginal word for water, and *millaa millaa* means "much water." The rain can last solidly for ten months of the year.

The farm where Clive dropped me off was on a winding road a few miles from town. My days began at quarter to six as the farmer, Joe, or his wife, Narelle, would wake me up to fetch the cows for milking. I had only been in the country for a week.

Stepping out of the house in the morning, I was startled by the strangeness of my surroundings: the exotic flowering trees and orchids, the brilliant butterflies, the lorikeets and parrots that streaked about in gaudy plumage. Everything was different and tropical. Spiders the size of a fist crawled up and down webs.

I was surprised to hear the call of the kookaburra for the first time. The maniacal laugh, *Kakakakakaka-oo-oo-oo-ooo*, rolling over the green hills was a sound I had always associated with Tarzan movies and Africa. And yet, it wasn't a monkey at all – it was a bird! Had Tarzan really lived in Australia?

I rounded up the cows on a four-wheel motorcycle, reveling in the opportunity to travel down winding tracks fringed by tree ferns, alone. The cows started for the milking shed before I arrived. I mowed the lawn around the main house, fixed fences, endured the twice-daily milkings, marveled at the stupidity of cows, fed the calves, and cleared fence lines with a curved axe called a scrub axe. Tiger leeches lived in the tall grass and fixed themselves on any flesh above my rubber boots. After a day of clearing, I'd take my raincoat off in the shed and feel a sudden itch on the back of my neck. Sure enough a blood-gorged leech would fall off at my touch. Even squeezing all of the blood out of the creature and grinding it into the concrete was no consolation. The bite would itch for days.

One day in February I stepped out in a heavy rain to find the lawn swarming with poisonous cane toads. Introduced in the 1930s to combat a beetle that was decimating sugarcane crops, the cane toads went on to be a pest in their own right. With no natural predators, they were everywhere. The younger children played a game called cane toad golf. The idea was to knock a toad as far as you could with a golf club. The children gleefully exclaimed "Fore!" then clubbed the hapless toads into oblivion.

Joe was nice enough, but he wasn't much of a conversationalist. When I admired a huge tree covered by epiphytes and orchids, he merely said, "Good piece of timber, that."

This part of the country was very English, from the mists rolling over the pastures, to the pictures of Queen Elizabeth II and Winston Churchill hanging up in the Returned Services League hall. On the television entire weekends were dedicated to the game of cricket. Here was a continent with leisure time. A short match lasted an entire day, a long one five days. The Australians played the West Indies, after which a woman newscaster interviewed a seven-foot-four Jamaican. Tongue in cheek, she asked him if he was "all in proportion."

"Good heavens no," he replied with a wide smile, "if I was all in proportion I'd be eight foot six."

* * *

In a way, Australia seemed the natural combination of my mother's English background and traditions and my father's youth in California in the thirties, when the land was young and anything seemed possible. My mother had told me stories about the shark nets off Australian beaches, and the disappearance of Australia's prime minister while swimming. We sang songs about the kookaburra in the old gum tree.

My father was born in 1927, the year Al Jolson starred in the first talkie and Lindbergh flew solo across the Atlantic. In the age before jets, Palm Springs was two nights from Chicago on the *Super Chief*, the fastest of all Pullman streamliners to California, traveling the Santa Fe Trail.

As boys, my father and his brothers spent time beside the pool at Charlie Farrell's Racquet Club with the likes of Don Ameche, Joan Fontaine, Louis Hayward, Dorothy Lamour, Robert Preston, Peter Lorre, Bill Tilden, Ingrid Bergman, Judy Garland, and Marlene Dietrich. My father had a crush on Judy Garland.

In the evenings my father and his brothers rode their horses through hills covered with the waxy white blossoms of Spanish bayonet, sage, greasewood and creosote bush, desert gold, lavender, and evening primrose flowers. They watched ruby-throated hummingbirds suck nectar out of ocotillo flowers and kept tarantulas in glass jars. My father remarked that when he was young he could ride his horse from Palm Springs to Encinitas on the coast and "not see another soul."

One morning my father got a call from the police chief who recognized his horse. Blackie had escaped his corral in Chino Canyon and was eating Mr. Sinatra's petunias. That America has passed in a single lifetime, but you can still find pieces of it in small-town Australia.

On clear nights even the stars were upside down. A constellation I recognized from the northern hemisphere, Orion, appeared to lie on his side. It was called the Saucepan by Australians. One constellation in particular drew my attention: the Southern Cross. It looked like a kite in the sky.

At night I sat down to dinner with Joe and his family. The perpetual evening mists rolled in. Joe did not look up as he passed the corned beef. The politicians on the television set spoke with Australian accents.

Apart from Joe's wife, the only females I had seen in the past three weeks had four legs and went "moo" when you approached them. Everything and everyone I knew was immeasurably far away. Three things impressed me most: the quiet, the brightness of the stars and moon, and the fact that I could drink water from any stream in the forest.

My first contact with the town of Millaa Millaa came on a Friday night after several weeks on the farm. The local primary school had barbecues on the back verandah of the pub every other Friday to raise money. Suddenly there was smoke and noise. Joe disappeared to talk to some fellow farmers. I stood beside the bar, determined to drink beer legally for the first time. The drinking age in Australia is eighteen.

Harvey, the owner of the pub and several other business interests around town, was the friendliest face in the crowd. The clientele tended to be cut of a coarse material: miners, loggers, stockmen, dairy farmers, veterans, plain drunks – men with the bark still on. It was among the latter category that I found myself after assuring Joe I would find a way home.

Harvey wiped the counter. "What'll it be?" he asked in an Irish accent.

I didn't want to seem out of place.

"I'll have a glass of Fosters, please," my American accent suddenly conspicuous.

"Pot of Fosters, right." Harvey retrieved a glass.

Heads turned. Though I was dressed in the Blundstone boots and King Gee shorts of a native and smelled vaguely of the backside of a cow, I might as well have been wearing a sundress. No one in Australia drinks Fosters. Especially not in Queensland. This was XXXX country, Queensland's own beer. It got the job done.

Where I came from Fourex was a brand of condom, but I didn't think it appropriate to say that here given the fiercely proud, almost pioneer-like spirit of the men sitting on stools around me. Besides, I had read in the newspaper that Sir Joh Bjelke-Petersen, Queensland's premier at the time, had deployed a tactical squad specifically for the purpose of ripping condom-vending machines out of public toilets in the city of Brisbane, seven hundred miles to the south.

"Hey mate, you're a Yank!"

"That's right."

"I've been to America. Wisconsin – beautiful country in Wisconsin, mate." The young farmer took a swig of beer.

It is a strange fact that what is near is considered common. He was living in what most would consider a tropical paradise, but to him the forest he cleared for pasture was just scrub.

"Don't think much of your Yankee beer. Like sex on the beach."

"What do you mean?" I asked. Sex on the beach sounded pretty good to me.

"Fucking near water, mate!" He laughed. "It's not beer!" He took another swig and declared solemnly, "I can tell you that *nobody* in Wisconsin sells XXXX – I know because I looked!" He pushed a full pot of beer in my direction. "Your shout next. Here – get that into ya!"

Through the door, palm trees huddled in the tropical rain by the quiet highway. The air was hot and humid. Several young men played a game of pool drunkenly in the corner. A sign over the pool table declared the rules: no smoking, no tossing coins on the felt.

So this was small-town Australia. I had never been in a smaller town.

On my left Don, a retired timber cutter, drank Bundaberg Rum and Coke and discussed his days in the battle for Australia in the Coral Sea. He disliked the Japanese intensely, a sentiment I discovered among many older Australians who had fought in New Guinea and the Solomon Islands during World War II. Several regulars at the bar had been interned in the infamous Changi prison and had worked on the Burma railroad. One of the men, nicknamed Quandong (a type of rain-forest nut), had built a bridge over the River Kwai.

"No not *the* bridge," he said when I looked at him open-mouthed. "This was a smaller one, further up ... The Japs were cunts."

On my right, Robbie barely reached the edge of the bar. He sipped a pot of beer and smacked his lips appreciatively. Old Robbie was the last of the original Millaa Millaans; an Aboriginal less than five feet tall with thin bones and birdlike hands. Robbie was a member of a tribe of pygmy Aboriginals who had inhabited the narrow corridor of rain forest beginning at the edge of the dry eucalypt savannah twenty miles to the west.

Their small frames required less energy and moved through the undergrowth faster – an adaptation to circumstances that had ultimately done them no good. His body was small and lithe, bred for generations to slip through holes in the undergrowth of the dense jungle in pursuit of small game, berries, and nuts. Now he looked somewhat out of place at the edge of the bar, wearing a tattered shirt.

I learned more about Robbie from Old Jack, who was cutting down trees on the property adjacent to the farm. I discovered Jack one day when I went to investigate the noise filtering through the woods. There, crouched over a chainsaw ripping into the base of a tree, was Old Jack. The tree pitched forward and crashed to the ground. Jack turned to me and wiped the sweat running down his face. He was a stout man with friendly eyes.

"Black ash, ideal for furniture." He stepped back to admire his handiwork. "I'll bring the tractor round." He stopped. "Who are you?" He looked inquisitive, friendly.

"I just heard the noise and thought I'd investigate – I didn't know there was anyone back here."

Jack looked delighted. "Well, I'm here. Where you from?"

"Tranter's, over that way." I pointed. "I'm helping them with the milking, but we're done for the morning."

"I'm just finishing up myself, actually. Yes, well, if you want, hop in the truck. I want to go and look at some more trees." I got in and Jack drove up the side of the hill, the suspension squeaking painfully. He stopped by a tree bearing fruit.

"Cherry guava," he said. "Very tasty. Wonderful for making jam. Pick some."

While I ate cherry guavas, little sweet fruit with juicy pulp centers and crunchy seeds like passionfruit, Jack pointed out big trees.

"Good timber there, black ash, Queensland maple, worth four dollars a super foot. That's one foot by one foot by one inch. That tree there –" he pointed through the "scrub" to a big tree – "worth fourteen-hundred dollars."

"See there–" he pointed to a cluster of leafless trees. "Lightning strike. Not too long ago either."

We passed gigantic stumps of old trees from a previous harvest.

"That's water gum, don't see too many of them anymore. When I was growing up the big trees were all over. Those were the springboard and axe days, before chainsaws."

We stopped in front of a stump, its core turning to soil, but the circumference wider than any tree I had ever seen. Jack stepped out of the truck.

"In those days you'd cut a notch into the tree with an axe, and then you'd put your board in it. To get above the buttress, you see.

Standing on the board, it might take me two or three days to cut down a tree like that."

I imagined what this land looked like before logging, when the huge kauri and bunya pines dominated. Underneath the canopy of overarching tree limbs, the jungle floor was dark and humid. Only those plants that needed very little light would survive. Though the forest we drove through was disturbed, it still seemed very wild and beautiful.

"Watch out for that right there." Jack pointed to a tall leafy plant. "Stinging tree. Very painful. Lasts for weeks. Best not to touch it." The stinging tree had grown up in a place where the canopy was open and sunlight filtered through. The stinging plant and others like it that grow up in disturbed forest are called pioneer growth.

Even Jack, who casually referred to the great cyclone of 1918 and the great fire that engulfed Mount Father Clancy in 1923, was a pioneer – a man standing with one foot in an earlier time.

"You run into Robbie yet?" he asked me. "He's the last native of these parts. When I was growing up you could find Abos all over the place. I learned to speak the language of Robbie's tribe, but he's the only one left."

Robbie thoughtfully rolled a cigarette at the edge of the bar.

"I'm the last blackfella in these parts, mate," Robbie said when I asked him about his family. The last member of the tribe, a true Aboriginal.

Robbie's "cousin," Vinnie, coal black and more than six feet tall, had been looking for gold.

"Nah, nothin' yet. Few flakes is all. Place too hard to get to. Not worth it." His sweet face furrowed below dark eyebrows. "You lookin' fer places? Gotta mate says plenty nuggets out west."

Much of the talk at the edge of the bar was about gold. Most of it was talk merely, but some pursued gold in between jobs. Gold certificates were for sale in the only bank in town. For eight dollars one could legally pursue the yellow metal anywhere one could find it. Gold ran through the streams, and a person might make forty dollars a day with a dredge, with the possibility of hitting the jackpot. Not a bad wage, and the lifestyle appealed to some. After a few weeks in the bush, people were said to go feral.

After almost a month of cleaning out calf pens and herding cows, I was getting my bearings. I paid Harvey and walked out onto Millaa's main street.

The surrounding hills were dark and quiet. A road train headed down the range, the growl of its jake brake throbbing through the rain. I was alone in a strange land. That meant keeping your wits about you, and standing on your own two feet.

Joe announced the next morning that his two eldest boys were coming back from school at the end of the week, and my services were no longer needed on the farm. I was stunned. Where would I go now?

CHAPTER 5

WILD BILL

In Australia alone is to be found the Grotesque, the Weird, the strange scribblings of Nature learning how to write.

Marcus Clarke

66 **T**here's no pay, but you'll learn about these forests and I'll put a roof over your head." The man speaking wore rubber boots and clenched a machete in his right hand.

Bill Laurance was a biologist in Millaa Millaa, undertaking his PhD thesis in "heterogeneity and patch characteristics in non-volant mammals in a fragmented rain-forest system." He was a big, outspoken man from Idaho, a graduate student from the University of California at Berkeley who seemed more mature than his twenty-nine years. I had asked if he needed an extra hand.

The next day I moved off the farm and into Bill's little house on Coral Street in town. I slept on a couch next to jars of formaldehyde containing a carnivorous centipede and several mammal specimens.

The house was occupied by four other travelers who had signed on with Bill, and a dog named Tully. Martin from Yorkshire spoke with a terrific accent and played Van Halen on acoustic guitar.

Bridgette was a plump Londoner who told me that she was 167th in line to the British throne. I felt compelled to tell her that my father was a janitor in the U.S. Capitol building, even though it wasn't true. Steve was an Australian and a skydiver who had been working as a machinist in Townsville before deciding he didn't want to fit pieces of metal together for the rest of his days. And John was a Californian from Berkeley, a free-spirited biology major who often wore a sarong – which greatly discomfited some of the locals. One of them called the police every time he saw John wearing a "dress" on the main street.

Our job was to place live-capture traps, each carefully baited with vanilla essence and oats, at scientific intervals along transects Bill had cut through the rain forest.

"You can bet Betty Crocker never thought of this," Bill said over coffee as we rolled the oats into little bait balls. Each morning at first light we headed into the small islands of rain forest surrounded by seas of cleared pasture to check and reset our traps. We never knew what creature a trap might hold. We weighed, sexed, and described the species of small mammals we captured and then let them go, dutifully recording all the data. It was "hard yakka," as the locals say, and dangerous.

The forest sites were often on steep hillsides, and the red mud was extremely slippery. Worse still was the threat of stinging trees, lawyer cane, leptosporosis, the occasional bite from a very large rat, tiny paralysis ticks, a host of fungal infections, venomous red-bellied black snakes, and Bridgette's singing. We endured leeches and heavy rain.

A dyspeptic camaraderie developed. After all, the team was comprised of travelers – not the easiest sort to send off into leech-infested rain forests early in the morning to catch what essentially were rats. Because I was the lowest on the pole, I became the "tag man" and carried a field vest loaded with halothane, needle-nose pliers, bags, and cotton balls. I was also the most likely to be bitten.

We called ourselves the Rat Patrol, studying the almost two-pound *Uromys*, the several smaller species of *Melomys*, *Rattus fuscipes*, and other creatures, including the carnivorous marsupial *Antechinus* and the musky rat kangaroo. Most of Australia's native mammals are marsupials, carry their young in pouches, and are thus more ancient than and distinct from placental mammals. We noted whether the animals were juveniles or adults, male or female, if they had mites or ticks, and whether or not males were "scrotal" or not. If an animal was scrotal, its testicles were greatly enlarged and it was ready for mating.

The purpose of Bill's project was to take a census of the rain-forest mammals and to compare the mammal populations in the disturbed rain-forest islands with those of larger tracts of control forest. The question was how much intact habitat was required to maintain a healthy forest with all its expected inhabitants.

Bill steamed ahead, wielding a machete. He stopped and held out a long thorny tendril that grew from a type of ascending palm, and pointed to the barbs growing on either side.

"See, the barbs go inward, like a hook. Aussies call it lawyer cane," he said.

The plant grows abundantly in disturbed forest and is also known as a wait-a-while, because once tangled up in it, you won't be moving anywhere for a while. The rain forest, I came to understand, is an extremely inhospitable place, and no place you'd want to get lost in.

On the track, a dollop of purple excrement filled with seeds was half the size of a cow pattie. Martin studied it carefully. "What's this?"

"Cassowary shit," Bill whispered.

"Good lord, you're not telling me a bird shat that? It must be huge!"

"He's probably watching us right now. They have excellent camouflage."

This flightless bird, the size of an ostrich, has bright blue and red neck wattles, long black quills, and a crest of bone like a conquistador's helmet.

"Is it dangerous?"

"Well, it's got a murderous third claw which it uses to dis-embowel predators . . . but no, we're not in any danger," Bill said quietly. "Not unless he's got chicks."

Like most megapods, the male cassowary raises the young chicks and may attack if threatened. In a solid case for biogeography, this giant flightless bird has relatives in the rest of former Gondwana-land, including the ostrich of Africa, the rhea of South America, the now-extinct moa, and the still-living but much smaller kiwi of New Zealand. Some plants in the forest will only germinate after passing through the gut of a cassowary. It is, however, an extremely shy creature, and we never did see one in the wild.

We collected field data in the wet forests during the day and spotlighted on clear nights. My job was to keep notes on the creatures we encountered while Bill scanned the trees with a spotlight connected to a motorcycle battery in his backpack. He swept the trees and canopy with the light, looking for eyeshine.

All creatures give off eyeshine as light is reflected from their retinas, for the same reason that a flash mounted on a camera will cause red eyes in a photograph. Even spiders' eyes glowed brilliantly in the dark, as long as the spotlight was held within a few inches of our own eyes. It was a terrific way to locate creatures in the dense canopy.

Bill hardly spoke except to whisper the species name, and give an estimate of how high up in the tree it was. Tonight we encountered several species of lemuroid possum in the rain forest:

three coppery brushtails, one Herbert River ringtail, and two green possums. A tiny sugar glider had gigantic eyes that glowed bright red in the beam of the spotlight. Most of the animals simply stared at us, or casually sauntered down their branches in the opposite direction. But one animal in particular had evolved a bizarre form of escape.

High in the canopy, the spotlight picked up the eyeshine of a tree kangaroo. This creature resembles a small kangaroo with a black face mask similar to that of a raccoon.

"Lumholtz tree kangaroo," Bill whispered, "sixty-five feet."

In the next instant the creature leapt from the branch and crashed to the forest floor. It landed with a thud.

I stared at Bill in wide-mouthed horror. Had the creature just committed suicide? Moments later I heard the "thump, thump, thump" from the dark forest as the creature hopped off into the bush.

"It doesn't matter how high up they are, they jump," Bill whispered. "Landing doesn't seem to bother them."

The tree kangaroo represents an interesting case of evolutionary recapitulation. Fossil evidence indicates that marsupials originated in ancient North America. But recent research has shown that the ancestors of kangaroos, and indeed the entire branch of Australian marsupials, evolved in the trees of South America some seventy million years ago – when the two continents were joined together as part of Gondwanaland. A small marsupial, *Dromiciops australis*, still lives in the forests of Chile and is a direct link to the kangaroos of Australia. The tree kangaroo Bill and I heard stomping through the rain forest had returned (albeit somewhat tenuously) to its arboreal niche, while its cousins had taken over the dry grassland habitats in Australia.

One day after an arduous morning of checking traps, John and I stripped naked and went for a swim in a clear pool in the forest at Zillie Falls. By the time we turned around, Bill had grabbed our clothes and was pelting up the trail, leaving nothing but our gumboots. We finished our swim, and then John and I calmly walked out of the forest stark naked. John even allowed that he might prefer to do field work *au natural*.

"For starters, it's easier to see the leeches," he said with a laugh.

We stood by the road nonchalantly with our thumbs out, in our rubber boots, waiting for the first startled farmer or his wife to come by. Bill leaped out of his hiding place and hastily returned our clothes. He was ever mindful of the local farmers' perceptions of him and his team, and he had to be.

At the time, the Australian government was considering giving much of the remaining 20 percent of Queensland lowland rain forest protection under the World Heritage Act. Rural Australians were up in arms over the meddling of the federal government in what the locals saw as *their* forests. Timber towns like Ravenshoe had a sign on every corner: CONSERVE ENERGY, BURN A GREENIE. As members of a biological team studying the rain forest, we were definitely considered greenies.

One of our sites had a resident platypus living in a stream in the forest. The platypus was thought to be a taxidermic joke when the first specimen was brought back to England, a beaver with a duckbill sewn onto it. This bizarre creature is one of only two living types of monotremes – an evolutionary stage between reptile and mammal. The platypus and the echidna, a sort of spiny hedgehog, are the only mammals in the world that lay eggs, and they occur only in Australia and New Guinea. It was, as Martin relayed one humid afternoon while we watched the platypus stirring up the mud, "the edge of science, the forefront of discovery."

On rare sunny days we discovered fourteen-foot-long amethystine pythons, named for the beautiful purplish sheen of their scales, and their smaller cousins, carpet pythons, dumbly perusing the forest boughs in search of sleeping cockatoos, wampoo pigeons, tiny sugar glider possums, and spectacled flying foxes.

On rainy nights Bill and I played frenzied games of ping-pong while flying foxes squabbled in the guava tree outside. The flying fox, I was surprised to learn, may be man's closest biological relative in Australia because it is one of the few placental mammals on the continent.

Friday nights Martin and I played pool down at the pub. Most other nights Martin spent with Bridgette moving furniture in the next room.

"A man has needs," he explained to me, "and so, by God, does Bridgette."

Martin was right, I thought, as I sat at the bar sipping a beer. Millaa suffered not just from a paucity but an absolute dearth of young, attractive women. I was, in the scientific parlance of the team, decidedly scrotal.

So it was with growing amazement and then finally astonishment that I watched not one, not two, but half a dozen young, blond, comely women enter the pub and seat themselves in a far corner.

I don't know if I shouted hallelujah in the noisy bar, or just whispered it. The locals were also quite taken aback. In Millaa, the polite women of the town drank in the ladies' lounge, separated from the men's bar.

As it was late in the evening and I was feeling social, I introduced myself. It turned out the young women were part of a group of American college students receiving credit as part of the School for Field Studies. The program was expensive, about ten thousand dollars per semester. They lived at a farmhouse a few miles out of town called Rawson's Pool, and took lectures on the rain forest in the main house. It all sounded tame compared to what we were doing with Bill. But they were getting academic credit for it, and they seemed nice enough.

The next day as the Rat Patrol drove back from trapping, Bill spied a ten-foot carpet python in the grass beside the road. He caught it and put it in a pillowcase in the back of the truck.

"It'll be a good learning experience," he explained. We drove out to Rawson's Pool. The students had just finished a lecture and were having lunch.

"Special delivery," Bill said, and shook the open pillowcase onto the living room floor. There were blank stares as the python slithered out. Several of the students screamed. The snake curled up under an armchair. As we left John said, "Don't worry — they're not venomous and they don't have fangs, but they bite like hell!"

Millaa Millaa is home to one of the most perfect waterfalls in the world, Millaa Falls. It is an inspirational place, a cascade pouring down a face of columnar basalt into a broad pool set amid leaning tree ferns, lilies, and flowering acacias. I often swam there after trapping.

Australians, I discovered, do not suffer from that peculiar American fear of nakedness. There were apparently few Puritans among the people who landed at Botany Bay, and just about any swimming hole is clothing-optional.

One morning as I was stripping down to swim naked in the falls, an entire troop of girl scouts, headed by a sturdy-looking matron, emerged suddenly from the wild ginger. I leaped for my underwear as the group plowed through the foliage and assembled near me at the water's edge – expecting at any moment to hear shrill blasts from the whistle around the matron's neck.

"No, no, don't worry about us," she said. "Go for your life. That's the only way to swim. Just watch out for the freshwater eels." I was a little taken aback about the eels, but I leaped in. It is almost impossible to be underdressed in Australia.

And for all the town's 1950s provincialism, there was a set of alternative types.

I discovered them one Sunday on the field in front of the movie theater. A dozen long-haired men played a game of soccer. Their girlfriends sat on the grass or occasionally joined in, smelling of patchouli, reefer, and rolled cigarettes.

It turned out that Far North Queensland was Mecca to, for want of a better word, hippies. The climate is perfect for growing marijuana, and many came here to get off the grid and "back to the land" in the seventies.

I joined the losing side and we kicked the ball back and forth to shouts of "Wine tasting!," "Get on with it!," and "Over here, you twit!"

The men had copious amounts of hair and names like Viking Steve, Dickhead Paul, Motorcycle Dave, Three-Star Rick (whose eulogy, later delivered by Rainforest Jane, went something like: He was a bastard – but we loved him), and Wise John. The women had names like Cyclone Wendy, Rainforest Jane, Cat's Eyes, and Mad Rachel. They were from small farms around the Tablelands and villages like Kuranda. The largest group came from a commune called Middlebrook, a few miles south of town and in the middle of the forest.

At the party after the game I struck up a conversation with Motorcycle Dave and a man named Lawrie, who lived in the old movie theater. We watched heat lightning down at the coast and stood under the eaves of the theater taking pulls on a joint. It was my first marijuana since arriving in Australia, and it was superb.

One afternoon a white jeep with Western Australia plates pulled into the driveway. A heavy-set man wearing a hat and sunglasses stepped into the house. He had a beard and a soft voice. Jeff had heard about Bill's project while at a hostel down in Cairns. Bill introduced him to the rest of the team.

Jeff seemed shy and a little odd at first. He wasn't just traveling around the country like the rest of us, he had been there for years. Bridgette didn't want him to sleep in the house, afraid he would murder us all in our sleep.

Jeff's only possessions were a backpack, a compound bow, some clothes, a few books, maps, and the white jeep. Jeff took my place on the couch on the verandah. I claimed a bed in the house.

The trapping and data collection continued. We were now working almost full-time, with the trapping in the morning and spotlighting at night. Bill had added a further dimension to the project. When we were done with trapping, we took inventory of all the seeds and fruits of the rain forest in the areas of study. It was rugged work. One day during fruit censusing Martin was stung by the infamous stinging tree. He turned white and sat on a log while we finished, in obvious agony.

Down the slope from our transect, I walked on the red soil picking up round Quandong nuts the size of golf balls. I grabbed a sapling to steady myself and suddenly there was shooting pain in my thumb. I looked up. The heart-shaped leaves were above my head – I was among a grove of huge stinging trees. The woody stems were not venomous, but my thumb had brushed a tiny bud of new growth. The pain was instantaneous and severe as the alkaloid poisons collected in the lymph nodes under my right arm. I was sick and could hardly breathe. It felt like there was a flaming bowling ball lodged in my armpit. I stumbled back to the truck.

"What? You too?" Bill shouted before giving Martin and me a ride to the ambulance service. There was little the ambulance driver could do. For six months I felt the twinge of the stinging tree whenever I put my hand in cold water or brushed it against something. Aah, North Queensland.

Bill wanted to know what size forest habitat was necessary to

54

maintain larger predators and, because I was the only one who really got along with Jeff, he and I were put in charge of predator trapping. Jeff and I called ourselves the Higher Mammal crew, and we trapped in different areas from the rest of the Rat Patrol.

Every morning we headed into the rain forest to check our live traps and put down raw chicken meat. We hoped to catch a species of spotted marsupial cat called the quoll, *Dasyurus hallucatus*, one of the larger carnivores in the rain forest. Mostly we just caught green catbirds, which seemed to like the meat and could peck quite hard when we tried to release them.

One day we inadvertently trapped a Boyd's Rainforest Dragon, a spectacular lizard with turquoise, yellow, and green scales, and white horned protuberances on its throat. A line of white triangular spines ran down its back.

"*Boydii* – it looks like a miniature dinosaur, doesn't it?" Jeff said, holding it carefully. "Dinosaurs were probably as colorful as this."

We studied the reptile beside a jungle stream.

"There were many orders of reptile-like creatures during the Cretaceous," Jeff said. "Now there are only four: crocodilians, lizards and snakes, turtles and tortoises make up three orders. The fourth is occupied by a single species, the tuatara. It lives on an island off New Zealand and is the last surviving species of the sphenodont order. It has a partially developed third eye. All other orders of reptiles were wiped out in a cataclysm about sixty-five million years ago – probably a large asteroid. If it weren't for that rock, man would probably still be little more than a terrified tree shrew."

Jeff despised smokers, hated cattle, and was a committed evolutionist. He was well-read and knew many things about New Guinea, Australia, science and biology, evolution, religion, philosophy, the United States, the natural world, wilderness survival, men, women, and reptiles. He called organized religion organized superstition, was appalled by Creationists who believe the Earth and its animals were created in six days by God, and often quoted his hero, Stephen J. Gould, on evolutionary theory and the "stone gospel": the fossil record.

Creationists point to gaps in the fossil record and the lack of intermediary stages in evolution as proof that evolution isn't really taking place. They've obviously never seen an echidna or platypus.

"That can be partially explained by Gould's theory of punctuated equilibrium," Jeff said. "Organisms go for eons without change, but then conditions change and creatures evolve rapidly over a few generations – punctuated equilibrium. And of course a lot of the gaps in the fossil record are waiting to be filled in by new discoveries."

At eighteen, I was asking all sorts of questions. "Why do women have breasts?" I wanted to know.

"Sexual selection. Men find women with breasts more desirable."

"But why?"

"Maybe because breasts resemble buttocks. I don't think anybody really knows."

On the jeep's tiny radio, we listened to the Australia Broad–casting Corporation's *Science Show* and the news of the world.

"Doesn't it strike you as odd that in the United States people put their hand on a Bible before swearing to tell the truth?" Jeff asked. "Or that the money says, 'In God we trust'?"

I hadn't thought much about religion up to that point, probably because my parents were scientists. I hadn't realized so much of the world *was* religious, and in particular in the United States. My own religious bent was along the lines of Henry David Thoreau: "Tell me the height of the mountains of the moon or the diameter of space and I may believe you, but profess to know the secret history of the almighty and I will pronounce thee mad."

As we walked old logging trails in the rain through forests alive with epiphytes, ferns, and delicate orchids, Jeff asked me what I had seen of Australia. He told me about a place called the Kimberley on the other side of the continent. He wanted to go there, and needed a partner to split the cost of fuel. He gave me a copy of the Sierra Club's guide to backpacking, *Walking Softly in the Wilderness,* and *The Panda's Thumb* by Stephen J. Gould.

"We can look for *Pseudothedactylus lindneri* in the caves of the Mitchell Plateau!" he shouted as we hiked into our trapping sites deep in the rain forest. "It's a kind of cave gecko," he explained when I stared at him blankly. "The point is, who knows what species are undescribed by science out there?"

The Holy Grail for any scientist is finding a new species, or rediscovering one that is thought to have been extinct.

"They only just published the first photographs of the warabi last month. That's the smallest member of the kangaroo family – found only in the Kimberley!" he said. Jeff seemed to know all the reptiles and most of the mammals in Australia, and their Latin names.

Jeff spied a ten-foot carpet python curled up on the forest floor. He seized the snake by the back of the head and tail. Holding the creature closer to me than I would have liked, he pointed out its features, the labial and rostral pits around its mouth that detected minute changes in temperature, the small teeth for grasping, the hinged jaw, the muscled body used to constrict prey. Pythons are basal snakes, so called because they arose early in the diversification of serpents. There are twenty-seven species of python in eight genera of pythonidae. The largest, the reticulated python of Southeast Asia, has taken the occasional rubber tapper out in the forest, but this snake was too small to overpower an adult.

"There's only one reliably documented case of a reticulated python eating someone – but it does happen. Snakes get a bad rap in the Bible. This is a yellow and black phase – jungle carpet." He held it while the tail coiled around his arm. "Beautiful. Australia has fifteen species of python, and probably more waiting to be discovered." I was intrigued by the idea.

Jeff had been to the Kimberley before, flying in with a fellow herpetologist named John Weigel to an airstrip at the abandoned bauxite mine near the Mitchell Plateau, an area of intense heat, ruggedness, and beauty.

"We were looking for the rough-scale python, *Morelia carinata*, Australia's rarest – only one specimen has ever been found. Scientists incorrectly identified it as a carpet python. It was collected in the Valley of Lagoons near the Mitchell Plateau and sat in a museum drawer for twelve years."

Jeff let the python go into the grass. "We didn't find it. *Morelia carinata* is the only python with rough scales. It could belong to an entirely new genus! It may be the longest snake in Australia! You and I could get the first live photographs!"

The serpent coiled up in the grass and hissed at us. "You'll need to buy a good headlamp and a compass down in Cairns."

Though I liked Jeff, I was a little unsure about traveling with a man I had only just met. I didn't even know how old he was, his real name, or his nationality. And he was, after all, a drifter.

I had applied to several colleges before leaving the States. One by one in May the letters started arriving. It appeared no one wanted me as a student. Bill laughed when I posted the rejection letters on my door and announced I would not be matriculating.

"You're just not Ivy League material," he said with a chuckle, even though I had applied to a number of back-up colleges.

I agreed to go west.

"Where will I end up?" I asked Jeff.

"I can drop you off at a station in the Tanami – they're always looking for hands," he said. "Or we can go to Alice Springs."

CHAPTER 6

PERRY FARM AND MIDDLEBROOK ROAD

Perry Farm had a rusted milk can for a mailbox. A dirt road led into the rain forest over a creek and past a shed. A sign nailed to a tree said: MAIN STREET. Two hundred yards up was the farmhouse.

I had met Peter in town one evening in front of the RSL hall. An Englishman in his sixties and a man of the world, Peter invited me to come out to his farm and have dinner with him and his wife, Maggie.

Mandarin, grapefruit, pawpaw, and lemon trees lined the drive. On all sides the forest encroached.

"I've been a farmer all my life," Peter explained. "I'm giving this land back to the forest. Land needs to rest."

Maggie was in the kitchen when we arrived, shooing six gigantic cats out of a plate of food.

"Tiger, you mustn't!" she said to one.

Over dinner Peter told me stories of life as a farmer and safari guide in Kenya, where he had met Maggie. She was from England and had moved to Toronto to work as a speech therapist before going to Africa and settling in Australia with Peter. They were both accomplished painters in watercolor and oils, and Peter was also a craftsman in wood. They kept chickens, two pigs, and the cats. Peter offered to show me a cabin he was building on the property.

We walked the trail from the farmhouse into the forest. One corner of the farm backed up to the Beatrice River, filled with rounded boulders, ferns, and clear pools. Wild ginger and huge trees grew along the banks.

The river had been named by the first white man to lay eyes on it, an explorer named Christy Palmerston. Palmerston had endured rain, leeches, and the dense forest to explore the Tablelands. Lost and starving, he had lived on the flesh of cockatoos and boiled fungus before breaking back to the coast and rescue. He named the river after his wife, Beatrice.

The cabin rose above the leaf litter on a foundation of wooden stilts. A pie plate set on the top of each post kept termites, snakes, rats, mice, and some of the larger insects from entering the house.

Steps and a small porch with a kerosene lantern hanging from a beam led to the front door. A series of decked causeways led to the outhouse and shower, both under construction.

The cabin was furnished with a wooden table, two chairs, and some shelves. A long extension cord from the farmhouse provided electricity to a single bulb above the table. A stainless steel sink and spigot offered water from a rain tank.

I had committed myself to going to the Kimberley with Jeff, but before heading west I wanted to be sure I had a place to come back to. Bill's project would be over and he'd be back in the States polishing up his PhD thesis by the time I expected to return. And I had some ideas about writing. It seemed like an ideal hermitage, if a little damp. I'd heard that the secret of writing is having a low overhead and few distractions.

A set of stairs led up to the loft. One end of the loft was a rough-framed window opening and the other was bare studs looking out onto tree branches. The roof was low, but high enough to stand under in the center. The rain forest was so dense from the front porch that I could have brachiated down to the main house like an orangutan.

"It's yours if you want it," Peter said. "One dollar a month."

I pushed some moldy mattresses into one corner, salvaged the least moldy one, and stuck it in the center. Peter lent me some blankets and a large mosquito net, which I hung above the bed. I had established a base of operations in Australia.

That night I slept in the heart of the forest.

At midnight I awoke to the sound of the rain coming down on the tin roof like buckshot. I felt wonderfully alive.

The morning dawned clear and sunny. Whip birds called in the forest with a sound like a cracking whip. I walked down to the farmhouse to find Peter standing under a pawpaw tree.

"There you are," he said. "Look just there." Peter pointed to the branches of a nearby tree.

A black bird with a metallic flash of iridescent green on its tail and throat fluttered from branch to branch, its plumage rustling. A long curved beak like a surgeon's scissors evinced the bird's love for fruit.

"Male rifle bird," Peter said, looking from the bird to two ripe pawpaw fruits solemnly. "Rifle birds love pawpaw. We'd better take these pawpaw in smartly or else he'll have them both."

Peter moved a wheelbarrow to the base of the tree, a skinny trunk with two yellow-orange fruits hanging ripe as rain. I stood on tiptoes on the wheelbarrow and with a hoe reached up and sliced the fruit at the stem, one after the other. They dropped from the tree and Peter, standing below, caught them with outstretched hands.

He picked a bush lemon and squeezed it over the pawpaw.

"Pawpaw is the second-best thing in the morning," he said.

* * *

Past Perry Farm the road turned to gravel, crossed several creeks on bridges constructed of old railroad sleepers, and was slick red mud as it plunged into the valley of Middlebrook Creek. Clouds floated above the steep sides of the valley, catching the last red of sunset. I parked a borrowed bicycle in the new dark by the shed and an abandoned bus, the end of the road for some of Kesey's antipodean pranksters, and walked in the fading light down to Motorcycle Dave's house. Above the trees, stars glimmered between patches of cloud.

Too steep for farming, the land had been purchased for a commune back in the mid-seventies. The people who remained had taken Joni Mitchell's advice to "get back to the garden." With fruit trees and vegetables, red and green king parrots, and white and yellow sulphur-crested cockatoos sweeping across the valley, it seemed like Eden to me.

The track was steep and led past pawpaw and avocado trees and stands of bamboo. Santana emanated from a simple A-frame home with stained-glass windows, mingling with the sounds of the jungle, the chorus of frogs, the smell of wood smoke and lemongrass. It might have been 1968.

Motorcycle Dave lived in the roundhouse at Middlebrook. He owned a 600 cc Yamaha and had promised to give me a lift down to Cairns in the morning. I needed to pick up a headlamp and compass before traveling west with Jeff, and I wanted to learn to dive.

Only a few people remained at Middlebrook, most in their late thirties, living the simple life. They had built houses according to their whims and the materials at hand. The A-frame was the most popular design, but there was also Dave's roundhouse made of concrete blocks with terrariums set in the walls. The houses had outhouses and bathtubs perched in the middle of the forest.

They tended their own gardens and lived with kerosene, solar power, and water from the creek. They chopped wood dragged in from west of the Great Dividing Range, as the wood of the rain forest is too damp to burn. They had bookshelves filled with Castaneda, Guevara, Solzhenitsyn, Leary, Kerouac, and stacks of old *National Geographics*. Their material needs were met quite simply, with no mortgage or power bills. They had made the fundamental choice between having time and having things.

I passed Dave's meditation platform that looked out over the valley. A child's swing hung from the branches of a five-corner-fruit tree.

Dave was downstairs, packing for the journey, when I showed up. We'd be getting an early start in the morning.

"Care for a cuppa?" he said.

"Sure, thanks," I said.

"There's hot water for the shower if you want one," Dave said, putting a few more logs in the stove.

"Love one," I said. I was always grateful for a hot shower.

"Here's a towel."

The tub sat beside an open window in a covered room beside the roundhouse. A breeze came through the window. I lit a candle and put it on the windowsill. The tiger-striped leaves of a monstera plant climbed one gutter.

I stripped naked and ran water out of the nozzle. Outside the hillside grew dark. Save for this candle, and the orange fire in the stove, the darkness was complete. The frogs raised a chorus — the yellow and black cannibal frog, the giant green tree frog with its one base note — while the thousands of peepers and creepers and scurrying things made their noises among the dripping leaves.

I stepped under the hot water and breathed in the smell of wood smoke and lantana while the warm water splashed over my body. The hot water was delicious. I stood listening to the sounds of the rain forest when I was done. The water dripped off my fingers and ran down my ankles.

Dave made lemongrass tea and we smoked homegrown reefer and played congas and listened to the rain roll in from the coast.

I had developed a sort of fatalism. I wasn't keen about riding on the back of a motorcycle down a winding mountain road, but Dave was a skilled cyclist and knew every twisting mud-slicked corner of the sixty-five mile journey to Cairns. We hurtled up the steep road out of the valley much faster than I would have liked, the rear tire slipping in the mud.

We reached the gravel, and then the paved road. As we roared along, I thought about the past few months. Australia had changed my view of the world. And for someone who had arrived in the country knowing no one, I had made a few friends.

Before going to the Kimberley with Jeff, I wanted to learn to dive on the Great Barrier Reef, which stretches almost a thousand miles down the east coast of Australia.

Alone on the road, Dave and I roared down the Gillies Range on a winding series of switchbacks. Halfway down the mountain, the coast spread below us, flat and green under a blue sky. The rain-forest mountains of Bellenden Ker and Bartle Frere rose to the southeast.

Once on the flats we rode through miles of sugarcane. We crossed the railroad tracks and came into town. I said goodbye to Dave and checked in to the Gone Walkabout Hostel. Dive class would begin at nine o'clock.

The sixteen members of the class were every bit as colorful as the fish out on the reef — tanned young men and women from Sweden, Switzerland, Denmark, Germany, Canada, Holland, and England, all traveling around the continent. I was the only American. There were so many Swedes in Australia that there was a joke: would the last person leaving Sweden please turn out the lights?

Robert was a Dutch truck driver. He and his friend Marcel were eager to "swim with the fishes." In class our instructor went over the potential for drowning, the natural hazards such as stonefish, blue-ringed octopi, marine stingers, sharks, sea snakes, the bends, cone dart shells, and the very real possibility of what the texts referred to as a "lung expansion injury."

"Does not sound good," Robert said. He and Marcel were traveling around the country in a Holden-Ford station wagon. They'd teamed up with Alister, a heavily tattooed Brit traveling on a motorcycle.

"My uncle is a tattoo artist," Alister explained when I gaped at the intricate depictions of Bengal tigers, hibiscus flowers, and dragons on his flesh.

Two days of classroom instruction included passing a physical, taking the PADI (Professional Association of Diving Instructors) course, and using the scuba equipment in the pool. I discovered among my fellow students a European rationalism that included an openness about sex I found very refreshing.

In the pool we learned how to use our buoyancy compensators, put on and turn on our tanks, and breathe underwater. We also learned how to clear our masks and reach for our buddy's spare air, called "the octopus," underwater.

In the evenings we gathered at the Backpackers Restaurant for dinner. At six dollars, the all-you-could-eat buffet was a bargain and typically fed me for the whole day. As most of us were on limited budgets, we didn't drink much.

I was astounded at the color and beauty of the reef and its inhabitants. The staghorn, fan, and brain corals were a fecund universe, home to hundreds of species of fish: the giant Maori wrasse, jade green with purple markings in the shape of a Maori tattoo on its face, the delicate yellow trumpet fish, clownfish nestled in sea anemones, bicolor angelfish, moorish idols, parrot fish, coral rock cod, saddle butterfly fish, regal angelfish, longnose unicorn fish, painted flute-mouths, harlequin tusk fish, bird wrasse, spangled emperors, ornate butterfly fish, clown trigger fish, yellowling goat fish, red squirrel fish, and giant clams with purple and green eyes and lips.

On the last night of the dive course I slept out on deck under a billion stars. The boat rocked gently. A Swiss girl, Caterina, was in her sleeping bag nearby. She had dark hair, was tanned and self-possessed, with a quick laugh, flashing eyes and smile. She spoke German, English, Spanish, and Italian, and when she'd had a little too much to drink, she spoke a delightful combination of Spanish and Italian. I was instantly in love with her. We stayed up all night on the ship, anchored on the reef, talking. Caterina was traveling around Australia with two girlfriends in a station wagon.

Back on shore we received our scuba certification and had a celebratory dinner with the others in the class. My dive buddy, Robert, the Dutch truck driver, pulled me aside.

"She likes you," he said. He and his traveling companions were heading north in the morning. Robert pressed five condoms into my hand as he said goodbye.

Caterina and her friends were also preparing to move on, south to Townsville.

"We're going to Alice Springs and then Ayers Rock and then we fly home out of Sydney," she said. "Come with us."

For the first time in my life I felt that I had met a soul mate. We had spent a week communicating almost without talking. She had a peacefulness in her, a steady calm that belied a real fire. But as much as I wanted to, I could not go with her. I had promised Jeff we would go to the Kimberley. And maybe staying with the girls would be too easy, too comfortable.

They dropped me off beside the highway in the evening in Innisfail.

"I am sorry we cannot go to your beloved Millaa Millaa," Caterina said, kissing me. "Meet us at the fountain in Kings Cross on the fifth of July if you are in Sydney."

Their tail lights disappeared among the fields of sugarcane. It was late and started to rain. I felt terribly lonely, but I was getting used to it.

"I am a fucking idiot!" I shouted in the wet darkness. They were gone.

The rain was pelting by the time I had walked up the highway a quarter mile. A car pulled over. Was I dreaming? Caterina rolled the window down, "Get in! We're not driving now – too much rain – let's go to the bar." I was overjoyed.

We all slept in the car that night, and I thought, Here I am in a car with three of the most beautiful, vivacious girls I've ever met, and the most beautiful and vivacious of them all is in the front seat kissing me.

The clouds hung over Millaa. Data collection would be complete in a few days. For all our trapping, Jeff and I had not succeeded in catching a spotted quoll. Either the fragments were too small to sustain them, they were too smart for our traps, or they had died out.

Bill was sequestered in his room, completing his thesis. Papers and data covered the ping-pong table. It was time for me to go.

I had arranged with Lawrie to leave my things with him at the movie theater in town. I would be carrying a small backpack only.

Bill was concerned when I told him of my plans to travel with Jeff. There was nothing out west, just a few stations, scattered towns, and roadhouses. Red earth and blue sky country.

I put my pack in the jeep. Bill leaned in the window.

"Where will you go after the Mitchell Plateau?" he asked.

"The Tanami, I guess."

"You know that's a desert, right? That's where those kids died. Don't disappear out there. Give me a call when you get back to civilization."

Jeff and I took the single-lane road west through Ravenshoe and the red dirt town of Mount Garnet – a boomtown in the days when tin and nickel were worth something.

"That's more like it," Jeff shouted when we crossed the Great Dividing Range into the dry outback and a plume rose off the tires, "dust!"

After five months of mud, we were heading into the dry country. We drove past endless termite mounds and scattered black iron–bark trees. We crossed empty creek beds with names like Battle Creek and Dinner Creek not far from places like the You and Me Mine. The mines and the great tin sluices were abandoned.

Mount Garnet had an impressive horse track and grandstand for a place that, as far as I could tell, had only five inhabitants – one of them a beautiful girl riding a horse beside the road just outside town. In the empty stables, chalk still marked the names of the horses that had been quartered there years before: Lunar Luck, Rum Trip, Cavalletto.

At the roadhouse in Mount Garnet I talked with an old woman who said she hadn't seen rain for four years "before last Tuesday." Go fifteen miles east, I told her, there's plenty of it in Millaa Millaa. Judging from the meat in my steakburger, times were tough for the cattle industry in Queensland.

After Mount Garnet the road stretched to the horizon. It was so flat we could almost see the curvature of the earth. We encountered kangaroos, flocks of galahs and cockatoos, several wedge-tailed eagles, millions of flies, and even a large flightless bird called a bustard, but no humans. We pulled off the road somewhere past the Burke and Wills roadhouse, a gas station and small store, a hundred fifty miles from The Isa, as the locals call Mount Isa, a mining town in central Queensland. Moribund trees rose out of the hardscrabble soil. Termites were everywhere. It was dead quiet. After a dinner of rice and sardines I strung my hammock up between two anemic trees, an inch above a termite mound. The termites waited underneath all night with antennae bristling in the moonlight.

I tried to get to sleep before Jeff started snoring. A single road train whistled by in the night. I heard it coming from a long way off in the stillness. Caterina would be driving past this way to Ayers Rock. Should I stand beside the road and flag her down? Maybe I'd meet her at the fountain in Kings Cross.

The next day we came into Mount Isa, a copper mine with two gigantic smoke stacks rising above the town, belching smoke.

"I have the Queen of England's smoke in my lungs," a man said to me outside the Kmart. Apparently the Queen owns a controlling interest in the mine.

"What the hell's a Kmart doing out here in the outback?" I asked Jeff.

"You have to buy your fishing gear somewhere. They've got one in Alice too."

CHAPTER 7

BY THE ROAD

Driving south from the Mitchell Plateau, Jeff and I passed through the tiny town of Turkey Creek. It was a place with a sense of humor. T-shirts in the window of the only roadhouse confidently proclaimed, Paris, Rome, New York, Turkey Creek. We headed toward Halls Creek, a small town near the southern edge of the Kimberley and the Tanami Desert. From there we planned to drive the Tanami Track to Alice Springs in the red center. Where I went from there I wasn't sure.

The Tanami Track is one of the longest dirt roads in the world. It stretches six hundred miles from just outside Halls Creek to Alice Springs. There is only one gas station along the track's entire length, halfway at a place called Rabbit Flat. I hadn't realized before what a crowded world I'd been living in. The outback was so remote that people actually waved by lifting an index finger off the steering wheel when they passed each other on the highway. It was called the Territory wave.

Australia at that time had a population of about sixteen million people. The country itself is almost as large as the continental United States. I began to realize then that freedom is a function of population. As one historian wrote a century ago, "The practical liberty of America is to be found in its large size and small population." The same could be said of Australia today.

A steady puree of insect parts and dust came from the air vents on the dashboard. Late in the afternoon, fifty miles outside of Halls Creek, the engine shuddered and died. We rolled forward twenty yards.

"Shit," Jeff said.

We stepped out into the silence of the Great Sandy Desert. I looked at Jeff. We both looked at the jeep. Jeff lifted the hood, and while I cranked the engine over he attempted to locate the problem. The engine turned over but would not start.

"Damn," Jeff said and put down a screwdriver.

"What is it?" I asked.

"Points."

For half an hour we adjusted the distance between the points with a feeler gauge and dumb luck. The engine fired and the jeep traveled fifty joyous feet before it quit again with a shattering sound.

"Not good," Jeff said. "Definitely not good."

With what tools we carried we attempted to rebuild the distributor, a small device that sends current to the spark plugs in a precise sequence. Several critical pieces had broken off.

Our reality suddenly became very small: a pair of pliers, a Swiss Army knife, a few broken pieces of wire, a sea of sand and stunted bushes stretching in all directions, and eight gallons of water in the back. Jeff stepped away from the engine.

"Good thing this didn't happen farther north," he said. I was not entirely reassured.

In the outback, when one sees a motorist by the side of the road, one pulls over to offer assistance as a matter of course. A person can be stuck for days, weeks even, once their vehicle has ground to a halt. As we had reached a main highway, we knew someone would come by eventually.

So we waited, reading, sleeping, or just thinking. I chased a flock of white cockatoos by the side of the road. They ascended into the sky, squawking and beating the air with their wings like indignant houseguests tossed out of a party by an ungracious host.

They flew off, leaving me to walk across the flat land in silence. For the first time in my life I wasn't in any hurry. Time was just something that went past.

Stars hung between the moonlit branches of a ghost gum. After one cold night and the better part of the next day a cloud of dust appeared followed by the sound of an engine. A pickup truck of stone-faced Aboriginals came to an abrupt halt. The driver, wearing cowboy boots and a hat with outrageously colorful feathers sticking out at all angles, leaped from the cab. He looked at Jeff and me and pointed to the car with a questioning look.

"Won't go?" he asked. We shook our heads.

"I'll tow you into town if you like." He retrieved a rope from the truck and tied it to the hitch. The people riding in the back, two snow-haired men and a young boy, did not shift position, nor did they direct their gaze upon anything but the flat, dry land stretching behind them as the towrope slackened and pulled. They looked right through us.

The boy was a few years younger than I, dressed in faded jeans and a long-sleeved shirt, sitting barefoot between the two old men.

"Law student," Jeff said, nodding toward the boy.

Coming from the northeastern United States with its law colleges of Harvard and Yale, I couldn't imagine a less likely law school candidate.

Jeff explained, "He's probably just been out with the elders to the sacred sites, learning the Dreamtime rituals and stories of his tribe. Learning the law."

The law, Jeff explained, was a law older than that codified by Justinian or Hammurabi.

72

The word *Aborigine* comes from the Latin *ab origine* meaning "from the beginning." They have certainly been in Australia a long time. Aboriginal law reveres continuity; and Aboriginal lore and traditions place great emphasis on their ancestors, the land, and coming generations.

The Aboriginal people had no written language, lived in a stone-age culture, and were still hunter-gatherers when an enlightened but perhaps overly optimistic Captain Cook observed them in 1779. He wrote:

> They may appear to some to be the most wretched people on Earth but in reality they are far happier than we Europeans; being wholly unacquainted not only with the superfluous but with the necessary conveniences so much sought after in Europe, they are happy in not knowing the use of them. They live in a tranquillity which is not disturbed by the inequality of condition; the Earth and the sea of their own accord furnish them with all things necessary for life; they covet not magnificent houses, household stuff &c, they sleep as sound in a small hovel or even in the open as the king in his palace on a bed of down . . .

That condition changed with the arrival of the first fleet of English convicts and soldiers in 1788. The English ruling class held strong beliefs about private property and transported man, woman, and child to the other side of the world for crimes against property. To the Aboriginals, this was absurd.

The English declared Australia *terra nullius*, empty land, and so justified their taking possession of the continent in English common law. This ruling has since been overturned in 1992 in the Native Title (or Eddie Mabo) land rights case. By a majority of six to one, the full bench of the High Court ruled that indigenous title to land is recognized in the common law of Australia, throwing out forever the legal fiction that the continent in 1788 was *terra nullius*.

From the High Court, Justice Brennan wrote: "There may be other areas of Australia where an Aboriginal people, maintaining their identity and their customs, are entitled to enjoy their native title." Further, he wrote: "The nation as a whole must remain diminished unless and until there is an acknowledgment of, and retreat from, those past injustices."

If the United States Supreme Court were to arrive at a similar finding of law, it would give Georgia back to the Cherokees.

Later I was to meet some urban Australians who complained about the money wasted in an attempt to bring Aboriginal living standards up to those of the industrialized world. What the modern Australians failed to recognize was the existence of an entirely different value system in Aboriginal culture. I was surprised that I had failed to recognize even the possibility of a different value system from the one I had grown up with.

It was as if I had stepped out of my world for a moment, and could look at it with an objective eye. I realized with a shock that what I thought of as my education, supposedly grounded in science and fact, was as much religion as education, as much ideology as science. Schools weren't really places of independent learning where people arrived at reasoned conclusions about the nature of the world – schools were the churches of an industrialized planet, complete with the factory bell.

"Americans are brainwashed," Jeff responded when I men—tioned my thoughts. "Forget about violence on TV. Do you know how many car ads you've seen by the time you're sixteen?"

There seemed to be no other way to explain the absurdities that I had accepted without even questioning: the efficient pro-duction of superfluities for consumption; the sixth mass extinction, which man has presided over; the overpopulation and pollution of the planet; the control of the airwaves by commercial interests, the profound materialism. The young Aboriginal boy would have been as mystified by my education as I was by his.

We passed a narrow dirt road off to our right, winding into the scrub.

"Wolf Creek meteorite crater is up that track," Jeff said. "A million years ago a large meteorite landed there. Outside Alice we'll pass a crater formed about ten thousand years ago. The Aboriginals still recount that impact in their oral traditions." Jeff smiled. "If you measure the success of a culture by its longevity – the Aboriginal people have everybody beat."

After hours of jolting corrugations and dust, the paved road began – we were coming into town. We passed the town oval, a field of dry grass for rugby, and ended up unceremoniously in the mechanics' yard. Hulks of rusted vehicles lined the lot, decaying into the red sand just before the garage. Jeff and I hoped it was not an omen. The man again leaped out of the truck, untied the towrope and, nodding at us, drove off with the elders and the young law student still staring into space.

I stepped out of the jeep. This was the first year of my "time off." I stood with Jeff beside the road at Halls Creek, surrounded by spatial and temporal immensities, wondering what happens next. It was like learning to breathe for the first time.

CHAPTER 8

THE ACADEMY

Man cometh forth like a flower, and is cut down.

Job 14:2

The distance from Boston is measured from the gold dome of the Massachusetts Statehouse. When I thought about all those miles between me and home, and how I would cover them when the time came, I wondered if I would ever make it back.

Five miles south of Boston, in a quiet town, lies the campus of Milton Academy. Founded in 1798 under the auspices of the academy movement, and intended to replace the old colonial Latin grammar schools in the fledgling republic, Milton Academy was one of the first academies chartered in the New World. In some years two-thirds of its graduating class attend Harvard.

Sam Adams railed against the academy movement in his inaugural address as governor of Massachusetts in 1795. He believed the academies were undemocratic and a threat to the new republic because "none excepting the more wealthy, generally speaking, can avail themselves of the benefits of the academies." To some, the academy movement represented an "enclosure" movement in education: just as the English aristocracy had fenced in formerly common land, the academies threatened to fence in education and take it out of the public weal.

I was sent to Milton in the fall of my fourteenth year to continue my formal education. I noticed that Centre Street, where campus was located, had the English spelling. My mother said goodbye to me in the parking lot, and I toted a footlocker up the stairs to my room in the alcoves of Hallowell House.

Hallowell House sat on one corner of campus and looked out across the sloping lawns toward the gymnasium and the brick dormitories of Robbins, Walcott, and Forbes Houses. Across the lawn was the Strauss Library, donated by the family of two victims of the *Titanic*.

Elms threw shade on the manicured lawns. Next to Hallowell sat the ivy-covered stone chapel, perched on a hill overlooking the playing fields and squash courts. From the outside it looked like a compact medieval castle with its commanding tower and ramparts.

I moved into a freshman alcove in Hallowell House with my fellow freshmen, boys with names like MacArthur, Mather, Bisbee, Sigourney, Tennille, and Freeman. The student body was principally composed of blue-eyed, yellow-haired Saxons, and slender, dark-haired Normans, with some African-American, Asian, and international students. Most of us had grown up in New York, Washington, and Boston. In the house system all four classes, from freshman to senior, lived together in the dorm under the guidance of a housemaster.

I knew that the academic curriculum would be intense, but I assumed that as I was now fourteen and hair was beginning to grow under my arms, practical aspects of my education would be addressed by degrees: issues of greater personal freedom and responsibility, the elemental and cultural realities of sex and alcohol, and some of the more philosophical and spiritual questions that occur at adolescence before the strangeness of the world has worn off. I assumed that I would be given the freedom to develop my own mental perspective on the world. I made one more funda— mental mistake: I assumed I would be treated like a man.

The seniors quickly recognized the more colorful characters in the class and tested them. In our first weeks MacArthur and I were dragged outside by upperclassmen. While a senior sat on our stomachs and another pinned our arms, they typed a letter home.

"Dear Mom," they intoned, digging into our chests with their fingers. "Ding!" they slapped us in the face to mimic the return key. "School is going great . . . Ding!" Another slap. "I am so happy here . . ." The letter continued for several paragraphs until we were red with pain. Remembering to breathe, I discovered, was the key to controlling pain. MacArthur possessed the rarest quality of defiance. When the letter home was over, he was dragged across campus by his heels, still cursing his tormentors. I picked myself up from the grass.

On the pool table, rather than lagging for break, one senior instituted a procedure called "lagging for wedgie." The freshman whose ball ended up farthest from the bumper received a wedgie. We had to compete, and went one at a time while the seniors looked on, studiously measuring the distance between balls – as though it were all very proper and logical, with explicit rules – before ripping the unfortunate's underwear up and off. It was a microcosm of what was taking place in the school at large.

MacArthur was a New Yorker, with longish hair and the sort of questioning and irreverent attitude that immediately made him a target of upperclassmen, insecure teachers, and, ultimately, the dean. He garnered the respect of the seniors by punching out various sophomores who, by virtue of their rank, thought he would not resist them. MacArthur's character was such that he returned from Christmas break with twenty new pairs of underwear that year. Then he stopped wearing underwear altogether.

Due to the house's antiquated water system, the first two

students to take showers in the morning received hot water. The other thirty-eight stepped into cold showers every morning before setting out into the frigid New England climate. For those of us who paid attention to the absurdities, prep school was a strange, strange experience.

The rules of the school were enclosed in the "blue book," a thin, puritanical guide to the prohibited activities of the school.

"Girl visitors are allowed on Friday evenings and Saturday if they are signed in, lights must be left on, and four feet must remain on the floor at all times. Is that their idea of foreplay?" MacArthur leaned back at his desk and flipped through the blue book. "Do they expect me to graduate from this place a virgin?"

MacArthur was failing Latin, and his father had insisted he retake Latin over the summer. He returned in sophomore year to tell us that he had had intercourse for the first time, with his thirty-four-year-old Latin tutor.

"No way!" I looked at him with a mixture of surprise, circumspection, and envy. MacArthur was unpacking his clothes and books, preparing for the academic year.

"I'm telling you, man, it happened." MacArthur unpacked all manner of cultural objects retrieved from faraway places: a carved head, ceramic bowls, a decrepit stuffed freshwater crocodile from Indonesia. His room bore the look of an Arabic harem, with tapestries adorning the walls.

"How was it?" I asked, awed that this gulf had now been thrown between us. He had crossed the last great threshold of youth: carnal knowledge — what one classmate described in a poem as the "dark triangle obscured by miles, trees, and smoke."

He smiled. "It was good. I felt kind of weird at first, screwing my Latin tutor, but I got used to it."

I bet you did, I thought, looking at him. Could you tell just by looking at someone if they were a virgin or not?

"That's unbelievable."

"She wrote me letters about it."

"No way."

"I can show them to you – they're right here." He unzipped a duffel bag and pulled out several pages of writing. In the letters I made out words and phrases – "love you," "miss you," "want to see you", "let's get together" – my God, I thought, it's all true. The sexual hypocrisy of the adult world was laid bare. I considered taking Latin.

At the academy, public displays of affection, what we called touching, were prohibited by the PDA rule. Being out after curfew was prohibited. Alcohol and drugs were prohibited, but in that closed society of money, privilege, and parental indifference we had access to all kinds of drugs: marijuana, cocaine, LSD. Children of busy parents are subject to whole ranges of experience their parents know nothing about, and dormitories are great places to distill such experience.

Nonetheless, I did well in my studies. In the fall of my sophomore year I walked across campus. The salty smell of the ocean rolling up the Neponset River lifted me out of my routine. Any Milton graduate will remember this smell.

It was this salt air that propelled the Forbes brothers to take to the sea from Boston, New Bedford, and Nantucket, in their Cape Horners, Yankee Clippers, and Indiamen, and return with a fortune to Massachusetts. John Murray Forbes and his brother left these shores in 1830 as penniless teenagers on a sailing ship, and returned from the China trade with an endowment for the financially strapped Milton Academy. A third brother drowned in Canton harbor. Any institutional education should include a history of the institution.

At Milton I attempted to step back and assemble a larger picture from the discrete units of information I gathered from my courses, without success. There was no holistic approach to my education, no coherence. I wanted to know why I was studying pre-calculus, chemistry, advanced topic history, English. Biology? I wanted to experience some of my own, first hand, and report back to my fellows. At fifteen it was the most important part of becoming a man. But as long as I did the work and passed the tests, it didn't matter. Getting into the right college was the point of my education, as far as the institution was concerned.

I took the standardized tests, SATs, which purportedly measure scholastic aptitude. I sat in a room with two hundred other sweating students, filling in small ovals with number 2 pencils, regretting the industrial approach to my education. Did they want to create standardized humans? I would be evaluated by machine, another product of mass production, factory-assembled like Henry Ford's motorcars, rendered almost incapable of questioning the process itself: college, career, money, retirement.

And I was a student of privilege.

Every Sunday the boarders from the boys' dorms, about a hundred young men in all, had dinner in the dining room with the girls in their Sunday best from the girls' dorms, Faulkner, Hathaway, and Goodwin, a ten-minute walk on the road running past the Milton cemetery. We dressed in jackets and ties, the girls in charcoal wools, tweeds, and silk stockings.

In the November air, MacArthur and I walked in a loose procession with other friends from the dining hall, past the old brick dorms and the gymnasium filled with silver trophies marking the athletic triumphs of previous generations. We filed into the chapel past solemn teachers, and the dean of the school, a tall, curly red-haired man of dour expression and humor: Jack MacKinnon.

Sunday chapel, ostensibly nondenominational, was compulsory for the student boarding community. The hardwood pews, stained-glass windows, and a chapel organ lent credence to the words of the Christian hymn, "a mighty fortress is our God."

MacKinnon was quite a tall man, around forty, with red downy hair growing from every pore of his body, down to his fingers. He spoke in a raspy, almost choked voice, as though someone had his gonads in a vice. He had studiously cultivated the mannerisms of propriety.

He had picked out MacArthur and me, already the target of hazing by upperclassmen, as troublemakers of a sort. MacArthur had shoulder-length hair, and neither of us responded well to intimidation. We were still learning what sort of troublemakers we were.

MacKinnon looked severely at us. He sucked in his cheeks disapprovingly.

"MacArthur! Chaffey!" he said. We were taken out of line, to condolences or smirks from the faces that filed past on their way to the pews.

Over the splenetic sound of the chapel organ, MacKinnon pointed to MacArthur's ankles. "Where are your socks, Andrew?"

"I was doing laundry. They didn't dry in time," MacArthur said.

"You couldn't borrow a pair of socks from your friend here?" MacKinnon looked very annoyed. The obsequiousness MacKinnon had anticipated was not forthcoming.

"You're supposed to wear socks to chapel, Andrew," he said, taking him by the shoulder. "You will sit with me."

Memorial plaques lined the chapel walls – so-and-so lost at sea, so-and-so drowned in rapids near Ottawa. We all stood to the familiar strain of the chapel organ. "And did those feet in ancient time / Walk upon England's mountains green? . . . and was the Holy Lamb of God . . ."

Tonight we had a guest speaker who set the place on fire.

The Reverend Stith, a black pastor in Roxbury and Boston, stood up and said black Americans "*was* ready, *been* ready, *past* ready!" for an equal place at the table.

After his speech the gospel singers came on. Black women and men in robes with white satin collars. They were our neighbors, having taken the bus from Mattapan and Roxbury. If Mattapan was the wrong side of the tracks, then boarding school was another country.

The singers filed out in front of the gathered faces stretching into the far recesses of the chapel. There was a hushed and uncomfortable silence. They collectively took a breath, opened their mouths, and began to sing, swaying back and forth, rubbing shoulders and hips and singing together from a place deep in their hearts. A powerful voice converged in the space above our heads; the voice of shared human trial and hope, the message of joy, brotherhood, and the indomitable human spirit. Hallelujah! I had never experienced anything like it in school.

I felt a tremendous desire to get to my feet and clap my hands, but I didn't. One brave man, a sophomore in the second row from the front, stood up and began to sway with the voices. The girl next to him stood up and then the whole row got to its feet, joined hands and rocked back and forth. I stood up.

MacKinnon sat bright red in his chair. He was enraged. He saw my face turn around in the crowd.

After chapel we filed out in the dark to our dormitories. MacKinnon gave the boy a dressing down outside the chapel for all the students to hear as they walked past.

The student had violated the PDA rule. The student's behavior was "out of control." And apparently standing up was not allowed in chapel. What about feeling? I wondered as I walked past. What about spirit? Our education was not about such things. We were being instructed, whether we knew it or not, in a "non-denominational," Protestant, secular materialism.

The boy, whose name was John, didn't care what MacKinnon thought, and told him so. John left Milton that semester in the middle of his sophomore year.

We lost a lot of interesting characters by the end of their sophomore years. They were the students with self-possession, the forthright personalities and independent thinkers. I do wonder what raw genius, what bold visionaries and strong leaders were discarded or not "asked back" as a result of this homogenizing process. Those with views of the possible, those characters who considered what the world might be or ought to be, the eccentrics and dreamers of the aristocratic classes who attended prep school, were removed from the very institutions that might have promoted them. The best of them never made it into Harvard.

"Quiet – someone's there." We crouched near a bush by the chapel door. A teacher walked by near the squash courts. We watched him disappear through the woods over by the faculty housing.

"All clear," MacArthur whispered. I lifted a pane, and we slipped in through the window. The chapel was silent. A dim blue light fell through a stained-glass window. We moved quietly up to the second floor. MacArthur lifted the pin of the locked door to the belfry by the chapel organ. Strictly off limits.

We walked the narrow causeway inside the tower, our footsteps amplified.

"Shh," MacArthur held his finger to his lips somewhere in the thrilling darkness. Up the rickety wooden stairs to the cupola, past the bell, we felt our way.

There was a ruffling explosion above our heads.

"Whaa – what the hell was that?"

"Pigeons."

"Jesus."

We pushed out of the darkness through a trapdoor in the roof and onto the top of the chapel, a castle parapet overgrown with ivy, bathed in moonlight. We were free. No one would think to look for us here.

Through the jagged ramparts atop the chapel roof we contemplated the stars, and the lights of campus below. The height of the chapel roof offered a different perspective on the institution. We looked toward the John Hancock Building rising over downtown Boston, carrying our gaze through 360 degrees. The gleaming towers of glass and steel pointed to the sky.

"That's Orion right there, the Hunter," I said. "And there's the North Star. See, the two stars of the Big Dipper point to it." A cloud wheeled toward the crescent moon and a single planet, and for a moment it seemed the cloud was still, and we felt the Earth itself revolving in the heavens.

MacArthur and I studied the campus below in the cold night air. We had learned to hate sitting inside at our desks. We were being broken in to the mundane, the routine, before the most fundamental of our questions had been addressed – questions of self-knowledge, of faith, of sacred and secular knowledge and understanding, of direction and meaning.

The chapel roof was where we oriented our own compasses, made our own observations on the world. This was our other education, our education in being young and free. We tested our strength and stealth and daring by climbing up every roof on campus. We tested our courage by walking alone through the graveyard long after dark. Such activities, if discovered, would result in immediate expulsion because they were against the rules but, more importantly, meant that the institution's attempts at controlling our inner lives – what William Blake called "the mind-forg'd manacles" – had failed.

We stood in the November wind, hoping to chart a course across the wide, strange maelstrom of youth. The chapel roof was a sacred vantage to us. It was a place from which we examined our lives in the context of a wider reality. The roof of our church was the sky.

"We'd get kicked out for this," MacArthur said, looking over the ramparts. "It's as if they don't want us to think for ourselves."

"We don't even have *time* to think for ourselves."

It would have been impossible to explain to our teachers, or the dean, or more importantly the Discipline Committee, how much we learned from these excursions, in moments of comprehending joy, when we discussed our life's dreams, engaged in wild speculations about history, free will, destiny and fate, philosphy and religion, when we considered our Utopias, when our companions were the night air, the moon and stars and planets, and we could think, for a few precious hours, our own thoughts.

That summer MacKinnon used his discretionary powers to kick out MacArthur and several other students from the dorms. Though MacArthur had committed three years to the school, was liked by his peers and teachers, and did well in the courses he was interested in, he was also a strong character and so he had no place at Milton. I exhorted him to stay and graduate, to be defiant as he had been for so long, but MacArthur had had enough of Jack MacKinnon.

"What's the point?" MacArthur said over the phone, "I don't want him to fuck with my life anymore." I hung up realizing that I was the only undesirable left.

Now that MacArthur was gone, the dean could concentrate on getting rid of me. One night I gave him his chance. Riding on a bike after curfew, drunk on wine and acceleration, I went to join some friends at a gathering. The next thing I remember was lifting my head off the road and watching my blood pool onto the concrete.

MacKinnon could hardly conceal his glee when I walked into his office a week later, having sufficiently recovered from my injuries to return to school. I felt like I was dying.

"You know this is a very serious offense, Will. You're supposed to be an example for the students." MacKinnon had me right where he wanted me. He and I both knew it.

That afternoon I sat before the Discipline Committee with four broken teeth, a fractured eye socket, blood leaking into my eye, cuts on my head, face, and legs, a split lip, and a broken wrist. After a four-hour dressing down and with an admonition that the results of this DC would accompany my high school transcript when I applied to college, I was told I could leave the room. I had learned the most important lesson prep schools teach: how to exercise power without remorse.

MacKinnon studied me for a moment, a young man struggling with issues much larger than the ones they taught in school, who in a single stroke had discovered his own mortality. I had learned conclusively that I was not a god, that we lead finite lives. Many young people don't survive that lesson: they die in car accidents; some kill themselves.

With feigned sincerity the dean asked, "How are you, Will, really?" He was adept at playing the role of paternal friend.

I looked out the window, wishing that for five minutes he could be just a man and not a dean, so that I could tell him how sad I was, how much this hurt, youth.

"I'm all right," I said. "I'll survive."

MacKinnon had one other great power. He wrote the dean's letter that accompanied our sealed transcripts to college admissions offices.

CHAPTER 9

FRANK AND EARL

The violence of raging thirst knows no parallel in the catalog of human calamities.

Owen Chase

Frank and Earl wiped the grease off their hands and looked at us. Jeff and I did not relish the thought of being stuck in Halls Creek for three weeks, waiting for parts. My plan was to continue with Jeff to Alice Springs and then head south to Melbourne to look for work. I had only a few dollars left.

Frank and Earl might, had they been the unscrupulous sort of mechanic one is likely to encounter at the junction of three vast deserts, have taken advantage of the fact that we were more than a thousand miles from a second opinion. I have heard of a man who was charged four hundred dollars by such a mechanic in Nevada for replacing a set of spark plugs – but not Frank and Earl.

Though bathed in grease, Frank and Earl moved as if in meditation. They knew exactly where every piece of equipment in the shop was, even though it might be at the bottom of a pile of other equipment.

"Bush mechanics," Jeff explained when Frank and Earl were out of carshot.

A wall calendar for the year 1974 with a bikini-clad blonde hung in one corner of the garage.

"She was a particularly good year," Frank said when he saw me studying the calendar. Time was a relative concept out here. So were women.

Shifting the linkage of a gearbox, Frank paused to look at me in the shade of the garage.

"Where're you from?" he asked, pulling a piece of steel out of a pile.

"Boston." I replied.

"Boston," Frank scratched his head. "Huh. Let's see, I got a postcard the other day from a woman in Saskatchewan. Anywhere near Boston?"

"Not really," I said, "that's in Canada."

"Saskatchewan. Imagine naming a place Saskatchewan." He scratched his head.

I didn't remind him that Australia had towns like Oodnadatta and Innamincka and Koombooloomba.

"So you're a Yank," he said matter-of-factly. It still felt strange to think of myself as a Yankee, a term likely derived from Yengee, which was how the Massachusetts aboriginals pronounced the name of their new neighbors: the English.

"Pass me that spanner there," he said, pointing. "Is there much outback round Boston?"

"No," I said, suddenly surprised to think in such terms. "Not anymore."

"Don't really know much about Boston." He wiped grease on his overalls. "Wait a minute, they had some sort of tea party?"

The epochs of history did indeed have fewer contours out here in the desert.

It seemed strange to trace the fact that I was speaking English with this man – and not Dutch or French – to the Lexington Green and the Concord North Bridge. Australia's colonial beginnings are linked *directly* to the American Revolution that began in New England with "the shot heard round the world."

It is not commonly written of in high school textbooks, but initially America was the principal dumping ground for English convicts. After losing the American colonies, the English needed a new place to put criminals. After looking at Africa, they decided on Australia in 1788, in no small part due to the encouragement of Joseph Banks, recently returned from Captain Cook's voyages of discovery. Australia never fought a war of independence and is still a member of the British Commonwealth.

"Boston, Massachusetts, isn't it?" He shook his head in wonder.

"You're a long way from home," Frank said, stepping over a half-assembled engine, pistons strewn about like metal ribs. "What're you doing here?" He removed some spark plugs from a truck engine with a long wrench while I leaned on a bumper. I didn't really know what to tell him.

"My friend and I were bushwalking up north, near the coast."

"You want to be careful up there," he responded gravely. "Dangerous country. Especially near the coast. Crocodiles taking you Yanks by the mouthful lately." He examined the contacts on a spark plug. "You heard about that girl?" he asked.

I nodded, aware that a young American woman, Ginger Meadows, who had traveled to Australia for the America's Cup, had been taken by a crocodile three months before.

"Hey," he said, "how do you separate two fighting crocs?"

I shrugged.

"Give them a Yank," he said, laughing. "Get it?"

He stopped laughing. "They found those two boys, though. Guess you heard about that. We knew they'd turn up sooner or later." He looked over at Earl in the yard. "Real tragedy."

I had heard about them on the news while still in North Queensland. The boys, James Annetts, sixteen, and Simon Amos, seventeen, had been working as jackaroos, or ranch hands, up on Flora Valley Station. On their way to Alice Springs for Christmas, they had disappeared along with a white truck they had been driving. Their intention had been to take the Tanami Track from Halls Creek into the back door of Alice Springs, just as Jeff and I were hoping to do.

An extensive land and air search had been conducted without turning up a trace of the boys. There was so much empty space out here. Speculation arose that they had met with foul play.

"Couple of surveyors found their truck last month. Suppose you heard about that," Frank said.

The images on the television screen had been stark and riveting: a white truck, a small speck in an ocean of sand and scattered shrubs. It was five months since the boys had gone missing.

The footage, shot from an airplane, showed the wheels buried in sand and, as the camera moved closer, an arrow fashioned out of stones pointing in a direction away from the truck. Ten miles in that direction searchers found the remains of Simon Amos, shot through the head with a .22 caliber rifle. James Annetts' body was found little more than a mile farther on. He had died of thirst after carving a final message into the water jug he carried.

Apparently the older boy had committed suicide, or Annetts had killed his friend, dying of thirst in the one-hundred-ten-degree heat and no longer able to continue, out of mercy. The empty water jug was found beside James Annetts. He had scratched his last words into the plastic: "My follt. I allways love you mum and Jason Michelle and Joanne. I found peece." Footage showed authorities loading the boys' bodies into the back of a truck in black bags.

"We were part of the search," Frank told me. "Everybody was.

We looked for two weeks, but there's no way we would have found them because we were looking in the wrong area. They missed the sign to Alice and headed off on a surveyor's track. Got stuck in a sand dune."

Jeff and Earl were outside examining the jeep's engine with the grave, disgusted air of men conducting a postmortem. Those boys probably wished to God emphatically, any god, sitting in the shade of their immobilized truck, lost and thirsty, for some intervening miracle to get them unstuck. The parting of the Red Sea, the visitation of angels, what was that in comparison to the trifling removal of a truck stuck in a sand dune? I imagined their despair as the wheels turned in the sand. Please God . . . Nature is indeed no sentimentalist.

One time I fished for blues off Cape Cod with a friend in a sixteen-foot aluminum boat. We had been fishing for several hours about three miles out to sea, and had seen a large shadow pass under the hull. My friend and I were both twelve years old. When we attempted to start the Johnson outboard in the afternoon, it only coughed and died. Frantically, we pulled the starter, manipulated the choke, checked the fuel line, cleaned the spark plug – to no avail. The anchor slipped in the sand. Land drifted out of sight. The afternoon fast became evening, and the waves picked up. We prayed for some intervening miracle, some trick of physics for the engine to run, but it would not. Fortunately, a passing fishing boat towed us to shore.

Without help, the boys waited by the vehicle, probably for four or five days. After all, it was on a road – people should be passing through that way, right?

"It's not likely we would have found them," Frank said. With a stick he drew a circle in the sand. "We were looking south of Halls Creek, toward Alice, whereas they were really in the northwest. Here." He touched the stick outside the circle. "They were just young boys from Adelaide."

"Even if they'd had lots of water, they wouldn't have made it. The body loses a liter an hour in that heat. They didn't drink the radiator water, which is surprising. When you get that thirsty, you'll drink anything." Frank looked at me, sizing me up.

"Tell you what they should've done," he said, pausing to take a handkerchief out of his back pocket. "Once they'd decided they couldn't get the truck out, they should have waited for several days. One of them had called his mother before leaving, and she expected to hear from them when they reached Alice – so they could count on people looking for them when they didn't show up. After a couple of days they should've set one of the truck's tires on fire – there was plenty of fuel left in the tank. It's not likely, but it's possible that someone might have seen it from the air. If they'd lit one every couple of days, they might have been rescued."

Instead, they had made a cardinal mistake: leaving the vehicle to walk perhaps a hundred miles to a more heavily traveled road. They did not make even a tenth of that distance.

"Whole thing seems a little strange to me, I must say," Frank continued. "There's going to be an inquiry. I heard they found several hundred dollars of the boys' earnings hidden in their room."

Frank put a boot on the bumper of the jeep. "Now tell me, if you're not planning on coming back, do you leave your money behind?"

"No," I said.

"'Course not," he continued. "Maybe somebody got angry and hit one of the boys, hit him so hard he killed him – then they've got to cover it up. But I'm not saying that's what happened, I'm just saying it doesn't add up."

Frank paused and looked over at Earl and Jeff in a corner of the yard. "It's a different world up here. People from down south don't understand that. You Yanks don't understand it, either.

"People forget what the sun can do to them once the air-conditioning stops working. Bring spares when you travel through this country, and plenty of water. A dead battery can kill you." He picked up a piston rod. "You were lucky this didn't happen further north. The heat up here will kill a person in one day without water, even by the side of the road. At Christmas time it's so hot you can hardly move." He wiped the grease and grit off a cylinder head and looked hard at me. "This country is *fatal* in the wet."

CHAPTER 10

TANAMI

Coming out of Halls Creek, we almost missed the sign, a hand-painted piece of wood on a fuel drum by the side of the road with the words ALICE SPRINGS in yellow letters. A little arrow pointed toward Alice. It was this sign that the two boys who died so horribly had failed to see.

"You can see why," Jeff said, as we turned down the track from the road to nowhere.

It was so quiet out here, along the Tanami Track. Frank and Earl had succeeded in fixing the distributor of the jeep. Before we left, Frank stood at one end of the garage and studied the desert.

"I'll tell you a trick," he said. "If you ever find you've got a dead battery out in the bush, jack up one of the rear wheels and get it spinning real fast, then you pop the car into second. If the wheel's spinning fast enough to overcome the compression of the engine, it'll turn over. If it doesn't . . . well, time for plan B."

He studied the red sand stretching to the low hills on the horizon. It was clear from his expression that plan B involved a great deal of suffering and probable death.

Frank and Earl charged us forty dollars to rebuild the distributor.

"We can't give you a guarantee on those parts, but they should get you to Alice," they said as we drove out.

* * *

I stood on the hard earth by the road and stretched my hands toward the sky. Another day's drive across the red desert and we'd be in Alice Springs. Jeff pulled the jeep off the road and out of sight into the scattered bushes while I followed on foot. He was still paranoid, but I was getting used to it.

I cooked some rice on his small stove and opened a can of sardines while the sky turned red.

Rousseau wrote of the "savage" that "his placid soul is wholly absorbed in the feeling of his present existence, with no idea of the future, however near it may be; and his plans, as limited as his intentions, scarcely extend to the end of the day." I was discovering a sense of this myself. Life was beginning to regain the magical quality it had possessed when I was a child.

"Why did we bring nothing but sardines and rice?"

"It's traditional," Jeff said.

"I'm getting really sick of it. We've got a stove. My God, we could be eating beef stroganoff, or spaghetti."

"Could be."

Frost was on our sleeping bags in the morning. On clear nights the temperature in the desert drops quickly after sunset as the heat radiates back into space. The antipodean winter was approaching.

I spent part of the trip trying to come up with a suitable palindrome to commemorate the journey down the Tanami.

"Able was I ere . . . No . . . A man, a plan, a thousand miles of bulldust and corrugations. No, that's not it."

"Tan am I, ere I'm a Nat," was all I came up with.

"Too bad your name's not Nat."

"My skin is pretty brown, though."

Rabbit Flat, Australia's most remote roadhouse, appeared out of the shimmering sand the next morning. We stood by the fuel pump and contemplated a sea of stunted bushes stretching away from us in all directions. It was liberating to think you could strike off into the desert at any point of the compass and not reach a paved road or habitation for thousands of miles.

The sign offered gasoline for eight dollars per gallon, the country's most expensive. Jeff bought only enough to get as far as the Aboriginal community at Yuendumu, a hundred miles on.

"It's cheaper there," he said. I pointed out that any potential savings had to be offset by the possibility of running out of gas and dying of thirst.

"Why not fill the tank up halfway at least? In case we miss it."

"I've been there before. You can't miss it – there's a big sign. It's not far."

"Is it really worth a few dollars?" I only had forty dollars left, but I would have spent it all on fuel for our jerry cans.

Back in the jeep the needle registered little more than a quarter tank.

We drove in silence over the sand for two hours. As the needle dwindled, my stomach turned.

"It's up here – not far." Jeff sounded less than assured. There were dirt tracks leading off from the Tanami Track now. Any one of them might have been to Yuendumu. One of them looked well traveled.

"Maybe that's it?" I said.

"No, probably just a station track. There's a big sign . . ."

Half an hour later the needle was in the red and Jeff clenched the wheel.

"Where is it?" I asked.

"We passed it."

I tried not to look at the fuel gauge as the jeep spun a U-turn in the sand.

"What the fuck happened to the sign? It was a big, *solid* sign."

We were running on fumes when the jeep turned down the heavily used track to Yuendumu and the gas pump.

Gas was about half the price it had been at Rabbit Flat.

"I'm still not sure it was worth it," I said as Jeff fueled up.

"What happened to the sign?" we inquired of the people we met. No one knew.

Outside Alice, two police cars were pulled over beside the road. A police officer waved us down and approached the jeep. I was surprised to see he was carrying a gun.

"Where you blokes coming from?" the officer asked, peering into the back.

"Up around Halls Creek – Gibb River Road."

"What were you doing up there?"

"Fishing," Jeff said. The police officer nodded and looked at the license plate.

"Western Australia, huh? Where'd you register this vehicle?"

"Kununurra," Jeff said.

The cop looked at me. "What's your story?"

"Just traveling," I said. "Over here from the United States."

The policeman stepped away from the car. "Why are you taking this road into Alice?"

Jeff shrugged, "It's the quickest way from where we've been."

It seemed reasonable enough.

The cop looked back the way we had come.

"There's a killer up there," he said. "Killed five people that we know of so far, including the former mayor of Fremantle and his son-in-law. They were on a fishing trip, just like you."

Jeff and I thought about the last two weeks.

The police officer continued, "The killer finds people in remote spots along the road and shoots them. I recommend you stay in town for a while. I can't let you go north again." He looked down the road toward Alice. "You'll hear all you want about it in there."

Jeff and I rode in silence for some time. Suddenly the incident at Drysdale River Station with the suspicious caretaker made sense. Whoever it was killing people up there needed fuel to move. The couple we had seen at the abandoned mining camp on the Mitchell Plateau had had their petrol siphoned out during the night by the killer. For some reason, the killer decided not to shoot this man and his wife, just leave them stranded. Five others had not been so lucky.

"We were right there," Jeff said as we pulled into town. "We would have heard the shots."

I remembered with a sick feeling how we had spent one night and a day stranded beside the road outside Halls Creek.

"He could have driven past us."

In the Alice Springs library, I leafed through the newspapers. The "Kimberley Killer" or "Top End Killer" was front-page news, and still at large. The largest manhunt in northern Australia's history was under way. The Special Air Service, an elite branch of the armed forces, had been called in.

"They won't let that fella live," a man said to me as we watched the news in the pub. "They'll kill him out there for sure. Killed five people, they reckon. That's what they've found so far. They've alerted every station by radio now, everyone's got their rifle out." He took a sip of beer. "Must've gone troppo."

"Little early for it," an old-timer offered from the bar.

Apparently, "going troppo" was a phenomenon of the Far North: in the heat and humidity building up to the wet season, people just went stark raving nuts. October and November were known as the suicide months.

The first victims, a father and son, Marcus and Lance Bullen, were found buried in shallow graves at a fishing spot near Timber Creek in the Northern Territory. From what police could determine, the victims had been told to strip naked and run for their lives. They had been killed with a .308 caliber rifle.

Then the bodies of three young travelers were found floating naked in the Pentecost River in Western Australia on June 15. After being hunted down and shot, they were apparently thrown to the crocodiles. The killer then stole their fuel and set their cars on fire. The police followed a trail of burnt-out vehicles and bodies along the Gibb River Road.

Then nothing. It appeared the killer had slipped away.

Speculation rose that a disgruntled Aboriginal was involved, as an unidentified Aboriginal man was seen near the site of the first murder.

"No way," Jeff said. "That's not their way at all."

Fear began to set in as everyone looked for the killer who they believed must have slipped back into town.

Then two men mustering horses flew over a vehicle camouflaged in the scrub near Fitzroy Crossing. They alerted police. Members of the Tactical Response Unit based at Home Valley Station sixty miles away moved in.

The man in the bar's prediction came true: the killer was shot to death in a gun battle with police and army units. Hundreds of rounds were exchanged. The killer tried to set a bushfire to cover his escape, but to no avail. He was hit by more than thirty rounds.

It emerged that the killer was a former West German army sharpshooter named Josef Schwab. He was twenty-six years old and had arrived in Australia just two months before. In Brisbane, Schwab had purchased thousands of dollars worth of rifles and ammunition before heading to the Kimberley. He told people in the gun shop he was going on a hunting safari.

He approached people in remote camping areas, told them to strip naked and run for their lives.

"You wouldn't have a chance," Jeff said. "Even if you didn't get shot, you'd die of exposure."

I now understood Jeff's purpose in staying out of sight. The couple we had met briefly at the mining camp may have been spared because the woman was also German. They were bizarre events, these killings. The wilderness was indeed a dangerous place, more so because man's rules governing his own behavior did not apply. I felt lucky to be alive.

Jeff and I were holed up in Alice and safe for the time being. I made friends with a helicopter pilot, two visiting Irish nurses, and several station hands in the little motel where we were staying. When we all pulled in to a local sandwich store with a full tank of gas the next day, there in the back of the pickup next to us was the sign for Yuendumu.

CHAPTER 11

GETTING OUT OF ALICE

The Todd River, which runs through Alice Springs and the gap between the MacDonnell Ranges, is dry most of the time. The river becomes instead a twisting swathe of sand and coolibah trees, its waters exhausted long before it reaches the ocean.

Just south of town the MacDonnell Ranges rise from the flat desert like a petrified tidal wave. Once higher than Mount Everest, the ancient mountains have been worn down so that they now rise only nine hundred feet above the surrounding plane.

In the riverbed the occasional loud shout or shriek came from beside the campfires. Above the light and sparks, black faces stumbled over the sand to urinate or vomit.

They did not see me as I walked in the darkness beyond the spheres of light, my footsteps falling softly in the sand. It was June and early winter in Alice Springs, a town almost in the dead center of the continent.

Alice hadn't changed much in real terms since its early days as a relay town for the overland telegraph line from Adelaide to Darwin, linking north and south. It remained a small island in an ocean of desert. The old telegraph house, where a man once tapped out a message to his wife in Adelaide before dying of spear wounds, still stood on the outskirts of town.

I did not approach too near the campfires as I walked, not wanting to be seen and perhaps asked for a cigarette or a drink. The Todd River bed is sacred ground to the Arrernte people around Alice Springs, and no white man is allowed to take wood from it. But that does not mean they treat it with the same respect as other sacred places. It is littered with empty beer bottles and wine casks. Many Aboriginal people have not yet adjusted to what Nietzsche called "the two great European narcotics, alcohol and Christianity."

I had twenty dollars to my name and few prospects for gainful employment. It appeared I might be stuck in Alice. It struck me as I walked across the riverbed under a million stars, on the edge of this edge of civilization, that I was quite alone. If the telephone had rung at any time of the day or night in the simple motel where I was staying, it would not be for me.

Sitting down on a fallen tree along the riverbed, I buried my feet in the sand and listened to a road train whistle south to Adelaide. Jeff and I would be parting ways as soon as I could find a ride out of town. The jeep's engine had exploded the day after we arrived.

"It's cactus," Rod, the helicopter pilot, said at the sound of the piston ring shattering. The motor court turned suddenly quiet. Jeff walked away from the jeep with a look of grim disgust. He had been stuck in Alice before.

I called home for the first time in five months that evening, a collect call via the operator whose Australian accent seemed so out of place in my conception of home. My father was alone in the house and accepted the call.

I told him about central Australia and the Kimberley, trying to convey a sense of the magic of this land, how much I loved Australia. I asked how everyone was at home.

"Mom and I are fine. Andrew, well, Andrew seems all right."

There was a sigh at the end of the line. "He just got out of the hospital last week. He had an accident on his motorcycle." My father referred to them as donorcycles, since so many organ donors were motorcyclists.

"Is he all right?" My older brother was not adjusting well to civilization.

"Well, he seems OK. He lost part of his foot."

"Oh no," I said, suddenly sad to be so far away.

"It's all right. They've re-attached it, but he'll be on crutches for a while. He's going to have poor circulation in that foot for the rest of his life, though." My father's voice was calm and matter-of-fact. Doctors are conditioned to disassociate themselves from pain.

"He's talking about selling his motorcycle," my father said. "That would be a relief for everyone."

When I hung up the phone, I wondered how my parents would receive the news if I were to die somewhere out here. Would they fly out to see the place where I died of thirst, fell off a cliff, or just disappeared?

The air was cold. I stared at the phone after hanging it on the hook.

I wondered about Christine, doing an internship with a law firm in Washington, D.C., now. I left so suddenly – one day working with a steady income and a steady girlfriend, the next on a plane for Australia. Should I call her?

She must have finished up her first year at Boston University by now. I remembered her apartment number, 41 Linden Street in Brighton, and her kissing me all over the face with red lipstick before I got on the train from Boston.

We had exchanged a few letters, but I had spoken to her only once since departing. She was having a party in her apartment with her roommate and some friends when I called. She seemed distant and distracted, occasionally putting her hand over the receiver. I heard laughter and commotion in the background.

We did not have any agreement when I left. I did not know when I would be returning. We were both young and evolving, but that didn't help when I imagined her mouth speaking into the receiver, her eyes looking across a room full of people.

Over the noise and sheer geographical distance I could not make her understand where I was. Maybe we didn't communicate very well on some levels after all. Here, standing by the side of the road, wearing the same clothes as I had for weeks, I realized that thinking of Christine or home was self-defeating. When I hung up the phone I would be surrounded by empty space, Christine by a room full of friends and maybe lovers. I didn't want to think about that.

I walked toward the brick bunkhouses of the motel. The fires in the riverbed were reduced to glowing coals, barely casting a light. A man cold enough to wake up threw another piece of wood on his fire.

The motel was on the southern edge of town, just inside the gap in the MacDonnell Ranges. The linoleum floor of the room I shared with Jeff was cold to my bare feet. I crawled into bed and pulled the covers over my head. Jeff had started to snore on the other side of the room.

CHAPTER 12

ALICE TO MELBOURNE

Michael Sanby, the owner of Toddy's Motel, made a fine living flying hot air balloons filled with tourists over the red and orange deserts surrounding Alice Springs. He had the largest balloon in the southern hemisphere. It carried twelve passengers, each paying a hundred fifty dollars for the privilege of floating above the desert for half an hour. The balloons launched early, before the wind picked up, and by nine in the morning Michael would be off to the bank with a sack full of cash.

His younger brother, John, was in the process of getting the hours required for his commercial license. Because of his inexperience, John had trouble finding people to go up in a balloon with him to practice landings and takeoffs. Even the prospect of a free balloon flight did not lure many people into his basket.

I had found a job. I was employed as ballast.

It was still dark when Rod came into the room.

"Get up, Will. It's time to go."

A purple dome of light grew out of the east as we drove toward the launch site, balloon in tow. John was behind the wheel. Beside him sat Vic, a Melbourne-based photographer who tipped the scales at 310 pounds. Vic was eager to take photos from the air.

"You can never have too much ballast," John said, when I mentioned quietly that maybe he had enough weight in the balloon already. "Besides, I'll need your help on landing."

"It's really no problem," John continued, in his South African accent. "The important thing to remember is, when we land, don't *immediately* jump out of the basket – because that will cause the balloon to take off again."

I wondered why previous passengers had been so eager to leave John's basket upon reaching solid ground.

By the time we assembled in the desert there were almost forty of us. We dropped the wicker gondolas off the trailer and unfurled the two nylon balloons across the ground. Michael's balloon would carry twelve paying passengers. John set up a powerful fan. I held the envelope of the balloon wide open until it was filled with air. John lit the propane burners and blasted flames into the throat. The roaring sound of the burners stopped and the balloon turned upright slowly and lifted in the sudden quiet, tugging at the ropes tied to the chase vehicle. John climbed into the basket and together he and Rod helped Vic in.

The basket was designed to fit four people comfortably. In this case it fit John, Vic, and four cameras in varying stages of extreme telephoto that Vic had strapped to his body and of which he was very protective.

"OK, hop in, Will," John said. Nearby, Michael's balloon lifted into a pink sky.

John fired the propane burners as I squeezed in beside Vic. "OK, Rod, let us go." Rod released the ropes, and we pulled away from the ground, colliding harmlessly with the top of a desert oak. Gray and pink galahs scattered from the branches.

The desert oaks grew smaller against the orange soil. John flicked off the propane burners and we drifted silently toward the MacDonnell Ranges. Vic fired away with his cameras, almost knocking me out of the basket when he turned suddenly with a three-foot-long telephoto lens. A family of red kangaroos bounded from under the trees below.

The MacDonnell Ranges turned from pink to red to orange. Whatever else you could say about Alice, the desert light was surreal.

John checked off items from his pilot's list.

"Check envelope for burns or tears. Any burns or tears? No. Check. Altitude 1,100 feet. Bearing east-northeast. Radio on. Check."

The other balloon grew tiny in the distance. We gained altitude and drifted over the MacDonnell Ranges, dotted with white ghost gums and desert oaks. The road south stretched into the flat distance. It was a long way to Adelaide.

"Not too bad up here, is it?" John said. We floated silently over a dirt road and began to lose altitude.

"Coming in for a landing, bend your knees," he said, firing the burners as we descended a little too fast. I looked at Vic to see if he was as surprised as I was at our lateral speed into the trees. We ducked into the basket and caromed off the top of a dead tree, tearing off branches. "Let's try that one again," John said, firing the burner gamely. "Here, this looks a little better!"

The basket cleared the trees and then hit the ground with a thud before bouncing into the air. Suddenly we were turning sideways. Vic scrambled to defend his lenses. John pulled mightily on the rope to vent hot air out of the balloon.

Descending again, we collided with a termite mound, which tipped us up so that I was suddenly in the bottom of the basket underneath Vic, my face inches above the dirt. We dragged for thirty yards while Vic smothered me painfully.

"Fence!" John shouted, as the wind pulled us toward the barbed wire. We stopped just before we hit it. The half-inflated balloon hung over the desert like a nylon scrotum.

"Not a bad landing, eh?"

"Will we be doing that again?"

"You're good for another practice landing, aren't you, Will? I've got twenty more to go before my test."

"Twenty?"

We crawled out of the basket, knocked the sand out of our ears, and began rolling up the balloon. I spat some dirt out of my mouth. "How's your telephoto, Vic?"

"I've got all the pictures from the air I need, thanks. I'll take pictures from the chase vehicle." Vic had already taken out a can of compressed air and was blasting the dust off his camera equipment.

"What's your twenty?" Rod's voice blurted from the radio.

"Half a mile past bugger all!" John stood up to see where we were. "No, actually we're inside the gap." Rod found us fifteen minutes later, and soon we were eating breakfast with the tourists and laughing about it all.

Rod and I spent our mornings launching, flying, and retrieving hot air balloons with John and filling up propane tanks. In return for flying with John, I received free accommodation at the motel and a chicken and champagne breakfast every morning.

But I needed to go south. I wanted to see more of Australia, and I had to find a paying job.

Travelers said Alice was the hardest place in the world to hitchhike out of. In the hostels in town, no one was advertising for fellow travelers to split gasoline costs to either Adelaide or Darwin.

Rod was sitting at the picnic table in the courtyard of the motel when I returned from the railroad tracks on the western side of town.

"Couldn't get on?" he asked.

"No," I said, dropping my pack.

I had never jumped a train before, much less the fabled Ghan. It seemed something one must do before turning twenty.

"It's too dangerous."

The hoot of the train wafted from the railyards near the gap.

"You can still catch it!" he said, laughing.

When Rod had learned of my intention to catch the Ghan out of Alice Springs, he referred to the whistle that marked the departure of the train two days a week as the Adelaide Express.

Rod was preparing to leave Alice to work down south. He had been working as a helicopter pilot for a cattle musterer in the Territory. The previous pilot had come in too low while mustering and got the skid of his helicopter caught in the curled horn of a cow and flipped over.

"What happens then?" I asked.

"It's called a dynamic rollover," Rod said.

"Is it dangerous?"

"Bloody oath it's dangerous – you've gotta front the boss and tell him you wrecked his half-million-dollar chopper."

Rod had family in Melbourne and a job running snowcats up Mount Buller in the Snowy Mountains. Rod could take apart an engine, fly a helicopter, and pull a wheelie on his 600 cc motorcycle. He could eat more than any man I had ever met. We became fast friends.

I ventured to Rod the possibility of riding on the back of his motorcycle when he journeyed back to Melbourne.

"Not a chance. Bike's too small. That ride is excruciating as it is."

"It would be an adventure."

"It would be an adventure we would never want to discuss," he said flatly. Despite our friendship, there was no way Roddy was going to take me to Melbourne on the back of his motorcycle.

Rod moved onions and sausages around a barbecue at the back of the motel. He watched me eat the same meal I had for the past two weeks: a plate of pasta with a dab of butter and some black pepper.

110

"Any good?" he asked.

"Not bad. Tasted better the first week."

"Want a sanger?"

"Please."

Rod tossed me a sausage. "How are you going to get out of Alice?"

"Bus," I said.

My new plan was to ride on the roof of a charter bus from Alice to wherever I could jump off without being noticed – somewhere in a place like Adelaide, or Melbourne. Adelaide was supposed to be a beautiful city. And I was traveling light. I walked to the bus terminal and studied the buses. It wouldn't be easy to climb onto the roof, but I could do it. And why not ride on the roof, if I could? Making your way through space creatively was the essence of travel. Rod thought it was a crazy idea.

"You can't ride on the top of a bus, you'll fall off," he said.

I abandoned the plan when the glass-carrying suction cups in the hardware store came to more money than I had. There would be no staying on the roof of the bus for eight hundred miles without them.

"Can I borrow some toothpaste?"

"No. You can have some. I don't want it back," Mike said. He was an American staying at the motel who distinguished himself by carrying the largest pack any of us travelers had yet seen. An electronics engineer, he was also riding an 1100 cc Suzuki motorcycle. I was out of everything but soap.

"The fastest production motorcycle made up to that time," he said through a mouthful of suds in the common bathroom of the motel. "Also the heaviest. You want to buy it?"

He called it the Iron Bull, and he'd been trying to sell it for a month.

"It's simple," Rod said to Mike as we watched another day disappear from the top of Anzac Hill. "You lend Will your bike, he rides it down to Melbourne, and we sell it." Rod was matter-of-fact. "I'll guarantee it."

Mike had a plane ticket out of Alice in two days.

"He needs to get to Melbourne," Rod said. "You need to sell your motorcycle. He's dependable."

Even though we were friends, Mike had only known Rod and me for two weeks. Were we that dependable? I'd borrowed the motorcycle a few times for jaunts around Alice, but a thousand miles of bad roads, narrow shoulders, kangaroos, and road trains?

In town, I'd never gone above thirty-five miles per hour. The growl of the engine and the way the bike handled around corners showed it was capable of fantastic speeds. A road machine. A donorcycle.

"I'll tell you what," Mike said, "I'll think about it."

Stones flew out from the back tire of Rod's motorcycle up ahead as Alice disappeared over our shoulders. The Stuart Highway isn't much of a road, defined more by the space around it than its blacktop. Named after John Stuart, the first white man to explore these parts, it stretches in a straight line from Darwin to Adelaide. Even at eighty miles per hour it was hard to escape the conclusion that the center of the country was immense and empty. Fortunately, there are no speed limits in the Northern Territory.

"Just send me the money," Mike had said. "And don't sell it for less than fourteen-hundred dollars. Or I'll find you and break both your legs, twice. And watch out for roos."

Rod and I roared across a vast plain heading for the distant metropolis of Melbourne – the big smoke. With the mustering over, Rod was heading south to work in the Snowy Mountains.

We turned west after the roadhouse in Erldunda. I insisted we visit Uluru, formerly Ayers Rock, the largest monolith in the world.

"What the hell's a monolith?" Rod wanted to know.

"A big rock."

From atop the weather-sculpted summit of Uluru, busloads of industrial tourists appeared like small steel larvae wending their way from the air-conditioned glass and concrete of Yulara, the nearby hotel complex. The rock rose abruptly almost a thousand feet above the surrounding red plains and shallow dunes dotted with desert oaks. The orange top of Mount Connor and the round shapes of the Olgas were visible in the distance.

The rock lies along innumerable Dreaming trails, almost in the dead center of Australia, and is of great spiritual significance to the local Pitjantjatjara and Yankuntjatjara Aboriginal tribes. I wondered how their experience of the rock differed from that of the thousands of tourists who flocked there at sunrise and sunset in the air-conditioned tour buses.

We rode the Lasseter Highway past Mount Connor and turned south at Erldunda toward the town of Coober Pedy. A swirl of red dust carried back for two miles as we entered the debris field of a road train. Designed to overcome the great distances between the cattle yards and the markets, the road train can be almost as long as a football field and consists of the cab and three trailers hitched together.

The last trailer swayed back and forth across the road like a steel whip. Passing it was like choking up the rear of a sandstorm. Rod went first, his body flinching as rocks the size of fists flew out from the fifty-two wheels.

I pulled out from the slipstream and peered down the road – ochre sand and shimmering heat melting into the blue sky, the cab rocking beside me at seventy miles per hour. With a twist of the throttle the bike roared past.

We left the trains behind and approached Coober Pedy, an opal-mining town whose Aboriginal name means "white man's hole in the ground." Conical piles of white sand from the diggings cast long shadows beside the road. Like other outback towns it offered just a few gas stations, a news vendor, half a dozen roasted chicken outlets, a pharmacy, and the lonely space on the edge of town. Some townspeople lived underground to escape summer temperatures of one hundred ten degrees.

"Want to buy an opal?" Rod asked. "I'm going to get a roast chicken for dinner. We'll take it out of town with us."

I wandered around Coober Pedy. Not much happening. We rode thirty miles from town before sundown and pulled the bikes off into the scrub by a single dead tree. The sky above Woomera held a billion stars.

Like White Sands in New Mexico, Woomera is a missile testing range. A woomera is an Aboriginal device similar to an atlatl, a piece of notched wood that acts as a lever to impart extra force to a hurled spear.

I collected sticks in the dusk and with some matches and dried grass started to kindle the fire.

"What are you doing, Will?"

"I'm lighting a fire."

"Like that?"

"What do you mean?"

"It's getting cold." Obviously, the fire wasn't starting fast enough.

Rod went to the back of his motorcycle where he had a spare jerry can of fuel. He flicked the top off and splashed some gasoline onto the dry sticks. Standing back, he threw a lit match out of the darkness. Instantly the pile was ablaze.

"That's how you light a fire in Australia."

Rod warmed his hands. He pulled his camera out and snapped a picture. It was the day after my nineteenth birthday. Here beside the road with a thousand empty miles in all directions, I thought I would be nineteen forever.

Rod pulled out the roast chicken. "Not bad for the middle of nowhere, is it?"

I nodded. The air was becoming cooler as we moved south. Maybe after all this time it was reminding me of home. I was facing another year "off." I wondered if going to Melbourne was such a good idea. What if I didn't find work?

Rod fell asleep quickly after dinner and began to snore.

In the morning the ground was bone cold. I rolled over in my sleeping bag.

"Coffee!"

"Are the eggs ready?"

Within minutes of sunrise the desert became warm and bright. Rod and I tied our sleeping bags to the back of the motorcycles and put on our helmets.

We rode out over the dry ground to the empty highway and instantly accelerated to Port Augusta. The road ran straight for five hundred miles. Near the coast the lights of Japanese squid boats glowed far out to sea.

Coming into Port Augusta, we were suddenly greeted by golden arches. I had not seen a McDonald's for almost six months and thousands of miles. Suddenly, in a landscape I had found so magical and different, I was back in the McWorld. Rod insisted we stop for a burger. He paid for it with coins with imprints of Queen Elizabeth II on the front and a tribal elder under the Southern Cross on the back. I remembered the buffalo nickel and where the buffalo went. I was heading for the big smoke. I had forgotten Australia had these things as well.

The city of Adelaide passed by in the dark. Our headlights illuminated a sign saying Devil's Elbow, ten miles per hour. Surely the road was as straight as it had been for the past eight hundred miles? We hit the turn at fifteen miles per hour and instantly drifted across four lanes. Fortunately, there was no traffic. "I've never been on a sharper turn," Rod said later. "I almost came a cropper!"

The road narrowed down to a single lane again, running along fence lines and paddocks. At midnight, just past the town of Horsham, Rod's chain slipped off the rear sprocket.

"Hold the light steady, Will." Rod had a wrench in his hand. A single truck whistled through the night, the only other traffic on the road. Rod stepped away from the bike.

"We'll be sleeping by the side of the road tonight. I can't fix this in the dark."

There was a field nearby, and the stars gleamed between the leaves of a tall blue gum. I had the feeling I could sleep anywhere in Australia.

Headlights were upon us. The truck had turned around. A man leaned out of the window.

"Having trouble?"

"Yeah," said Rod from beside the truck. "Chain's come off."

"I saw you with the spanner when I drove past before. Where you heading?"

"Melbourne."

"I'm going there too. What part?"

"Murrumbeena."

"Going right past it. I'll give you a lift." The man stepped down from the truck and opened the back door, revealing empty bread trays. "Think we can get your bike in there?" he said, pushing the trays into the back of the truck.

Rod smiled. "Good onya."

We tied the motorcycle securely inside the truck. Rod hopped up in the cab while I mounted the Suzuki and we roared off.

Outside Melbourne, we stopped and switched places. Rod rode the 1100 while I watched from the truck's cab. I stared in awe at the square glass skyscrapers looming on the horizon. In the suburbs the blue light of televisions flickered in countless living rooms: news, sport, weather . . .

At Caulfield Station we passed a convertible wrapped around a telephone pole. The sound of metal was still ringing through the air as people ran across the street to the car. Two bodies lay among the wreckage, dead. We didn't stop. I read in the paper the next day that they were nineteen.

It was July 4, and Rod and I were exhausted from the journey. We slept most of the day. I didn't make the six hundred miles up to Sydney for the rendezvous with Caterina by the fountain at King's Cross on July 5. Perhaps that is the way of travelers.

CHAPTER 13

MELBOURNE

After several days of searching, I found a job as a laborer on a building site in Toorak, digging footings, mixing concrete, and moving bricks. The other workers were a recently naturalized Englishman, two Irishmen, a second-generation Greek-Australian, and an Italian.

I joined the working class, building a mansion in the richest suburb of Melbourne. We had smoko at ten and two o'clock, an hour for lunch, holidays, and Melbourne Cup Day off in November. Australians get four weeks paid vacation per year and why not? I wondered why Americans worked so damned hard at the expense of everything else in their lives.

I learned the difference between standard of living, which measures the amount one consumes, and quality of life, which is by its nature much harder to measure. It has to do with whether or not you can see the stars at night, or tour the Botanical Gardens, or walk a deserted beach, or drink water from a creek.

I slept on a cot in the spare room, living with Rod and his family in Murrumbeena. Rod and I ate at Italian, Lebanese, and Greek restaurants and toured the Royal Botanical Gardens, St. Kilda, and the Melbourne Zoo. We swam at the Harold Holt Memorial Swimming Pool in Malvern. (Australians have a sense of humor – who else would create such a memorial in honor of a prime minister who had presumably drowned?) We rode the trams and purchased pavlovas on Lygon Street, known as Cake Street. The pavlova is an Australian creation of egg whites and cream covered with strawberries and kiwi fruit, and is named after the great Russian ballerina who toured the country in the twenties. Rod knew every bistro and bakery in the city.

On weekends I rode the Great Ocean Road along the southern coast and spear-fished with Rod's younger brother and his friends, who were surf lifesavers by day and worked security at the Lorne and Portsea hotels by night. They thought nothing of swimming two miles up a beach behind the breakers, or swimming out to a reef a mile from shore to spear fish. At nineteen, it didn't occur to me to be concerned about stepping into water in which my buddy was carrying a .303 bang stick and a tourniquet in case of shark bite.

I spent months in Melbourne, building the mansion and for a time working in a windowless warehouse sorting stationery, saving up to buy a good camera and travel north again. I applied to more colleges in the United States.

One day at the loading dock the company retired a man after thirty years. Management said a few words of appreciation. The man had grown gray inside those walls. I had spent the morning sorting romance books and packing bonbons into boxes. I knew I didn't want to do that for much longer.

I had a plane ticket back to the States that left from Cairns. I hadn't seen my family in more than a year. Maybe it was time to head home.

The phone rang one morning at Rod's house. It was Jeff, calling from a trailer park in Warrigal, two hours away. When I gave him Rod's number before leaving Alice, I'd wondered if I'd ever see him again. Jeff told me of his good fortune in getting out of Alice Springs. The day the jeep had broken down was the very last day the engine was under warranty. The company had shipped him a brand new engine from Sydney and paid to have it installed! It must have seemed like a miracle. He'd driven the Gunbarrel Highway to Perth before heading across the Nullarbor Plain. He had since sold the jeep for reasons that were not clear and had divested himself of most of his possessions except the bow and a Sony Walkman, and now he was living in a tent.

We talked about the magic of the Kimberley and how much we missed it. Something about it had captured both of us. Life was simpler out there.

Jeff said, "Let's walk the Prince Regent River in the wet season. It's the Grand Canyon of Australia! No one's ever walked there. We can sell the idea to *Australian Geographic*. You write it up."

It sounded like a perfectly logical idea. I arranged to meet Jeff the next day.

Over a beer in the Warrigal pub, we studied topographical maps of the Prince Regent River. On the manicured lawns outside, elderly men and women in white sweaters, crisp pants, and sun hats played lawn bowls.

We spread the maps out over the bar and studied the terrain. The Prince Regent River is Australia's wildest and most remote, flowing along a nearly straight fracture line in the Gardner Plateau. Hatched lines marked massive escarpments on either side of the river. Near its source, the waters flooded a stone maze of gorges and side canyons. Captain Phillip Parker King had designated this river above all others, naming it after a future king of England.

Contour lines indicated rocky hillsides and open eucalypt country punctuated by vast wet-season swamps leading up to the headwaters. Blue ink marked rivers, creeks, and pools. Where the river reached the sea, dense mangroves lined its banks. To walk the river would be to step back in time, to see things no white man had ever seen before. It seemed a long way from where we were.

The plan we agreed on was to hitch a ride on the mail plane from the town of Wyndham into the Drysdale River Station. The station itself was a pretty remote place, but the river flowing past it started in the same canyons as the Prince Regent. From the station we would walk west to the headwaters of the Drysdale and, from there, to the headwaters of the Prince Regent. The great part of the plan was it didn't require a lot of money, just time, which we both had in abundance.

"We can spotlight for python *Morelia carinata* along the way," Jeff said. "It might take us two weeks to walk to the headwaters of the Drysdale. Then we find a canyon leading into the main gorge of the Prince Regent River and just keep walking. Think about it! The headwaters of the Prince Regent! There are isolated remnants of rain forest in there. Who knows what we might find? Lost tribes? There could be dinosaurs still out there!"

After exploring the Prince Regent River and whatever side canyons seemed most interesting, we would make our way to the King Cascade, a picturesque waterfall flowing into the Prince Regent below the tidal zone. Without airdrops or resupply, we'd have to supplement the food we could carry with fish and forage.

"How do we get out?" I wondered.

"Hitch a ride out on a boat at the King Cascade. It's the only place to get fresh water on the whole coast. Boats are always going in there. We just wait there until one shows up."

It seemed a reasonable, if somewhat capricious, way out. I'd heard about the King Cascade. It was supposed to be beautiful, a waterfall plunging into a green lagoon on a tropical coast. It was a place where intrepid yachties traveling the remote Kimberley coast stocked up on fresh water. It was also where a crocodile had eaten Ginger Meadows the year before.

The King Cascade was charted in 1818 by Phillip Parker King on his unsung but landmark journeys to map the coast of Australia.

He had named many features of the Kimberley coast, including the Prince Regent River, which he thought might offer access to the interior of the continent. On his second voyage in 1820, the King Cascade was a place where King found water when all other sources had failed him. Water was essential on that thirsty coast. As he wrote in his narrative:

> We then bent our steps to the water-gully, but, to our mortification, it was quite dried up, and exhibited no vestige of its having contained any for some time. From the more luxuriant and verdant appearance of the trees and grass, than the country hereabout assumed last year, when the water was abundant, we had felt assured of finding it, and therefore our disappointment was the greater.
>
> After another unsuccessful search in the bight, to the eastward of Careening Bay, in which we fruitlessly examined a gully that Mr Cunningham informed me had last year produced a considerable stream, we gave up all hopes of success here, and directed our attention to the cascade of Prince Regent's River; which we entered the next afternoon, with the wind and tide in our favour, and at sunset reached an anchorage at the bottom of St George's Basin, a mile and a half to the northward of the islet that lies off the inner entrance of the river, in seven fathoms muddy sand.
>
> The following morning, at half-past four o'clock, Mr Montgomery accompanied me in the whaleboat to visit the cascade; we reached it at nine o'clock, and found the water, to our inexpressible satisfaction, falling abundantly.
>
> While the boat's crew rested and filled their baricas, I as— cended the rocks over which the water was falling, and was surprised to find its height had been so underrated when we passed by it last year: it was then thought to be about forty feet, but I now found it could not be less than one hundred

and fifty. The rock, a fine grained siliceous sand-stone, is disposed in horizontal strata, from six to twelve feet thick, each of which projects about three feet from that above it, and forms a continuity of steps to the summit, which we found some difficulty in climbing; but where the distance between the ledges was great, we assisted our ascent by tufts of grass firmly rooted in the luxuriant moss, that grew abundantly about the watercourses. On reaching the summit, I found that the fall was supplied from a stream winding through rugged chasms and thickly matted clusters of plants and trees, among which the pandanus bore a conspicuous appearance, and gave a picturesque richness to the place. While admiring the wildness of the scene, Mr Montgomery joined me, we did not, however, succeed in following the stream for more than a hundred yards, for at that distance its windings were so confused among rocks and spinifex, that we could not trace its source.

That afternoon I began writing a letter to Dick Smith. He had made a fortune in electronics stores, sold the business, and started a magazine, *Australian Geographic*. He was also a world-class adventurer, having flown his helicopter solo around the world.

Over several drafts, Jeff and I laid out the plan: to begin at the Drysdale River Station, follow the Drysdale upriver to its headwaters, and then follow the Prince Regent downriver on its descent through a massive sandstone canyon to the ocean. On our journey to the coast we would spotlight for creatures unknown to science, including the rough-scaled python, and would document any Aboriginal artwork and artifacts we encountered. It promised to be a good adventure, and, if we were lucky, we might even get the first live pictures of Australia's rarest animal, and the only keel-scaled python in the world.

CHAPTER 14

BACK TO MILLAA

The bus to Sydney took fourteen hours from Melbourne. *Ishtar* was playing on the small TV above the driver's head. I stumbled off the bus and checked into a youth hostel near the fountain at King's Cross. I was traveling solo again. I had eleven hundred dollars in the bank and a new Nikon camera. I had sold Mike's bike in Melbourne and wired him the money.

I thought how nice it would be to meet a familiar face in Sydney, but it wasn't going to happen. I wondered about Caterina and the travelers I had met, now all gone home. I had been in Australia for more than a year.

Sydney reminded me of New York. I planned to get north of the city and hitch a ride to Cairns at a truck stop. But it was a long way to go.

I was a little down about traveling alone again. The water fountain at Kings Cross reminded me of the July 5 rendezvous that had never happened. I sat in the foyer of the empty hostel recording my doubts in my journal.

Amy walked through the door and sat down nearby. She was twenty-three and had been working as a recruiting coordinator in New York. She was good-looking, with dark hair and a bright smile. We talked about New York. She had more money than time.

I hadn't had a girlfriend for months. She had a flight to Brisbane in the morning.

"Get your ass to Brisbane and meet me at the Amex office. We'll rent a car and drive to Cairns," she said. "You can be my guide."

In the various motels we stayed in, Amy would say things like, "This shower is just the right height for fucking in." You never know your luck.

Traveling up the east coast of Australia reminded me that there was a suburbanized world with plastic signs and billboards and fast food. It didn't leave much of an impression. I do remember looking at a refrigerated sixteen-foot Great White Shark (the world's "largest preserved White-Pointer") in Vic Hislop's shark museum in Hervey Bay. I would never have gone spear-fishing in Victoria if I had seen that before entering the water.

At a hostel we met up with two Swedes and a Brit who were heading north and wanted to split fuel and vehicle rental costs with us. All went well until our trip up the coast was halted by Cyclone Charlie, which shut down the main highway. In the little town of Airlie Beach, there was only one room available for rent. For four days we sat in the little shared room while it rained incessantly and the wind howled. I cursed the Swedes for their ignorance of the unwritten male code. The Brit understood but was reluctant when I finally laid down the law.

"You're not going to send us out into a cyclone just so you can have sex with your girlfriend, are you?"

I nodded. "It's only gusting to seventy miles per hour. And don't even think of knocking on this door until three hours have passed . . ."

The cyclone kept building strength out to sea, but as it neared the coast it weakened. Finally, we went out to the local pub for the crab races. There I met a young Australian who said, "If I have a kid, I won't name him Charlie, because when he gets it up, he can't keep it up; and when he keeps it up, he can't do anything with it!"

We made it to Cairns and the Tablelands, and after a week of doing the sights, Amy and I said goodbye on the Esplanade. It was time to head back to Millaa, on foot. Jeff would be getting there soon too, if he hadn't already arrived.

Millaa hadn't changed. It was raining when I got a lift into town. I picked up some waiting mail at the post office and swung by to see Lawrie at the old movie theater. He wasn't there, but one of the School for Field Studies students was. His name was Dave Sacks, and he was a premed junior at Brown.

"You want these?" Dave asked, holding up a pair of gum boots.

"Sure."

The study program had ended, and he didn't need them anymore. Dave had moved in temporarily with Lawrie at the old theater. We talked about the rain forest, life in Millaa Millaa, and the slower pace of life in Australia. Dave was planning to go down to the coast and meet up with his girlfriend at Cape Tribulation.

We watched the rain drip off the eaves. I told Dave that Jeff and I were planning on climbing Mount Bartle Frere when the dry season arrived. He liked the idea and wanted to go with us. The mountain is only 5,200 feet high, but covered with thick jungle and slippery boulders. I told him it was too early in the season: "You'd get to the top and wouldn't be able to see a thing except rain and cloud."

I liked Dave. I told him about the people living down on the commune off Middlebrook Road. I asked him if he wanted to go down there with me and see the houses and the way they lived in the rain forest. We arranged to meet at ten the next morning.

After Beatrice Creek bridge, the road turned sharply past some boulders and a waterfall. Last week, Amy and I had made love there, leaning into the current. Now she was gone. As I pedaled by Whiting Road on a borrowed bicycle, a colony of flying foxes ascended out of the treetops in their thousands, looking like the winged monkeys sent by the Wicked Witch of the West to capture Dorothy in *The Wizard of Oz*.

I leaned left down Middlebrook Road, turning off the back road to Ravenshoe that Jeff and I had traveled all those months ago. I'd come full circle in Australia.

A rusty mailbox announced Perry Farm, the dirt road leading into the forest. The front tire slipped into a rut of red soil.

No more stars tonight. I parked the bike in the shed and walked under the low-hanging branches of the forest. The lights were out in Peter and Maggie's farmhouse.

It had been a long time since I had seen Peter and Maggie. Bill was gone, back to California. I had seen the big smoke: Melbourne, Sydney, Adelaide, Brisbane. I had learned many things since leaving here, grown some too. It made returning to Millaa and the wild places all the more precious.

Millaa had become home. The deserts around Alice Springs were beautiful, but a place to get stuck in. Melbourne and the south coast were experiences, but, in the end, too urban. The stars were not bright nor the air clear enough. Millaa was a jewel, a place where the mind came alive.

Jeff was sitting on the verandah of the cabin in the yellow glow of a kerosene lantern when I walked up through the darkness. He was reading a book. He looked up at the sound of footsteps coming through the trees.

"Hey!" he shouted from the verandah. He'd shaved his beard. We'd both changed a bit. I no longer viewed Australia as I had upon first arriving, as one vast wilderness continent punctuated only by small towns and isolated roadhouses.

"You made it," I said and walked into the crude kitchen. The house was two stories, with no walls on the upstairs loft, no hot water but what was boiled on the gas stove, no flush toilet.

I sorted through the bundle of mail, a few letters from home, one from Roddy in Melbourne, and a letter on *Australian Geographic* letterhead. I pulled it out, "What's this?"

I read it with growing amazement.

The letter said that our application for sponsorship of a proposed two-month trek into the Kimberley had been reviewed. The editor, Howard Whelan, wrote that *Australian Geographic*'s Science and Exploration fund would be sending us a check for two thousand dollars to help in our attempt to photograph the python *Morelia carinata*, and to complete the first traverse of the headwaters of the Prince Regent River to the King Cascade.

"Fantastic!" Jeff shouted. "We'll have to get ready right away!"

I was stunned. For so long I had felt on the outside after leaving high school, on walkabout and getting my education from truck drivers, old soldiers, Aboriginals, bush mechanics, stockmen, retired timber cutters, pilots, miners, farmers, pig hunters, pub–licans, and old men fishing off piers: Italians, Greeks, Germans, Brits, Aboriginals, Torres Strait Islanders, New Zealanders, Maoris, Samoans, South Africans, and Australians. Elders. And I was doing my best to educate myself by reading.

The ties that had unfurled like a string behind me on my way over on the plane, in those first uncertain moments, had snapped like a line drawn too taut. This letter meant I had finally been accepted somewhere.

I looked at the simple cabin. This was home. Without indoor plumbing, refrigeration, hot or cold water. With sunbirds on the front verandah, whip birds calling from the forest, possums, a green tree frog living above the soap dish, and a leaf-tailed gecko under the sink. With the rain hammering on the roof, I turned down the wick on the lantern and trudged up the stairs to bed with my flashlight, elated.

The next morning I rode into town to meet Dave Sacks. It

was an unusually sunny day for Millaa. The theater was empty, but there was a note on the door: "Will, waited until 10:15 but no sign of you. Decided to climb the mountain. Be back in a few days (!) (?) Dave."

I looked at my watch, it was 10:20. I rode out to the main road, but there was no sign of Dave hitchhiking. He must have got a lift right away. Bad luck.

That afternoon the rain swept back in. It would be six weeks before the sky cleared.

I rode back out of town. Jeff and I had a lot of things to do if we wanted to be on the mail plane to Drysdale River Station in two weeks.

CHAPTER 15

SWAHILI SPOKEN HERE

"You'll want something to dig with." Peter looked up from a box of silky oak he was crafting from recycled bits and pieces of timber he collected at the local dump. "To dig for water."

He was right. Beyond the maps, with their thin orange contour lines, the hatched black lines marking escarpments, the light blue of permanent pools, and the green of vegetation, I was not sure how much water we would find out there. Australia is the second-driest continent in the world (after Antarctica, which has its water locked up in ice and snow), and the sun is so hot in the wet season that it can kill you in a day. I almost learned that from experience.

At least we had maps to go on, though Jeff said they would probably be inaccurate. Certainly in the gorges there would be water year round, but what of the boulder fields, escarpments, and vast eucalypt plains we would have to cross? Would we find ourselves two days from water? Three days?

The Kimberley's southern portions are characterized as a "dry hot climate where winter is drier than summer," and the northern coastal area as "hot moist climate with a marked dry season in winter." On the map it merely said "subject to extensive seasonal flooding." But what about after the rains had gone? Would there still be water? We wouldn't know until we got there.

It suddenly occurred to me that I had never really been on an expedition this serious before. Two months in the Australian bush? All that time away from television, electricity, radio, the internal combustion engine, hot and cold running water, other people?

There would be poisonous snakes, crocodiles, and lightning storms. We would be sleeping on the ground, exposed to the elements. To be bitten by a snake was unlikely but a possibility. So was a bad toothache or appendicitis. Or even malaria.

"The Africans have a saying," Peter said, "*Kukufwa ni dakika mbili pekiake* – dying takes only two minutes."

"Pass me that thing there, will you," he pointed to an adze leaning up in the corner.

He leaned over the box and carefully beveled the edge of a board of silky oak with ripples of glossy wood.

"You see the wood? It's quarter-cut to bring out the grain." Peter held the wood out. "You see this tabletop here?" he asked. "Yellow walnut. Rain-forest timber. Jack's old floorboards!" Peter laughed. The table sat on two halves of an old carriage wheel found at the dump. "It's a question of seeing things from different angles. You must take in a wide range of experience, otherwise you don't know what makes you happy.

"When I was a boy, the Battle of Britain was happening. I was shipped out into the country. I'd grown up in the city, but in the country I met a farmer who taught me a thing or two about living a good life. Changed my life, really. Otherwise I might have lived in London, riding the Tube to work, instead of having the life I've had."

His hair was silver like the shine on the blade of the adze.

"That's it," he said, carefully putting the wood in place on the edge of the box and tamping it. Glue leaked out of the joint. "Now, just here I have something for you."

Peter had worked as a safari guide in Kenya, Uganda, and Tanzania for thirty years. He had also been a farmer in Kenya, raising corn, sunflower, and tea in the shadow of Mount Elgon.

I followed Peter across the shop, littered with hammers and mallets and callipers and forging tools. A handmade forge of metallic coke was hooked up to an old hair dryer that, when turned on, served as bellows.

"It's somewhere over here." Peter disappeared into a shadow of the shed, next to a porcelain sink and cans of grease and screws and old nails and fan belts hanging from a roof beam.

"Here it is." He reached into an old coffee can.

"Whoops, that's not it." Peter wiped grease off his hand with a rag. "Here." He held a piece of steel the size of a child's shoe, with a hole in the center in which to stick a piece of wood as a handle.

"That's what you need. For digging, you see." He made a motion up and down with the steel. "Rocks, sand, roots . . . whatever is between you and the water. Because the water is there, you just have to get at it! The creek might not be running over the sand, or the rocks, but it's flowing underneath. And you'll want something to dig with."

He handed me the steel.

"It could make all the difference. You can cut a handle for it out there. Taper the wood, so the head won't slip off."

I held the steel in my hand and tried to picture myself in the months to come. Would I be in a narrow creek bed, cutting through dry earth, digging for my life? I remembered how hot the sun was, so hot it makes you sick. For a moment I thought of Crystal Creek and those two boys outside Halls Creek and the prospect of endless, breezeless country in all directions. The arrow fashioned out of stones beside the truck, the boys' bodies ten and eleven miles farther across the sand. "I allways love you" scratched into a water jug.

"And this here," Peter said, holding a piece of wire about six inches long. "You never know when you're going to need this. You might need it to chase lizards out of cracks for food or something.

It is good to have a piece of wire with you. You can sharpen it and make a barbed spear if you have to." Peter ambled across the shop.

Before I left, Peter showed me how to make solar stills, a method for collecting water in even the most arid conditions.

"What you do is you dig a hole in the ground, preferably a dry river bed, about three feet deep and two feet square, and collect all the leaves you can find, and put them in the hole." Peter looked up from where he was throwing seed out for the chickens. "Then, if you can, you pee in the hole, and put a cup in the center of it. You can use your urine once. Lay a sheet of plastic over it, put a pebble on the plastic above the cup, and water will condense and drip into the cup. You might need to make several of these stills, so take enough plastic with you."

He moved away from the chickens and puttered about in the shed. Peter's attitude was that if something was not strong or intelligent enough to survive, then it should not.

"Right, that's all I can think of for now. When are you leaving?"

"In two days," I said.

The next morning Peter held up five small cotton bags with cinching ties. "You'll need these, expedition bags. Put your things in here, your fishing gear, batteries, etcetera, and label them. Then you won't be forever pulling things out of your pack. You need to know where everything is. You don't have energy to waste out there. And you don't want to lose anything. It is all essential."

Jeff had retrieved at the airport in Cairns a half-pallet of food and equipment donated by a Sydney outdoor store, Paddy Pallin. We stood for hours with the equipment spread about the floor of the cabin, fitting it into our packs.

We carried no tents or sleeping bags.

"It's so hot there now that you wouldn't get any sleep in a tent anyway," he said.

I was reminded of the quote by Antoine de Saint-Exupéry, "Perfection is achieved, not when there is nothing more to add, but when there is nothing left to take away."

We could not pare down our material any further. Each pack weighed eighty-five pounds, and 90 percent of the weight was food.

I carried: a plastic cup, plate, fork and spoon, three candles, a headlamp for spotlighting, aluminum foil, binoculars, good boots, fifty-five foil packets of freeze-dried beef and beans, four pounds each of rice, flour, muesli, and powdered milk, seasoned salt, several blocks of chocolate, sixty packets of tea, freeze-dried coffee, a Swiss Army knife with tweezers and folding scissors, sunscreen SPF 25, glacier glasses, a wide-brimmed hat, a spare hat, a long-sleeved shirt for nighttime and a T-shirt for daytime, a pair of army pants with side pockets, a pair of hospital scrubs for sleeping in, a nylon jacket, a small bar of oatmeal soap (I figured I could eat it if necessary), two razors, three pairs of socks, a pair of shorts, underwear, a signal mirror, spare bootlaces, one orienteering compass with folding mirror for sighting landmarks, one simple back-up compass, a whistle, five Bic lighters, a small cooking pot and lightweight frying pan, a small folding saw, fifteen aspirin, a small bottle of iodine water-purifying tablets, a sleeping mat and sheet, a waterproof space blanket (to serve as groundsheet, tarp-shelter, and emergency blanket), a mosquito net, insect repellent, six collapsible one-liter water containers, a canteen, a journal, four pens, a 35-millimeter Nikon camera with 35–70 millimeter zoom, polarizing filter, collapsible tripod, flash, and twenty rolls of Kodachrome film, a piece of wire, a sewing kit, two compression bandages in case of snakebite or sprained ankle (in addition to the full medical kit with sutures, painkillers, and antibiotics that Jeff carried in his pack), a whistle, a sharpening stone, a small flashlight, four spare AA batteries, spare bulbs, a telescoping fishing rod and reel, two spools of forty-pound test line, five lures, forty fishing hooks and sinkers, a powerful slingshot, an MSR XGK stove, Peter's piece of steel, two one-liter bottles of white gas, a sparker, spare flints, one stove maintenance kit, ten one-gallon Ziploc bags for holding food, eight heavy-duty garbage bags (for waterproofing, carrying water, and solar stills), twelve elastic bands, a hundred fifty feet of lightweight nylon parachute cord, fifteen Band-Aids and waterproof tape, a diving mask, lip balm, a tiny pocket dictionary, a journal, four pens, 1:100,000 series topographical maps of the Prince Regent River and surroundings, half a roll of toilet paper, some concentrated butter, toothpaste, dental floss, and a toothbrush. Jeff brought along a small tube of shampoo, the only luxury.

We arranged with a mapping agency in Perth to send additional topographical maps to the post office in Kununurra, where we would pick them up. Jeff and I carried laminated maps of our planned route into the Prince Regent River, but we wanted all the maps to the north, south, and east of the area just in case we didn't get picked up by a boat.

"Make sure you bring plenty of hooks," Peter said to me one day. "Burke and Wills died because they didn't bring enough hooks."

In 1861, Burke and Wills had reached mangrove swamps in the Gulf of Carpentaria, having started from Melbourne. Their intention had been to explore the limits of the country north from Victoria and find suitable lands for grazing and minerals. The expedition had split into two groups, the one led by Burke and Wills pushing on to the northern coast, while the other waited with extra provisions at a place called Cooper's Creek. After several months Burke and Wills reached the coast, then hurried south to the rendezvous point at Cooper's Creek.

The back-up team had waited an extra month for Burke and Wills to return. But when the two explorers stumbled into camp they discovered that the team had left that very morning, leaving behind a few provisions buried at the base of a tree with the word DIG carved on it. Burke and Wills were too exhausted to follow, even though the others were only several hours journey ahead. They fired rifles into the air, hoping to alert the departed team. Despite a subsistence diet of what the Aboriginals called nardoo flour, all the members of the party died except for John King, who was befriended by the local Aboriginal people and later rescued.

I came home that evening to find a cork on the table with all sizes of hooks sticking into it. I packed it away. We would be leaving in the morning.

We wore rip-stop nylon army pants with side pockets and thick-soled leather hiking boots. I came to view my backpack as a sort of life support system, enabling me to cross distances I otherwise would not survive. How did Aboriginal tribes do it? Without maps or compasses? Barefoot, carrying only spears and sharp flints?

That night the phone rang in the farmhouse. Peter called me down from the cabin. It was Lawrie from the movie theater.

"What's up, Lawrie?"

"Dave's still on the mountain, mate."

"What do you mean?"

"I haven't heard from him in a week. I just went into his room and all his stuff is still there. The only things I know are missing are his tent and his flashlight."

I couldn't believe that Dave would go missing. True, he had gone hiking by himself, which is always a mistake, and it had been raining since he left. But the trek across Mount Bartle Frere takes two days at the most. The trail leads down to a place near the coast called Josephine Falls.

"He's fine," I said. "He's walked down to the coast and gone up to Cape Trib to see his girlfriend. Probably lost your phone number."

"Don't think so, mate."

I was not worried. In the note, Dave had been vague about when he would be returning, and he had told me about wanting to meet up with his girlfriend, Pam, in Cape Tribulation.

"He's fine," I repeated. "Find Pam in Cape Trib, she'll be with him."

"I'm going to call Constable Spear," Lawrie said. "He's missing."

CHAPTER 16

WEST

The bus from Townsville took two and half days to reach the Western Australian town of Kununurra. Through the window, mile after endless mile of desert oak and saltbush passed by. The bus made a few stops to pick up passengers, mostly stockmen, miners, and Aboriginals out of places like Cloncurry, Camooweal, Mount Isa, and Tennant Creek. I sat next to a young jackaroo who had broken a leg and spent six weeks laid up in Cunnamulla, playing solitaire. "Cuntamulla, I call it," he said.

The road was a single lane in places, and kangaroos and cattle roamed beside and across it. A young bull went into the grille of the bus with a heavy sound, like a sack of grain falling onto a concrete floor. We didn't stop. We passed rusted Southern Cross windmills bringing bore water up into cisterns by the road. Flocks of pink and gray galahs scattered at our approach. We left behind the silence and the heat.

As I looked out the window, the landscape filled me with loneliness. I was not sure if I would ever see my family or friends again. That pile of orange rock in the distance would remain unchanged while generations passed. Time could only be measured on the intergalactic scale: the impact of meteorites, the changing distances between continents. Something resembling human time did not exist. Not out here.

The bus stopped several miles before the connection with the Stuart Highway running north and south. A torrent of water from a passing thundercloud swept across the road. On the other side of the wash two four-wheel drives waited. The driver lit his pipe and looked at his watch. This being the only road west in the interior of Australia, I was surprised that there was not more traffic.

The town of Kununurra services the cattle stations and the Argyle Diamond Mine on the southeastern edge of the Kimberley in Western Australia. The town sprang into being in the 1960s to serve Australia's most ambitious land and water scheme: the Ord River irrigation project, a dam that was intended to provide thousands of acres of arable land and to draw settlers by the thousands. Because of its heat and remoteness, only a small number of Australians actually settled here.

The bus dropped us off near the post office in town. Even after the rain had stopped, in the glow of the sun following an afternoon shower Kununurra was a bleak place. Tin houses clustered together as if to keep out the heat and indifferent space. The land was too rugged for most Europeans, and many of the Aboriginal inhabitants had moved to the missions at Kunumunya and Kalumburu several decades before. To them it was still holy land. In the heat and silence, I began to understand why.

I called the owners of the Drysdale River Station from a pay phone and told them of our plan to take the mail plane.

"Do you have a radio?" Anne Koeyers asked.

When I said we did not, she suggested I contact the Royal Flying Doctor Service, to see if they had a loaner. It was a wise suggestion.

I didn't explain to her that we didn't want a radio. It would be too heavy, an encumbrance of the modern world. We wanted to be completely responsible for our own survival or demise in this landscape, with what we could carry.

"People walked through the wilderness for years without a radio," Jeff said.

"Yeah, look at Burke and Wills, if they'd had a radio . . ."

"You can die anywhere – on your back verandah sipping mint julep when your neighbor's lawn mower kicks a rock at your head," he said. "If we die, we die. Better than dying around here." He was right about that.

We walked over to the post office to pick up the extra maps and unrolled them one by one on a picnic table.

"What's this?"

The maps depicted areas around Halls Creek and the Durack Ranges, far south of where we intended to be.

"Shit," Jeff said. The agency had sent us the wrong maps.

"We'll have to get them sent up express," I said.

"They won't get here in time."

The mail plane would be leaving Wyndham in two days. After that it would be two weeks before another plane could depart, if at all. Neither of us wanted to wait in Kununurra for two weeks.

"We won't need those other maps. We're getting out on a boat, remember?"

"That's the plan," I said. "It's always nice to have a plan B."

We bought extra candles and canned spaghetti bolognaise for dinner in Kununurra and walked to the western edge of town in the evening. We would hitchhike in the morning to Wyndham.

Jeff walked a few yards behind me in the fading light.

"Hey," he said, "you almost stepped on this."

Under the tube of maps he had pinned a common western brown snake, just as my leg might have done. "Look at that. You just missed it!"

The snake bit the cardboard tube several times, twisting its head and sinking its fangs in before Jeff shook it off.

"He wouldn't have any trouble striking above your boot, would he? You're lucky," he said. "You must have just stepped over it."

Poisonous snakes can inject two types of venom. One is a hematoxin that kills the cells in the location of the bite, turning the flesh blue and lifeless. I had seen a picture of a man's hand after being bitten by a king brown. His thumb and forefinger were purple-black with necrosis, as though from severe frostbite, and had to be amputated.

The other type of venom, neurotoxin, affects the nervous system and causes death principally by hypotensic shock and paralysis of breathing. Such a bite would probably be fatal out here.

"The first symptom of a taipan bite is that you die," Jeff said nonchalantly. "One hundred percent mortality before the development of antivenom."

A snake's lethality is measured not only by the potency of its venom, but by the amount it can deliver. Some sea snakes have extremely poisonous venom, but because it is delivered by teeth in the back of the mouth, it is unlikely that one would receive enough venom to actually die from a bite.

Unfortunately, we carried no antivenom because it requires refrigeration and would have to be species-specific. At night, sleeping in the open without tents, the possibility of being visited by a snake was real, though unlikely. I remembered that rock painting at the Mitchell Falls, the life-size image of a human figure, with a snake striking at the foot.

We carried bandages to restrict the flow of venom through the lymphatic system if struck. Hematoxins would kill local skin and muscle cells, but a bandage wrapped tightly around an afflicted limb would prevent the flow of neurotoxins to the heart and lungs, for a little while. In any case, a snakebite would be a very unfortunate event in this wilderness. But there were other things to worry about, given the terrain and our heavy packs.

"Accidental falls are the number one cause of death in the wilderness," Jeff reminded me from under his hat.

It began to dawn on me that there was no guarantee either of us would make it back from this adventure.

We pitched camp in the dark on a patch of sand in the tall grass near the quiet highway, with the lights of town in the distance. I thought back to our first camp in central Queensland, with my hammock strung between two sickly shrubs above the ants. That seemed an age ago, and we were still out here. If I'd been accepted at college, I would be finishing up my sophomore year now. Was I crazy to be out here?

At dawn we woke up next to a mound and a wooden cross, with the words JIM's GRAVE etched on it. We had not seen it in the dark.

"That's kind of grim," Jeff muttered as we packed camp and stumbled to the silent highway.

Hours passed in the heat by the side of the road. There was hardly any traffic. The high sound of an approaching car could be heard for miles – a hopeful smile, thumb out – then the low sound as the car continued by. Jeff and I split up to increase our chances of a ride. Two local girls stopped and gave us each a cold Coke. They weren't going to Wyndham, but we were grateful anyway. I held the Coke against my face before gulping it down. Then two young Germans in a white station wagon picked us up at noon by the side of the road.

"Wyndham, ja, we're going to Wyndham. What the hell's in Wyndham?" the driver wanted to know.

Not much, as it turned out. We rode the Great Northern Highway the fifty miles from Kununurra, through a landscape of orange stone and spinifex grass.

Wyndham, the northernmost and hottest town in Western Australia, is a few single-story buildings, an airstrip, a pier and a pub, stretched out over nine miles across a mud flat on Australia's northwest coast. Its highest point is less than three feet above sea level. Gray mud surrounds the town on three sides.

In 1872 the Colony of Western Australia, hoping to open up land, offered five thousand pounds "to anyone who discovered a workable gold field within 300 miles of any declared port in the colony." Wyndham was a port in name only. There was silence for thirteen years.

Then in 1885 Charles Hall and John Slattery found ten ounces of alluvial gold farther inland at a place they named Halls Creek, and Wyndham was designated a year later to service the newly opened mines there. The discovery of the yellow metal, which electrified the adventurers and prospectors farther south, was followed by another discovery: there was not much of it. In fact, hardly any at all. The number of prospectors dwindled dramatically. A few held on.

A steady trickle of ore, destined for ships heading north to Asia, kept Wyndham alive, barely. By 1896 the mines had produced only 1,400 pounds of gold. The last mine closed in 1953, though a few tenacious prospectors continued to work their claims.

But Wyndham held on. In 1919 a slaughterhouse was set up to service the emerging Kimberley cattle industry. The meatworks discharged offal and blood into the waters of Cambridge Gulf, attracting and sustaining several large saltwater crocodiles. A year before the town's centenary celebration in 1986, the meatworks shut down.

Wyndham had the air of a ghost town. Crocodiles can still be seen from the town wharf, along with the wreck of the ship SS *Koolama*, which was sunk by Japanese Zeroes in World War II. The year before, a man had been "peeled" off the beach by a crocodile while he slept, drunk, too close to the water.

Fittingly, there was a prison in Wyndham. The warden opened

the gates every morning at eight. When I later asked a guard if he was concerned that any of the criminals would escape, he looked around with a bemused expression.

"Where could they go?" he asked.

The Germans dropped us off beside the pub a few miles from the airstrip. The air outside was 102 degrees.

"Here's some advice for you," the driver said. "Get the fuck out of Wyndham!"

Jeff and I stepped in from the heat. The men scattered at the edges of the bar wore the traditional uniform of the Australian working class, faded T-shirts and green stubby King Gee shorts, battered hats and Blundstone boots.

We savored our last cold beer for a while, and the air-conditioning.

At the edge of the bar was a pay phone. I had a few dollar coins in my pocket. No point in carrying them out into the wilderness. I called Lawrie.

"Find Dave yet?" I said.

"No sign of him."

"You're kidding!"

"There's a search going on now," Lawrie said. "His mother and brother were out here. Pam hasn't seen him – nobody's spoken to him since he left for the mountain. Police found a farmer who'd given him a lift to the trailhead on his tractor."

"Nobody's heard from him?" I could not believe it. I was sure he'd gone up to Cape Tribulation with his girlfriend, after reaching the coast.

I felt terribly guilty. Dave was a friend, even though I'd known him only briefly, and now he was missing. And I was the one who had put the idea of climbing Mount Bartle Frere in his head. If only I hadn't been a few minutes late that morning.

"Any sign of him?" I asked Lawrie.

"They found a spot on the trail where he probably pitched his tent, but since then nothing. Dave's gone, mate. He had his tent, and he would have had plenty of water. If he were still alive, they would have found him by now. He's dead."

"Oh God, I hope not." I wondered if Jeff and I should go back and help look for him. I felt terrible that I hadn't reported him missing.

"We all feel bad. His mother and brother are leaving tomorrow. I think they know now that they're not going to find him alive," Lawrie said.

The search had engaged the efforts of local police and Special Air Service units. A farmer on the Topaz Road had given Dave Sacks a lift to the end of the road. That much was certain. But beyond that there was not much to go on. At one point a member of the Special Air Service was lowered from a helicopter into the camp of what turned out to be a marijuana grower, who ran off.

Lawrie lamented not bringing in an Aboriginal tracker. "They would have found him – if he could have been found."

It appeared that Dave had missed the trail to Mount Bartle Frere summit and continued along a disused logging track down into the Russell River Gorge. If he proceeded downriver, his disappearance was a foregone conclusion. The Russell River runs through impenetrable rain forest, teeming with vines, dense undergrowth, painful stinging trees, slippery boulders, and sudden cliffs. He would not have seen the sun for weeks.

Since he had a tent and water was not a problem, he must have run into serious trouble early on. If he'd sprained an ankle or become lost, it is likely that he would have waited in his tent for rescue.

It seemed more likely to me that Dave fell and injured himself severely after getting lost, perhaps after wandering around for several days. He might have been swept away while trying to cross the Russell River. He might have blundered into a stinging tree and been stung in the face and eyes, effectively blinding him. There were any number of ways to die alone in the wilderness. The slightest mishap becomes an insurmountable obstacle, for which two heads are almost always better than one.

At least Jeff and I could count on each other. Did it matter that I knew so little of his past?

Jeff was studying a chart of rainfall behind the bar.

"We had a bit in December but not much in January," the bartender said. "We're due for a good soaking, I reckon."

Jeff handed me a beer.

"You can shout me one when we get out. Bad news?" he asked when he saw my expression.

"Yeah. Bad news. Dave's gone."

"He shouldn't have gone out there alone."

"Doesn't help now. Jesus, I feel terrible. I should have stayed and helped with the search."

"You didn't know he was really missing. We should start walking to the airstrip soon," Jeff said.

CHAPTER 17

FLOOD: THE FLIGHT FROM WYNDHAM

Jeff and I walked the last three miles to the airfield with our backpacks and the roll of maps. We didn't talk much. The only sound was that of our boots scattering stones across the hot tarmac.

Floating towers of cloud rose in the distance – massive, silent infusions of solar energy vaulting twelve miles into the sky, scraping the troposphere. Tropical storms in northern Australia are the most intense and violent on the planet.

A sign with an arrow said, AERODROME.

A two-story house rippled in waves of kerosene heat on one edge of the runway. The tarmac stretched to the base of some low rocky hills. At the near end sat a tin hangar.

"Where are the planes?"

"Must be inside."

All the doors were locked. There was not a breath of wind. The house had a covered verandah on three sides and, improbably, a public telephone booth. I had to admire those engineers from Telecom Australia. I put down my pack on the verandah on the edge of nowhere.

"I hope there's a water faucet out here."

I found one on the side of the house and refilled my canteen with chalky artesian bore water. Water was now almost as vital as oxygen. A gallon of water weighs more than eight pounds. We went through a gallon every four hours. It was impossible not to. In this heat even the trees tried to hide from the sun: several species have evolved to turn their crescent leaves edge on to the sun.

Behind the runway stretched an empty country of red rocky hills and green and yellow eucalyptus. Today was our last day in civilization, our last few hours. After this flight, our journey began on foot.

Anvil-shaped clouds twelve miles tall drifted silently toward us in the afternoon sun. I watched from the verandah, awed. We walked for our own reasons.

"This'll be our last roof for a while," I said.

The white columns moved slowly across the afternoon. Black rain enameled their undersides. I counted silently for the thunder after each flicker of lightning, a thousand feet for each second. The lightning was still several miles away.

After tonight we would have nothing over our heads but the space blankets we carried. The fabric reflected body heat and was waterproof, but it would not make for a comfortable camp in a downpour. It occurred to me that we should have brought at least a rain fly.

Jeff and I busily prepared our beds: sleeping pads, a thin sheet, space blanket, and mosquito net. He picked one side of the verandah and I chose the other, thinking that someone should be around to do CPR if one of us were struck by lightning.

On the verandah, the yellow light of the telephone booth was the only beacon in an immense, humid darkness. A cable connected to a single telephone pole sixty feet away and disappeared into the distance toward town. Insects were drawn to the light by the thousands. A giant green tree frog stuck with suction cup feet to the glass. Should I make one last call home before I headed into the bush for two months?

I decided not to. No one could understand where I was right now.

The cloud approached suddenly like the hissing comber of a wave breaking over our heads. Bolts of lightning enfiladed the ridge at the end of the runway. In the flashes, the colors of broad daylight returned, the greens and whites of the eucalyptus leaves and trunks, the red sandstone in the distance.

I looked for somewhere to run but there was nowhere. Instantly the temperature dropped. Rain raced across the ground in a beaded curtain. Water spilled off the eaves in steel torrents.

Crack! Lightning struck a tree on the ridge at the far end of the runway. I counted the seconds before the peal of thunder. One . . . two . . . two thousand feet away.

The giant green tree frog stuck to the glass on the telephone booth, eating insects.

If there was a likely place for a strike, it was right here.

Jeff unrolled his sleeping mat and lay down on it. He turned away from the light of the phone booth.

"My God, you're not actually going to sleep, are you?"

"Why not?" he said. "We've got a long day tomorrow."

I stood in bare feet with my uncertainties. We're going to have long days for the next two months, I thought. Rain was driving almost horizontally into the verandah. Jeff didn't have a family that would miss him if he didn't come back, or if he did, he never spoke of them. I didn't want to disappear out in the bush like Dave Sacks or any of the others. It was all very real now. There was still time to change my mind. I didn't have to ride the mail plane tomorrow. No one was making me do this. I had known Jeff for little more than a year. Was that enough time to know the limits one might be pushed to after two months together in the wild?

I watched the stricken tree burn in the rain. One of us could actually die out here, *tonight*. I counted silently after each flicker of lightning. One . . . Kaboom! The thunder rolled off.

CRACK! A streak of white etched a line of light from the top of the nearby telephone pole to the sky. I was lifted off my feet by the thunderclap. Bright sparks flew from the shattered insulators at the top of the pole.

"That was close!" Jeff shouted, sitting up.

The storm raced over us, leaving the runway under several inches of water.

By midnight the thunderclouds had swept back out to sea. We listened to the sound of distant thunder. The tree frog was gone.

The next morning dawned clear and bright. The sun hadn't even cracked the distant ridge and already it was ninety degrees. Within an hour the rain evaporated from the runway. The sound of a car stirred us from sleep. The pilot parked in front of the hangar and walked over to us.

"Comfortable sleep?" he asked with a bemused expression. He was a young man in his mid-twenties, wearing sunglasses, collared shirt, shorts, and knee socks: the uniform of Australian taxi drivers, bus drivers, postal workers, and pilots.

"So, you blokes want to go to the Drysdale, eh?" he said amiably, pulling back the metal door of the hangar. "I think we can do that. I'm Richard."

He walked over to the single-prop plane, with space for the pilot and three passengers. The tin roof creaked in the heat.

"Lot of mail this week, someone needs a gearbox – but I think we can fit you in. Might be a bit heavy to start."

Great, I thought, bit heavy to start.

He pulled out a bathroom scale and weighed several packages from a pallet beside the plane before arranging them in the rear of the cabin. Then he motioned to us. Jeff and I stepped on the scale in succession. I was starting the journey with a body weight of 176 pounds, Jeff at 183. Neither of us had much to spare.

"OK," the pilot said, motioning to Jeff, "you sit in the back, mate, and you're up here," he said, pointing to me. I squeezed into the copilot seat while the pilot walked around the plane, inspecting wires and ailerons. He hopped in.

He moved the ailerons right and left, the elevators up and down. Jeff and I sat with the peculiar gravity passengers feel in the minutes before takeoff.

"Right, off we go." He flipped his sunglasses down over his eyes.

The sound of the single engine was high and small compared to the silence that engulfed us. He concentrated his gaze on the control panel: the altimeter, the artificial horizon, the oil and manifold pressure dials.

"We'll take off from that end of the runway," he shouted. "It's usually a good idea to take off into the wind."

Through the blurred circle of the propeller, the cracked lines on the asphalt passed under the nose wheel. This was it. If I had doubts, I wasn't about to get out of the plane now.

At full throttle the hull shook. The pilot looked intently out of the windshield. I leaned back in my seat, wondering if the journey was just beginning or just ending.

The painted lines disappeared faster and faster under the nose of the plane and the wings flexed against the metal hull as the white-green eucalyptus trees at the end of the runway grew distinct and with a sudden stillness we were airborne, soaring up over the treetops. As we turned in a broad circle, I saw the way we had come: the runway, the tin hangar, the two-story house with wide verandah growing smaller and smaller and in every direction empty country. To the west lay red stone massifs, to the north the silver sheen of creeks fringed by green mangroves running into the vast gray rippled space of the mud flats, and the small forlorn town of Wyndham disappearing out of sight as the plane was buffeted and lurched. We skirted the coast and flew over a red stone ridge, heading west. Already we were three days' walk from Wyndham.

To the north and east of us, large thunderclouds were collecting, rising in sheer columns into the blue sky.

"What are you doing out Drysdale way?" the pilot asked once we'd reached eight thousand feet.

"Going bushwalking," I said.

"At the Drysdale?" he asked. "What for?"

"We're going to walk from there to the coast along the Prince Regent River. If all goes well, we're going to get picked up by a boat at the King Cascade."

He didn't seem to understand.

"We've been sponsored by *Australian Geographic* magazine. We're looking for the world's rarest python."

He looked surprised. "Are you serious?"

The pilot studied the lines of rock jutting up out of green treetops, the ridges, massifs, and screes glowing orange in the morning light. He shook his head.

"You blokes have got to be crazy," he said finally.

It was a line we often repeated to ourselves in the days to come.

We droned along over the uplifted plateaus and crumbling ridges dotted with tiny trees, endless boulder fields, and silver creeks.

"Tiger country down there, mate," the pilot shouted.

"What do you mean?"

"Nowhere safe to make a forced landing down there, *any—where*. That's what pilots call tiger country."

The plane lifted and ducked in the turbulent atmosphere. Behind sunglasses the pilot was alert but relaxed, his shirt already soaked with sweat. Dark thunderheads towered fifty miles away, behind us. I looked backward in the plane at Jeff.

"Pretty exciting, eh?" I shouted, looking past Jeff's head at the disappearing coast. He nodded.

"Is it my imagination or are those thunder clouds gaining on us?"

"Don't know."

This was not going to be a walk in the park. Watching the lightning roll in from the edge of the verandah last night, I had begun to wonder if we would make it out. There was no imagined safety. Life and death were everyday events out here.

For an hour and a half we flew over empty country. No roads, no mines, no sign of man: nothing. From this height covering distance was easy. The pilot had a clipboard with a topographic map and a line in pencil drawn from the airport to the Drysdale River Station. He studied the compass heading: 267 degrees, almost due west. From there he had other lines drawn to Doongan Station, to the mission at Kalumburu. He would be dropping us off first, to conserve fuel.

The first sign of man appeared out of the dry, rocky country almost miraculously, a stripe in the orange soil and a windsock sagging on a post: the station's airfield. I looked down at the land below as we descended. The Drysdale River snaked through miniature paperbark trees across a wide sandy plain. The station buildings, the bunkhouse, the water tower with a splash of magenta bougain—villea creeping up a leak in its side, the corrugated tin garage, and the main house were surrounded by a vast orange plain dotted with eucalyptus trees.

A single vehicle waited in the tall grass beside the runway some distance from the station. Small figures stood beside it: John and Anne Koeyers, the owners of the station, and their two children. They had heard the sound of the approaching aircraft for some time, droning somewhere in the quiet sky.

Like all station owners in outback Australia, John and Anne

eagerly awaited this twice-monthly flight, weather permitting, for goods and mail from civilization. Earlier in the day they had checked to make sure the airstrip was safe for aircraft by driving their four-wheel drive up the length of the runway at forty miles per hour. This was standard procedure at outback airstrips – if they did not skid off the runway, it was dry enough to land on.

The pilot made a pre-landing sweep, studying the ground as it passed under the wings. Our shadow dodged and flickered over the treetops and rust-colored earth. As we lost altitude, I noticed all the little things, the wheel ruts in the soil, the faces of the children as we hurtled past fifteen feet above the ground, the trees at the end of the runway.

The plane bounced twice in the soil. We slowed and taxied over to the truck. The pilot killed the motor and we stepped out into the furnace of twelve degrees south latitude.

"You blokes have got to be crazy," he repeated.

"How you going, Richard?"

"Not bad, and you, John?" the pilot said.

"Been pretty quiet."

We said hello to John and Anne and their six-year-old son, Paul. Anne held a baby girl in her arms.

We helped them stash boxes of perishable foods and mail into the back of the truck. Jeff asked about the wet.

"Hasn't really started yet. This week's as wet as it's been," John said.

The rains had cut off all access by road, but the torrential rains of the wet season had yet to come.

We said goodbye to Richard as he got behind the controls. He brought the small plane up to speed and bounced down the runway into a lonely sky. Jeff and I watched the plane disappear with different thoughts.

John and Anne got into their truck and with a few words of warning about bulls and freshwater crocodiles headed off on a road back to the station with their children. The sound of the truck engine grew fainter until Jeff and I were surrounded by quiet. The sky was empty. I looked at Jeff. Now where were we?

"Welcome to nowhere," he said.

"You blokes have got to be crazy," I added.

It was half a mile from the station's airstrip to the Drysdale River crossing, a place where the road meets the river. We carried our packs, each overloaded with eighty-five pounds of equipment and freeze-dried food, down to the water. The white sand burned to the touch. The river was our way from now on, our home, at walking speed. Exactly where it would take us we did not know.

"I pity those poor bastards sitting in air-conditioned offices right now," I said.

"Yeah."

I threw my sleeping mat out in the shade of a leafy paperbark and had a nap. It was midday, and there was no point in moving anywhere. It was just too damn hot. I pulled my hat over my eyes. My circumstances were once again reduced to the bare minimum. What the hell was I doing out here? Was I wasting time?

A frilled lizard crawled near Jeff while he was dozing. He immediately awoke and grabbed the reptile. It had long legs and toes, and a fiery orange collar that it flashed at us while we photographed him. We let the lizard go and walked down to the river in the yellow light. Lying on our backs, we floated with the warm current, grabbing handfuls of wet sand to check our speed.

CHAPTER 18

FIRST STEPS

Before us lay the trackless immeasurable desert, in awful silence . . . we continued to march all day through a country untrodden before by any European foot. Save that a melancholy crow now and then flew croaking over head, or a kanguroo was seen to bound at a distance, the picture of solitude was complete and undisturbed.

Watkin Tench

The river curved lazily across the plain through stands of white paperbark trees. Pandanus leaned on curving trunks over the water, their spiky crowns sputtering with crimson finches. We walked against the current, backward on the river of time.

Beyond the fringing forest of weeping and silver-leafed paperbark trees, river red gums, and leaning pandanus, the yellow-flowering kapoks and grevilleas gave way to a grassy plain punctuated with scattered ghost gums, woollybutts, ironbarks, bloodwoods, tea tree and mimosa bush, casuarina and quinine trees with orange but inedible fruits, and the primitive cycad, a relic from the Triassic.

The Kimberley, isolated by deserts to the south, is not desert country. The habitat is comprised mainly of eucalypt savannah, with fifty of Australia's more than five hundred species of eucalyptus occurring here. The soil is eroded sandstone and basalt and though poor supports a rich variety of flowers, trees, and other plants.

The gallery forest along the river ricocheted with birds and the fragrance of eucalyptus. Collared rainbow lorikeets screeched through the foliage like colorful missiles. Willy wagtails flicked their tails back and forth with a ratcheting sound. Rainbow bee eaters flitted above the water snapping up insects. Freshwater crocodiles lay on the banks with their mouths agape to cool off.

We plodded over the white sand with our boots and heavy packs feeling utterly earthbound. Outer space began at the treetops.

Six miles from the crossing we passed a tractor beside the river, pumping water through a fire hose to the station water tower. It was the last machine we were to see or hear for months.

The river cut a natural highway through the landscape and, though it was by no means straight, we followed it because it was our only known source of water and our only point of reference. It moved alternately over sand and polished sandstone.

In the afternoon a flock of red-tailed black cockatoos, black with a dappling of brilliant red on their tail feathers, flew jerkily overhead, creaking on mechanical wings as though God, in a moment of whimsy, had let an outrageously colored windup toy out the window of Time.

"Raaaaak! . . . Raaaaak!" They alighted in the upper branches of a white gum tree.

"*Magnificus*," Jeff said. "You can see why. Absolutely stunning."

I stopped and had a long drink, closing my eyes and sucking in water from my canteen. Sweat had soaked through my shirt.

"This is hard yakka," I said.

"It's going to take a few days to acclimate."

"If we ever do."

A tree trunk lodged in the fork of a tree thirty feet above our heads indicated the height of a past flood.

"I wouldn't want to have been here when that wave came through." Jeff took off his hat and rubbed the back of his neck. "Man, that sun is hot!"

A freshwater crocodile lying on the bank rose up on its hind legs and plunged into the water at our approach like a startled nude sunbather. Everywhere the river was alive with splashes.

"Still too many cattle about," Jeff remarked. "It's not totally wild yet. Lot of flies, too."

The flies were numerous, constantly flying into our eyes, ears, and mouths, trying to suck up every drop of moisture. Jeff swatted at them continually with a pack towel.

We made our first camp in the pink light a few miles upriver, throwing our sleeping mats out on flat rocks while blue-winged kookaburras began their raucous chorus in a patch of trees fifty yards away. "Kookookookoo-ah-ah-ah-aah!"

Jeff put his MSR stove on a rock and lit it with the sparker. It flared and settled to a blue flame. He put a pot of water on for tea while we pulled burrs out of our socks and pants. The kookaburras grew silent. Yellow light struck the tops of the paperbarks and gilded the limbs of the ghost gums out on the plain. The flies disappeared, and the land was mystical and quiet.

I took two candles out of my pack and placed them on the stone next to my sleeping pad. Jeff boiled more water. He poured a cup of rice into the pot and let it sit for twenty minutes while he cooked his packet of freeze-dried lamb and peas. Once it boiled he took it off the heat and put my meal on. We sipped orange pekoe tea and waited for our meals to finish cooking, pleasantly exhausted. Jeff dished out the rice and the lamb and peas. We ate hungrily, savoring each bite between sips of tea. When we were

Jeff makes a river crossing in the Kimberley in the tiny Daihatsu. Later it would strand us beside the road in the middle of nowhere.

My first trip to the Mitchell Plateau with Jeff. The upper part of Mitchell Falls is in the background. At one point I climbed into the lower pool, which I would never do again without a rope. (*Adrian Cunningham*)

Jeff stands at the ledge camp jutting out over the waters of the Mitchell River. It was the first time I had ever fished directly from my bed.

A velvet gecko (*Oedura gracilis*) crawls across rock art in the Kimberley. (*Adrian Cunningham*)

A freshwater crocodile can grow to ten feet. Though they can be territorial and have sharp teeth, they are not man-eaters like their saltwater cousins.

Getting ready to take the mail plane to the Drysdale River Station. We were "a bit heavy to start," according to Richard, our pilot. Here, he weighs packages before arranging them in the plane.

A scene along the Drysdale River. The bird life was stupendous in the riparian forests alongside the water.

Me in the best shape of my life. A few weeks later I would be almost skeletal from hunger. (*Adrian Cunningham*)

Trekking through the broad eucalypt with thumbs up. I would lose almost a third of my body weight in the days to come. (*Adrian Cunningham*)

Because we had to carry all our food, there was no room for tents or other luxuries. Caves provided the only shelter from the heat and the rain. The grooves on the rock at upper right are where Aboriginal people sharpened their stone axes.

Bushtucker. I collected wild figs to supplement a lean diet of powdered milk, muesli, fish, and one packet of freeze-dried food with a cup of rice per day. (*Adrian Cunningham*)

Looking down into a gorge at the headwaters of the Prince Regent River. It took days to find a way into the main gorge.

The magnificent tree frog (*Litoria splendida*) we encountered while spotlighting in isolated pockets of Kimberley rain forest.

Jundudd, the lightning man with hair standing on end, indicates a highly charged electrical field. Thunderstorms in the Kimberley are the most violent on the planet. Lightning struck within a hundred feet of us on numerous occasions. (*Adrian Cunningham*)

From the cave Jeff and I watched the lightning storms roll in. Lightning struck a tree at the mouth of the cave.

I stand in the falls of Widjinari Creek. (*Adrian Cunningham*)

Our nightly spotlighting revealed numerous unusual creatures like this velvet gecko (*Oedura filicipoda*) but not the elusive rough-scaled python.

Jeff with a frill-necked lizard.

Cave wall at Oralee Creek. These Wandjina figures have no mouths, a detail that puzzled us initially. According to tribal elder David Mowaljarlai, a Wandjina has no need for a mouth because he sends his thoughts.

Me with a backpack and a roll of maps. Until we ran out of food, we did not miss the comforts of civilization much. (*Adrian Cunningham*)

Jeff prepares lunch, some sooty grunter fillets with salt. Not a bad meal after weeks in the bush.

Looking east on the Prince Regent River. Jeff and I retrieved water from the river warily as we neared the tidal zone — due to the possibility of saltwater crocodiles.

Jeff looks into the gorge of the Prince Regent River above the site of our last crossing. Below these rapids we encountered stripling barramundi and saltwater fish: saltwater crocodile territory.

I stand beside Rapture Falls.
(*Adrian Cunningham*)

Jeff and me upon reaching the valley of
Cascade Creek. We thought the walk
was almost over.

I jump into one of the best swimming holes in Western Australia.
(*Adrian Cunningham*)

Our goal, the King Cascade, named by Phillip Parker King in 1819 and a good place for mariners to get fresh water. At the base of these falls Ginger Meadows was killed by a crocodile.

The view from the face of the falls. I would have given anything to be rescued at this point.

A fifteen-foot saltwater crocodile like this one shadowed me for days as I grew thinner and more desperate while fishing from the slippery face of King Cascade. (© *Brandon D. Cole/CORBIS*)

I returned to the old homestead some years later under much more comfortable circumstances. The walls had been whitewashed by a squatter, but it was still deserted.

Thin but happy to be alive on Loch Street, Derby, Western Australia. I had been eating nonstop for days at that point, but that first cold beer in town tasted great and the first hot shower in two months was sublime. (*Adrian Cunningham*)

finished, I walked down to the river and cleaned the dishes in the wet sand.

"It's right about now that I wish we'd brought along a little whiskey," Jeff said, letting out a loud burp. "What's for dessert?"

In my pack was one dessert, a freeze-dried raspberry cobbler. I planned to surprise Jeff with it midway through the journey.

We settled down to sleep. I changed into my pajamas, a long-sleeve turtleneck and hospital scrubs, and rubbed mosquito repellant onto my face, hands, ears, and scalp. Jeff lay on his sleeping pad on a flat rock five yards from the one I lay on. A flock of cockatoos swept in from the plain and roosted in the tree branches above us. I counted forty-two corellas like white flowers perched on their roosts. Their feathers turned from white to gold to pink in the last of the sun as they chattered and cooed like excited children being hushed in a dormitory after lights out. They quietened down until one chortled, setting off a new round of chattering and chirping.

"The range of their vocal expressions is amazing."

"We'll never get any sleep if they keep it up."

Then with a sudden screech the whole flock rose into the lavender light and headed upriver going "Raaaaaak! Raaaaaaak!"

The screeching faded.

Dawn climbed down from the sky. A flock of crows found us early in the morning and let out cries of "Caaw! Caaaw! Caaaaaw!" After a breakfast of powdered milk, muesli, and instant coffee, we walked a mile before the sun cast shadows across the plain.

In the afternoon we stumbled up to a barbed wire fence strung across the river: the boundary fence. In Australia, every cattle property, no matter how large, has a perimeter fence.

We climbed over the barbed wire and stepped into the wide space beyond, into the wild.

* * *

The following evening we came to a wide green billabong lined with pandanus and set down our packs. An azure kingfisher flew downriver.

"We've been lucky with the weather so far," Jeff said, boiling tea on the stove.

From now on, fish and forage supplemented our diet. Jeff and I could only carry enough food to have a cup of muesli with powdered milk in the morning, and one freeze-dried meal at the end of the day. We fished for lunch and breakfast and collected fruits and berries, mainly bush passionfruit, wild figs, and bush grapes.

I cast a lure across the pool in the ambient light, standing up to my waist in the clear water, my bare feet in the submerged sand.

When the lure was halfway across the pool the rod bent, and I reeled the line into the waters at my feet. A two-pound fish struggled on the hook.

Suddenly a toothy snout appeared silently beside my toes. "Crocodile!" I shouted in surprise and jerked the fish out onto the bank. The six-foot *Crocodylus johnstoni*, a shy, retiring reptile, disappeared in a flurry of algae and sand.

We continued up the Drysdale, stopping frequently to apply more sunscreen or wipe the sweat out of our eyes. The river was clear and ran in places only two feet deep above the sand. I took off my boots and waded through the water to avoid the tangled underbrush on the bank and to stay cool. In a small eddy I spied a five-foot freshwater crocodile. He had obviously been kicked out of a nearby pool, as a section of his tail was missing and the wound was fresh. I photographed him before he lumbered off downriver.

In the shade at noon five ants trundled by, carrying a butterfly wing in their mandibles with the precision of five men moving a grand piano. Lying on my back in the leaf litter, I noticed a tiny black speck way, way up in the sky. A wedge-tailed eagle with a wingspan of over seven feet cored a thermal in rising circles. The second-largest raptor in the world, it searched for kangaroos and other prey.

Jeff arrived from his patch of shade. We shouldered our packs, pushing through tall speargrass with seeds like little harpoons. We studied each configuration of sand, rock, gum leaves, bark, and grass underfoot. The wet meant snakes on the move. But wherever they were sunning, on rocks, or moving in the grass, most snakes would sense our footsteps and slither away.

There were other dangers, however. Plowing through the head-high grass I came within ten feet of the rear haunches of a large animal. For a moment I was utterly confused. It wasn't a kangaroo but . . . what? It raised its head, displaying two long horns. The bull wheeled, snorted through twelve-gauge nostrils, and charged. Some bulls in the Kimberley, called cleanskins or scrub bulls, are missed by the muster every year. They do not learn to fear man.

Its hooves clattered on stone as I stepped sideways and twisted my body away from the horns and its wild eye. When the flanks passed my chest, I turned and ran for a tree, the bull close behind. I flinched as its horns clipped the other side of the tree.

The bull and I circled once around the thin trunk, then stopped and stared at each other for a moment.

"Fuck off!" I shouted in desperation. The bull snorted, tossed its head, and trotted downriver. Jeff approached some moments later with a scowl.

"Monster bull just went by, did you see it?"

"Bastard just about got me."

"Damn things are dangerous. Getting stuck in the chest out here would be really bad." He looked across the river. "You'd bleed to death very quickly. I'd like to have a gun to shoot them out of the canyons farther in, if they're in there. And the donkeys. Feral brutes."

In the following days the rain clouds roared over us. The river rose. We sank up to our ankles in mud as we walked to the headwaters of the Drysdale River. One afternoon I watched as Jeff, on the other side of the river, was swallowed up by a wall of black rain.

We pushed on through the orange mud, stinking hot and soaked to the bone.

"The wet has definitely arrived," Jeff said.

We camped in a grove of trees high enough to escape a flash flood and laid out our sleeping sheets. I staked out my mosquito net and went down to the water. A crimson finch bustled about its nest in the crown of a pandanus tree bobbing just a foot above the rising waters.

"You're doomed," I thought.

Cumulonimbus splashed with every hue of red from the departing sun marched out of the south in the closing light. The mosquitoes arrived. After a week, I did not feel mosquito or most insect bites, and went around in camp wearing only shorts.

The night wheeled slowly around from the east, sowing stars.

This landscape, so remote and so ancient, cleared the mind. The Western notion of time disappeared. Time became inextricably wedded to landscape, to the rocks and trees, to bends in the river, to the moon and stars and sun overhead. Next week was the red cliffs somewhere in the distance.

Jeff cooked rice on the stove. The beef and beans soaked in a pot while he boiled more water. "Your tea's there," he said pointing. "Uh-oh."

Thunderclouds moved silently in the blue-red light, bearing down on us. Streaks of lightning etched the cloud. Two dozen black flying foxes, several pink and gray galahs, a hawk, and ten sulphur-crested cockatoos flew upriver in the space between the fringing trees.

I put a plastic bag over my backpack and leaned it against a tree.

The downpour arrived. I hunched cross-legged under my foam sleeping mat to keep off the rain. Jeff sat with the water spilling in torrents off the brim of his hat. The stove went out.

The lightning rolled forward like creeping artillery, illuminating the world for an instant – the brilliant white paperbark trees and clouds, the green pandanus plants, the muddied river, the glistening sandstone: rock, tree, sky, water, life. A single cockatoo screeched downriver, the motion of its wings caught in each brilliant flash like frames of an old movie.

After the thundershower a colony of flying foxes roosted in the trees nearby, hanging by their feet and wrapping themselves inside their wings. They gave off an aroma not unlike that of buttered popcorn. By their fitful flapping, I figured they were getting as much sleep as I was.

For ten days we stumbled on, stopping only to sleep under our space blankets or in whatever bowers we could find. We grumbled about the vastness of this eucalyptus plain. Where was the canyon country? After a cup of muesli with powdered milk and tea for breakfast, we pushed on.

Here the river cut through the mahogany stone. I put down my pack and swam in the water with the freshwater crocodiles. In this abundant wet, the freshwater crocodiles were quite gregarious. Five pairs of eyes watched me cautiously as I swam out to the middle of the pool among the water lilies, the white petals tinged with purple.

I picked a flower and inhaled the fragrance, so far from anywhere. On a branch above the pool two sulphur-crested cockatoos perched side by side, cooing softly to each other in the afternoon. They preened one another with their beaks, nudging each other and chatting contentedly. Cockatoos mate for life. Clearly love is not the province of humans only.

The only signs of man appeared at night. A satellite moved overhead high enough to catch the sun's rays and disappeared as I watched through binoculars. My father was teaching physics at Sequoia High School in California when the first man-made satellite, Sputnik, entered orbit in 1957. He tuned his Hallicrafters radio in to the satellite, and with his class listened to the high-pitched "beep . . . beep . . . beep . . ." that announced the dawn of the space age.

The Milky Way stretched across the night sky, the stars like flecks of silver in an alluvial stream, the moon rising fifty minutes later each day. In the wilderness, over time, I saw the stars in a way I had never seen them before – not as pinpricks of light in two dimensions, but as stellar beacons, real suns of all sizes and colors in three dimensions scattered at various distances through space. Antares in the constellation of the Scorpion was ruby red. Suns on the horizon flickered white, blue, and red through a sea of atmosphere. Beyond the stars of our home galaxy lay other galaxies separated by an immensity of celestial outback.

CHAPTER 19

LANDMARKS

"The mountain should be in that direction." Jeff pointed to the southwest. I climbed the tallest tree beside the river. From the highest branch I saw nothing but endless treetops.

After another day's hard slog I lay in my sleeping sheet on a rock ledge above the river. Red-tinted clouds moved off toward the east. Tomorrow, if the weather cleared, we would climb an ancient mountain rising 2,130 feet above the surrounding plain and assess our entry into the Prince Regent River gorge.

We studied the maps again by the fire that evening. If we were right, the mountain lay only a mile away.

The next morning, with our eyes on our compasses, we left the river and crossed a eucalyptus savannah dotted with cycads out into the trackless stony plain. I carried six liters of water in my pack and a liter in my canteen. A casuarina tree screamed with collared lorikeets and red-winged parrots on golden stalks of nectar. After half an hour's walking, the mountain had not appeared. I felt like a sailor on a ship waiting for landfall.

"Land ho!" A house-sized boulder appeared among the sea of trees. In a previous wet it must have tumbled from the mountain and sluiced for several hundred yards through the mud.

Massive boulders began to rise up above the scattered trees. We were getting close.

The rocks at the base of the mountain fell together in a thousand different configurations. Jeff took his pack off.

"Rule number one is never leave your pack in the wilderness," he said. "Rule number two is never leave your pack without first making absolutely sure you can find it again."

We took note of the dead trees and strange rock formations, confident that we could return to the packs. It felt odd suddenly to walk without the weight on my shoulders and hips.

We climbed up the boulder heap. In between the rocks grew sticky, sweet-smelling spinifex grass and a few stunted trees. Within an hour we stood at the summit, the highest of three gigantic boulders, looking in all directions. In the cloudless afternoon we oriented our maps to the north, checking the lines on the map with the features of the landscape before us.

"That must be Mount Bomford," I said, taking a compass bearing on a distant pile of rocks.

"And that must be Mount Hann." To the northwest of us a flat-topped mountain of ochre basalt jutted above its scree, like a block of carved wood surrounded by its shavings.

"We're way out here."

No smoke rose into the quiet afternoon. There was no cairn on this mountain, no sign of man. Between us we laid claim to a hundred thousand square miles.

"Hey! I can see your house from here."

Below us, the Drysdale River flowed east in a great sweeping curve between three bouldered mountains, its progress marked by the meander of white gum trees and green pandanus. The water glinted through the foliage. I turned slowly in a circle, looking back to the east. From this height the trees were like matchsticks, disappearing over the eastern horizon. Civilization was weeks away.

At the farthest reaches of the western horizon, burgundy cliffs marked the headwaters of the Prince Regent River, four days walk at least. What would we find in the gorge?

"Somewhere in there is our entry into the Prince Regent."

"The promised land!"

"It looks like some very rugged country."

The eucalyptus march was almost over. Now for the canyons. As far as the eye could see, and a thousand miles beyond that, lay a silent wilderness.

As a child I had watched my father's slides of his raft trip down the Colorado. Every year he would project them on an old silvery screen and relive a part of his youth. In the heat of summer he showed the pictures of the rattlesnake he had encountered, poised, crisp, ready to strike the camera, the shaking rattle blurred by the slow shutter speed, the black columns of Vishnu Schist at Lava Falls that he always wished he had had a person in for scale, the photos of cliffs, stone dwellings, and light.

"You can't imagine – those columns are gigantic," he would say, stepping back to assess the photo of Vishnu Schist for what seemed the first time.

One picture we never saw: my father's only encounter with a human skeleton in the wilderness. He told us the story every time he showed his slides – how he and others in the party had searched for a headless Indian skeleton that was first mentioned by John Wesley Powell on his great expedition down the Colorado.

"Even in Powell's time, the skeleton was missing the skull," my father remarked. "We searched for a whole day up and down along a cliff face near where Powell had described encountering the skeleton, but we didn't find it."

The American west was so much younger when my father knew it, even then.

"I lay in my sleeping bag that night wondering where in the heck that skeleton could be. We'd searched everywhere. And as I thought about it, I remembered that just above the last ledge in the rock was a bench higher up. No one had climbed up there. It didn't seem likely to be up there – but I knew right then in my sleeping bag it was the only place the skeleton could be."

I watched the sun move across the sky, thinking of my father.

"The next morning at first light I hiked up to the place I had remembered. It was quite a ways up and guess what, there it was! Exactly as Powell had described it. A bleached skeleton lying in the dust without the skull," my father said.

"How many days walk to those cliffs, you reckon?" Jeff stirred me from my thoughts.

"Maybe three, four. It'll be slow going inside those gorges. I hope it's not flooded right to the edges of the cliffs."

We hiked back down the mountain and found the terrace where our packs had been. They weren't there. The trees all started to look familiar.

"Must be farther up," Jeff said, but I thought they had to be farther down. We separated and began to search the stone terraces, one by one. What the hell, I wondered, we'd been so careful about marking the packs and taking note of landmarks. At first I was only irritated, but as the minutes went by I became increasingly anxious. The water in our canteens had long been exhausted.

Finally Jeff called out from above, he had found them. We put our packs on in the afternoon and strode across the plain, reaching the river by nightfall, sure now of where we were. We cooked our dinner and fell asleep to the sound of freshwater crocodiles slapping their tails on the river, marking territory.

The following afternoon we reached a branch of the Drysdale River meandering from the northwest called Woodhouse Creek. Narrower than the main flow, it led more directly to the gorge at the headwaters of the Prince Regent River.

Rain poured down in the gray afternoon. I put my pack at the base of a tree and studied the muddy tributary.

Jeff came up and I shouldered my pack.

"I don't want to sleep in the mud," I said.

"No argument here."

We fanned out from the river, looking for a suitable cave, or at least a flat rock to sleep on. Ten minutes from the river we found a pile of boulders. Hopping over and around them, I found a slight overhang. We would have wet feet, but it was shelter.

Jeff and I unpacked our sleeping gear and gratefully took off our sodden boots. Everything was soaked through. Night arrived quickly with the rain. For as far as I could imagine, no light pushed back the darkness. I had never before beheld so much unelectrified space.

I found a few twigs and arranged them underneath the overhang. With a lighter I directed a flame at the tinder. The fire crept up hopefully through a few sprigs of dry grass and then went out.

I rearranged the tinder and tried again. The grass burned long enough for a small twig to catch. Then it went out.

Remembering Roddy's trick in the desert, I went to my pack and took out a fuel bottle. Normally, I would have carefully splashed some fuel onto the twigs and then put a spark to them. This time I lit the lighter under the tinder and poured the fuel directly onto the flame. It was a mistake I would not have made had I not been utterly exhausted.

The flame leapt into the mouth of the bottle. In an instant the entire cave was illuminated by orange light. I reared back, the bottle spurting flame like a Roman candle. Burning white gas spilled onto my hand. I looked wildly around for Jeff – two eyes crouched at the rear of the cave. I looked at our packs, wheeled, and hurled the bottle into the darkness.

My hand was still on fire. I slipped off the edge of the cave and fell three feet to the rocks below. Jeff came over quickly with a flashlight. It looked like we had been napalmed.

"Are you all right?"

"I think so. Oh, I cut my wrist."

Jeff helped me up. Flames lingered atop puddles of water at the mouth of the cave.

"What were you doing? Didn't you hear me? I was telling you to stop! I said don't! You didn't hear me. It was like you were in a trance."

My wrist was gashed. My fingers burned. What was I doing?

"I think I'll forget about the fire and go to bed," I said.

The puddles of fuel burned out in the rain and once again we were enclosed within an immense, dripping solitude. I lay on my sleeping mat, my feet in the rain and my burnt hand submerged in a pot of water all night. Jeff made me a cup of tea.

"You want to be careful. What if you'd spilled that fuel on yourself? Help is at least a week away. I'd have to leave you in the creek, and there's no guarantee you'd be alive when I got back."

Jeff bandaged my wrist while he counseled me on the perils of fatigue. From now on I would recognize early symptoms of exhaustion and rest. We continued slowly over the boggy plain.

Mist draped across the endless stony valleys. We entered the maze-like sandstone canyons in a steady downpour. The wet had set in. When the sun did come out, steam rose off the rocks.

We struggled to find our way down sheer escarpments that ran for miles, backtracked up narrow canyons, and stumbled over scree slopes, looking for a way into the main gorge of the Prince Regent River.

"I think a good title for the article could be, 'Rock Climbing with a Seventy-pound Backpack,'" I shouted.

On day three of the canyons we entered what Jeff named the valley of the cycads: a narrow creek hemmed in by sandstone ridges. Green cycads on fire-battered stalks grew up among the rocks and grass, relics of the Triassic. I half expected a juvenile *Tyrannosaurus rex* to appear at treetop height through the fog-shrouded trees.

"It's like the valley that time forgot, isn't it?" Jeff said.

I found a cave in the late afternoon high above the valley. I would have to sleep almost in an upright position, but it was shelter from the rain. I looked out over endless horizons of stone, alone and exhausted. Firelight from a small fire flickered on the cave ceiling. What am I doing here? I wondered. Jeff looked for a cave higher in the cliff. He disappeared, and for once I felt what it would be like to be completely alone in outer space.

I watched the rain. This habitat was recently home to *Megalania prisca*, a close relative of the goanna and Komodo dragon.

Megalania prisca, "the great ripper," resembled a Komodo dragon but grew up to thirty feet long. It preyed on diprotodons, a prehistoric forerunner of the kangaroo as big as a rhinoceros, until the end of the Pleistocene, some 12,000 years ago. The Komodo dragon still lives on several islands in the Indonesian archipelago, not too far to the north. Could a remnant *Megalania* from the Pleistocene be lurking in this primeval valley, waiting to ambush one of us near a waterhole? If so, it was a discovery we were unlikely to bring back to civilization.

It was thrilling to know that Jeff and I were the first non-indigenous people in these parts. Except for a brief survey in 1986, this land was still unknown to science. Jeff and I might discover something truly fantastic – a relic from a previous age, like the coelacanth discovered still living in the waters off Madagascar, or the hundred-million-year-old species of ginkgo tree discovered in a quiet canyon only a hundred miles north of Sydney.

I imagined a herd of diprotodons grazing in the valley below.

Just the possibility of discovering a new species, in a world where it seemed everything was known and stock values went up and down by one-eighth increments, was enthralling.

What about the land crocodile, the Quinkan? Could a surviving population remain in a valley like this, undiscovered? Or Australia's marsupial "lion," *Thylacoleo carnifex*, thought to have gone extinct during a period of great aridity 18,000 years ago? A remnant population wasn't likely, especially as there was no sign of any large herbivores for these creatures to prey on, but who knew?

Of all the species of creatures that might survive the Pleistocene and remain undiscovered because of its furtive habits, it seemed the giant Australian python, *Wonambi naracoortensis*, was a natural candidate. At over twenty feet long, it might still find enough prey among the wallabies and kangaroos to have survived the megafaunal extinctions that occurred with the arrival of *Homo sapiens*. Was *Wonambi* out here still?

For two days we sat above the valley in our caves, recuperating. I hoped the wounds on my hands would not become infected in the constant humidity.

Jeff occasionally came down to see how I was doing and boil some tea. Otherwise we kept committee with the wallabies who appeared on occasion. I cried for an afternoon in the middle of nowhere. Only I knew where I was, but I did know, and that was the important thing. A rock wallaby appeared among the boulders, and bounded away in search of food.

Night fused out of the shadows. The rain began. In the darkness I closed my eyes. I could be anywhere in time.

I sang to myself over the sound of the rain a remembered song, "Who'll Stop the Rain?" It seemed somehow incongruous in this place, which would outlive all of popular music, all human history. I wondered who would be the last person to hear one of Beethoven's symphonies. A thoughtful scientist had put such information on the Voyager 2 spacecraft, moving beyond the reaches of our solar system.

In the morning a dingo chased a kangaroo over the rocks. They disappeared, the dingo still trailing.

On the third day the sun came out. We studied the maps. This was adventure! I'd almost forgotten why we were here.

"We could be here, or we could be here, or we could be here," Jeff finally swept his hand over the map.

For a day we steered to all points of the compass, clambering down labyrinthine canyons cut into the escarpment, constantly seeking a vantage. In the rain we climbed a sandstone ridge. Mountains stood in the distance, lonely rocks in a lonely sky.

Finally, we followed a flowing creek as it cut through steeper and steeper walls, descending into the main gorge. Rounding a bend, the creek fell 150 feet down a sheer face onto a pile of boulders. We peered over the precipice.

"Not getting in this way."

"Nope."

We backtracked and climbed over a crumbling ridge.

A pair of wedge-tailed eagles spread their wings and took to the sky silently. Against the rocks and tiny trees of the gorge below, they appeared huge. We walked to the edge of the cliff and peered over. At the bottom of the gorge the river ran fast and brown.

"There it is, mate!" I shouted. "The headwaters of the Prince Regent River!"

We set down our packs and shook hands.

From the cliff below us a talus slope descended to the river.

"Hmm," Jeff mused, the tops of trees three hundred feet below. The gorge ran southeast to northwest, disappearing in both directions.

"How do we get down from here?"

I walked the cliff until I found a place where it had partially collapsed.

"This way!"

We boulder-hopped down the broken rock and then I climbed seventy feet down a cliff face with numerous holds. Jeff lowered the packs to me on a rope. In the bottom of the valley I stripped and swam in the river, the waters brown with silt. We had reached the river, the great river.

CHAPTER 20

THE RIVER

Massive stone walls towered hundreds of feet above our heads. We struggled through thick stands of pandanus and the lush growth crowding the water's edge, lost in time, cloud dreaming. The vegetation swarmed with biting green ants. Numerous smaller side canyons intersected the main gorge.

"I'm starting to realize there's a reason no one's done this before."

"We'll know for next time."

But in truth we were both astounded by the prospect of being somewhere no civilized man had ever been before. There was nothing ugly about the natural world. We encountered clear blue pools, artful configurations of rock and tree, orange and yellow leaves stirring gently in eddies, turtles, and clouds, graceful bends in the canyon. Each step brought a new world. We pushed through high grass on one side of the river, and plunged through enchanted forests of ancient trees and ferns.

At lunchtime I sat naked on the rocks and cleaned three freshly caught fish by the water's edge. Two freshwater crocodiles and a turtle, visible only by their brows, made their way against the current to feast on the scraps.

We pushed on along the bank of the river. Here the walking was easier, as the gorge walls did not encroach so close to the water. In the evening light I caught six more fish and built a stone cache to preserve them from the crocodiles until morning. The basalt cliffs of the canyon glowed red in the evening light.

Jeff and I stood on the bank of Pitta Creek watching a torrent of water roil into the main body of the Prince Regent in the pouring rain. As we watched, the creek rose and covered a line of boulders. It would be impossible to cross here with the river in full flood.

"Hope it stops raining this afternoon."

"Not bloody likely."

I climbed up a talus slope and crawled into a small cave. The ceiling was only six inches above our heads, and our legs stuck out into the rain. We lit the stove to make a cup of tea. Three weeks from the edge of nowhere, Jeff and I were as remote as either of us had ever been, soaked to the bone, hungry, and happy. Despite our crude habitation and meager fare, we felt like Caesars in this wilderness.

The next morning we continued up the canyon of Pitta Creek under gray skies. Water flowed off every rock. The creek had only risen higher.

"Nothing for it but to walk up and around it," I said.

We shouldered our packs. A couple of miles up, the river widened into a large churning pool, the bottom of which formed a rapid. Just above the pool the river narrowed and a line of pandanus stretched almost to the other side. It seemed a good place for a crossing. All morning I fashioned a raft of dead wood, but when it hardly broke the surface, I abandoned it.

"That was a waste of energy."

"I know. Don't know what I was thinking. We can just inflate our sleeping pads if we have to swim for it."

Jeff stood on the bank while I entered the river above the pool and pulled myself hand over hand along the line of pandanus stalks growing into the middle. The main current surged through a break only four yards wide in the pandanus. So close. Should I try to swim for it? The rapids rumbled 250 feet downriver. The current thrummed through the branches of flooded trees. I stuck a foot out into the raging water. I turned and looked at Jeff over the roar, shaking my head.

Something slid into the river from the opposite bank. A large tail disappeared into the water. I retreated to shore.

"Did you see that?" I asked.

"It looked like a very large freshie. At least I hope it was."

"Could it be a saltie?" I wondered. "This far up?"

"I suppose it could be. It looked awfully big."

"I don't like the crossing anyway. Let's look further up." The rain continued all afternoon. We found a small overhang in the cliff and prepared to wait out the flood.

"This is rough," I shouted from where I was huddled inside my space blanket over the sound of the deluge.

"Yeah," Jeff said. "Very rough. But think of Papillon!" We had both read the story of the prisoner Papillon.

"Eight years in solitary confinement, without light, without conversation . . ." Jeff's voice became more urgent, "Without books! Can you imagine, without books!"

In the late afternoon the water dropped. Two hundred yards upstream, a narrow line of pandanus held against the surging water.

"Make sure you undo your belt buckle, in case you need to get out of your pack," Jeff shouted over the rumble of rapids. We pulled ourselves across the flood on the stalks of the pandanus, placing our feet carefully among the submerged roots. Finally we waded through a paperbark swamp and began climbing up a gorge filled with vines and fruiting trees.

CHAPTER 21

THE CAVE IN
THE CLIFF

I hiked up the slope of a small gorge running into the Prince Regent and found a gallery of paintings. Rock cods, turtles, emus and kangaroos swirled in shades of red, white, and orange ochre on a white background: totems of the Ngarinyan clan who lived in this area with the tribes of the Wunambal and coastal Worora for thousands of years.

This was an "increase center." The elders maintained these magic sites to ensure the continuation of rain in the Kimberley, to maintain the cycles of flood and fire that caused the native fruits to flower and assured the availability of fish and wild game.

In that topography every spring of water, every prominent hill or valley is named and connected with a creation myth: the mythical trails that an Aboriginal uses to find his way across a landscape rich in meaning. For the Ngarinyan, who had no written language, these cave paintings were a gospel, painted in red and white ochre.

To look at the figures and out over the rocky hills was to know the passing of millennia. The oldest known sites of human occupation in the Kimberley date back twenty-four thousand years. Older sites, which would once have been near the mouths of rivers, have disappeared beneath rising oceans.

I considered the terrain surrounding me. In local belief, the mythological rock cod is thought to have formed the channel of the Prince Regent River, pushing out to the sea through the rocks to escape the Rainbow Serpent.

How sad, I thought, that the elders were no longer around to maintain their covenant with nature. The stones they had used to grind ochre sat in worn depressions in the rock below the gallery, as if they had been left there yesterday.

In local myth, creation began when Wallanganda let freshwater fall from space upon the Earth. Wallanganda means literally "Rain God" and is, according to tribal elder David Mowaljarlai, the sovereign of the galaxy and the force that made everything on Earth. Wallanganda came to Earth in the form of a Wandjina. Wandjinas are the mythical ancestors, the creator heroes in Aboriginal belief. Some took the shape of clouds, others kangaroos, turtles, and fish. Walking on Earth, the Wandjinas created the features and inhabitants of the landscape. Wallanganda created mankind on the orders of Ngadjar, the above one, master of all galaxies. Long before Edward Hubble, it seems, the Aboriginal people had an understanding that there are other galaxies beyond our own.

Wallanganda came from space to give life. His deeds are known as Yorro Yorro, meaning "Everything on Earth brand new and standing up." Yorro Yorro is perpetual creation and renewal.

In white and red ochre a figure of the Rainbow Serpent curved on the canyon wall. It is not surprising that rainbows formed a part of the spirit world for the Aboriginals here. To them, the perfect symmetry and colors of the rainbow were unlike anything in their world.

As rationalists, Jeff and I viewed rainbows as natural phenomena, the separation of white light into its components by the prismatic effect of water droplets. But, over time, I began to see a rainbow both as a natural phenomenon and as proof of the presence of a creative force some called God. Not an Old or New Testament God, something far older. Life, it occurred to me, must be a force acting throughout the universe, like gravity or the weak and strong atomic forces. Indeed, any grand unifying theory of physics must include life.

The Rainbow Serpent was Wunggud, who, according to Worora and Ngarinyan belief, lives today and always in the Earth. She is the primeval substance of which everything is formed. Before creation she was tightly curled into a ball like a python.

At the time of creation Wunggud stirred, forming waterholes, rivers, and other physical features of the landscape around us. Wunggud is still in charge of all cycles, and Wallanganda continues to send batches of energy to Earth in the form of lightning.

Wallanganda exists in a form that can be seen, but under law it can only be shown to men, and only after initiation. It lies embodied in the Milky Way, where Wallanganda lay down in the sky after creation.

These Wandjina paintings, though thousands of years old, displaced other older paintings, named after the pastoralist who discovered them in 1902, Joseph Bradshaw. Bradshaw paintings are intricate and depict figures as wearing clothes, which more recent Aboriginals of the area did not, with the exception of a human-hair belt.

Where the creators of the Bradshaw paintings went, who they were, and what they looked like, remains a mystery. The Wandjina paintings themselves show the encroaching influence of the Rainbow Serpent belief from eastern and central Australia. To the east, Wandjina paintings include the Rainbow Serpent, while those nearer the coast do not.

Rainbow Serpent paintings in other areas have been documented back to 9,000 B.C., which, according to Josephine Flood in *Archaeology of the Dreamtime*, makes the Rainbow Serpent myth the longest continuing religious belief on the planet. If religion, like culture, like education, is a tool for species survival, *Homo sapiens* has much to learn from the last generation of Aboriginal elders of the Kimberley.

"It must have been quite an affluent culture to support an artist of this skill," Jeff said, climbing up and admiring the pictographs.

Above the gallery I found a long cleft in the cliff wall, tall enough to stand in, a dry, spacious cave, high in the cliff. At the foot of the cave pieces of sharp quartz lay where they had fallen, flaked off by a hunter fashioning a spear point. It might have been yesterday or it might have been five thousand years ago.

"Nice cave."

"Definitely a four-star rating."

"Lot of flat rock."

"Awesome view."

From our vantage in the cave, we gazed out over the afternoon. Opposite, a cliff formed the other half of this canyon studded with palms and cycads. A hundred-fifty-foot waterfall thundered in the distance through the ghost gum trees, their limbs as smooth as stockinged legs. Below us a line of silver-leafed paperbark trees, black ironbarks, kapok with yellow flowers, cocky-apple, and other gums followed this flooded creek.

On the rock ceiling above our heads Jundudd, the Lightning Man, pointed a warning finger toward the sky. From the top of his head, red and white lines radiated like spokes, indicating a highly charged electrical field. The Wunambal, Worora, and Ngarinyan Aboriginal tribes of this area had a great fear of lightning. The native word *Garergula* means lightning or poisonous snake, a reflection of nature's sometimes fatal caprice.

Jundudd is a creator of child spirits in the Kimberley. Without lightning, there would be no conception, no new generation. According to local belief, all souls come from lightning strikes, bringing life to Earth in white flashes of illumination. Again, this native or intuitive belief approaches our scientific understanding.

Lightning has made life possible, not only in its interaction with amino acids in the primordial soup, which sparked self-replicating chains of proteins, but also because it helped create ozone over billions of years of lightning strikes and allowed life to emerge from the oceans sheltered from the sun's intense ultraviolet light.

As with Einstein's thought experiments, perhaps all the answers to the big questions lie in our own minds, if only we would spend the time thinking and imagining.

Cliffs, escarpments, and boulders stretched to the horizon. This was close to the original mind. Climbing a thin sapling, I collected wild grapes while hundreds of green ants swarmed over their larder and me.

It occurred to me that if you did not spend two months in the wilderness in your youth, you might never discover who you were: you might never discover your true self, stripped of all conditioning, ideology, and belief. I was the child of professional parents, who grew up in a suburb of Boston, and yet here I was, no more than an Earthling. Nature was the final context, and everywhere it seemed that context was being destroyed.

Clouds moved across the bluest sky. The sound of the waterfall spilled through the trees. If you sat in silence for thirty days, you would hear the voice of God.

In the afternoon I climbed around the cliff face to the waterfall and lay naked on the hot stone above it. A blue-tongued lizard, fat and stubby with a dark blue tongue, crawled across the sand. Two brolgas flew overhead on long wings, landing nearby with a curious staccato bleat. They approached upstream, the red splash of feathers around their eyes brilliant against gray feathers.

Exploring up the creek, I discovered a twig bower in the sand. Bowerbirds are a family confined to New Guinea and Australia. Constructed of twigs woven on either side by the male bowerbird, the bower forms an avenue for display and courtship. This bower contained small bleached bones and the white shells of land snails stacked at either end of the bower to entice a female. Nobody was home.

I climbed back to the cave. The rumble of distant thunder replaced the silence of midday. From the north the dark beating heart of a Wandjina rolled over us. The razor flash, the brilliant colors of the sky: One . . . two . . . three . . . *Crack!* The thunder pealed off like a giant wave. One . . . two . . . *Crack!*

Caves are not good places to be in a lightning storm. If a bolt struck the top of the escarpment the lightning could travel through rock until it reached the hollow of the cave. Then it would take the path of least resistance. That path could be one of us.

Our hair stood on end in the electrified air. *CRACK!* We were lifted off our feet as lightning struck a ghost gum at the mouth of the cave. Its trunk exploded into a thousand pieces and burned in the rain.

No wonder the Aboriginal people considered the clouds gods.

One . . . two . . . *Crack!* I counted the interval between flash and thunderclap with growing relief. The cloud was moving off. I walked down to the tree when the storm was over. Glowing coals still burned in the trunk. I was humbled with the realization that this was how mankind first acquired his most important tool, fire. With it he was able to scare off the large predators of the Pleistocene, transform the landscape, cook, and ultimately forge metal.

Back in the cave I pondered the brief window of time of which I was a part. With so many different possibilities for the biological and cultural evolution of the world, how strange to have arrived at this one.

It occurred to me, against the backdrop of all time, that I was standing in the early dawn of humanity's nuclear age, before the sun had even cracked the horizon. Five thousand years from hieroglyphs to $E = mc^2$ and the hydrogen bomb was no time at all. Not out here.

How strange that one element in the periodic table, uranium-235, had the capacity to be manipulated by man to his own destruction. Why had Nature given man this literal Tree of Knowledge? Was it a self-fulfilling prophecy, arising out of the Judeo-Christian tradition? Would the Hindus or the Buddhists ever have come up with the A-bomb?

Strange that the first atomic pile, truly man's first disobedience, took place in the squash courts of the University of Chicago. If "all nature's difference is all nature's peace," in the end, they will say, it was our schools that destroyed us.

My father was eighteen years old and laying a concrete floor on the day the bomb exploded over Hiroshima. He and the other workers marked the date in wet concrete. It wasn't some bizarre symbolic myth, it was all real.

In one Aboriginal legend, man in a fit of hubris allied himself with the animals and tried to take on the Creators in battle. The azure kingfishers, green-winged parrots, red-tailed black cocka-toos, and others were all arrayed for ancient combat. When man came to his senses, he put down his weapons. The battle between man and the Creators never took place, but the war paint remained, resulting in the brilliant plumage of the birds.

In the morning a band of black flying foxes flew past the cave, returning home at first light like revelers returning from an all-night party.

We stayed in the cave for four days, exploring the surrounding countryside, fishing, photographing, and wondering. After five weeks of silence, walking, heat, and the myriad wonders of the natural world, the Western duality of mind and body disappeared. Walking was meditation. Every configuration of leaves became a work of art. Every rock had meaning. Every passing cloud was a moment in the cosmic clock. I lived in a completely sensual world, beyond time; swimming, climbing trees, jumping off rocks into deep pools, fishing, watching clouds, thinking without words, both animal and God. After weeks in the wild, I understood how each piece of nature, each shadow, each birdcall possessed a mysterious significance.

Vermilion light poured through seams in the cloud and struck the escarpments in the distance.

"It makes you think we ought to be in a factory somewhere, making widgets, doesn't it?"

"Or at least thinking of ways to make widgets more efficiently."

The sky turned pink, then lavender, then black. The clouds silently retreated, and stars blazed in the first clear night in weeks.

"Hey," Jeff said putting on his light, "it's a Friday night." I laughed. Such distinctions meant nothing out here. Monday, Tuesday, Wednesday — names were just abstractions from reality.

We climbed out onto the escarpment above the cave by the light of our headlamps, seeking out the eyeshine of strange and wonderful creatures unknown to science.

Sloshing up a narrow creek bed, we kept our gaze on the overhanging branches above us. A yellow eye hovered in the dark.

"Look! Look there!" Jeff whispered. On a branch before us was a giant green tree frog, *Litoria splendida*. Carefully Jeff caught it and put it in a pillowcase.

Farther upstream we encountered a ten-foot python curled in the roots of a tree.

"Olive python," Jeff said, picking it up by the tail. The snake had a beautiful sheen and, unlike carpet pythons, did not attempt to bite us. "Isn't it beautiful?"

"Who knows — tonight might be the night!"

We hoped a final piece of the adventure would be to find

Morelia carinata, but we knew the chances were slim. In the heat and silence I shut off my light and stood in an enormous darkness. Jeff was a wavering beam of light in the midst of outer space. Near the edge of the escarpment our headlamps caught the eyeshine of a possum. As we approached it disappeared in the rocks.

"Might have been the scaly-tailed possum, *Wyulda squami-caudata*, endemic to the escarpments of the Kimberley. Can't say for sure," Jeff said. Returning to the cave he caught a velvet gecko on the wall. It had enormous black eyes and a banded tail.

The next morning we photographed the creatures and returned them to the escarpment before continuing our journey.

CHAPTER 22

ORALEE CREEK

To go back in time, you walk.

David Mowaljarlai, Ngarinyan tribal elder

We entered a small canyon that cut into the wider gorge of the Prince Regent River. The waters swirled around massive boulders. Atop the cliffs livistona palms kept lonely sentinel against the sky.

Five weeks' walk from civilization, I took off my pack and undressed on a flat rock under a bottlebrush tree, contemplating this junction of ancient rivers. A geological curiosity, the Prince Regent River runs in an almost straight line through a fracture in the beds of Leopold sandstone. The creeks running into the Prince Regent intersect the main gorge perpendicularly through other fractures in the Gardner Plateau. Captain King wrote:

Mount Trafalgar is a conspicuous object on the north-eastern side of the basin; and another hill, close to it, being equally remarkable was called Mount Waterloo. These hills rise precipitously from the plain; and being capped by a warlike battlement, bear a strong resemblance to Steep Head in Point

Warrender. Upon leaving the cutter we crossed St George's Basin, which appeared to receive several streams on the south side, and landed on a small wooded island for bearings; from which the summits of Mounts Waterloo and Trafalgar bore in a line. About two miles farther on, the banks of the river again contracted, and trended to the south-east on so direct a course, that, from the distant land being hidden by the horizon, the river bore the appearance of being a strait. We were now twenty-two miles from the sea, and as there was every appearance of this proving a considerable stream, it was honoured by the title of Prince Regent.

The sky was blue as I slipped off a boulder into the tributary and swam through the world of stone, sand, and water. The creek was clear and moved lazily here despite the rains.

I stood up on a boulder in midstream. Red walls streaked with yellow and orange towered overhead. A bank of soil remained between the base of the cliffs and the water's edge. Between the walls grew tree ferns, fruiting trees, stout buttress trees, tangles of vines, and other living examples of Australia's rain-forest past. I emerged from the water and climbed onto the narrow bank.

The Kimberley contains at least 1,500 clusters of these ancient rain forests, known as vine thickets or monsoon forests, most of them huddled around permanent water sources in the shadow of deep canyons – vestiges of a time when Australia was covered by rain forest and ruled by dinosaurs, long before the arrival of Aboriginal people. Rain forests are the dinosaurs of the plant world.

One hundred and forty million years ago, Australia and Antarctica were joined with New Zealand, South America, Africa, and India in the supercontinent Gondwanaland. At that time much of the northern and eastern sections of Australia and Antarctica was covered by rain forest in what was then a wetter climate. Tropical rain forest dominated after the emergence of flowering plants (angiosperms), pushing aside the ancient non-flowering plants (gymnosperms) like cycads, conifers, ferns, lichens, and mosses.

About fifty million years ago Australia broke off from Antarctica and moved northward at the rate of three inches per year. As it moved, about thirty million years ago, Australia's climate became drier. The rain forests retreated. Over time the rain-forest species evolved into the more drought-resistant species like the eucalyptus that predominate in Australia today. Rain forest now covers only about four thousand square miles in Australia, along the northeastern coast between Townsville and the tip of Cape York Peninsula, and in isolated pockets in the Far North.

I stood on the bank in awe. In the silence of the canyon stood the ancestors of all Australia's native tree species. The ancient and primitive Myrtaceae and Proteaceae families before me were the primeval progenitors of the eucalypts, bottlebrushes, banksias, and grevilleas. A cluster fig grew next to a giant rain forest bloodwood. Leaning over the water in the shade of the canyon was a buttress tree with wide surface roots that occurred in the eastern rain forests of Millaa Millaa and Cape Tribulation and no place in between. How did it get here, I wondered?

But the answer was obvious. It had been here all along, while the flora of the rest of the continent had been transformed. In these cool, wet places between the canyon walls, Australia remained as it had for millennia. This tree and its cousins in the rain forests of Millaa Millaa were separated not only by close to two thousand miles but by millions of years as well. Clustered in the shadow of the cliff, this remnant rain forest contained ancient species and was a redoubt of biodiversity surrounded by vast arid regions, quite distinct from the rain forests of Asia. It was waiting only for the next great wet to expand its range.

To move among these strange fruiting trees was to walk in an enchanted forest. A black-and-white Torres Strait Island pigeon flew silently through the choked vegetation and disappeared.

Butterflies fluttered in patches of sunlight. Rainbow pittas, with a streak of blue on their green-feathered backs, rummaged in the leaf litter. Here green-wing pigeons, yellow orioles, and other birds of the rain forest moved below the shady canopy.

The wafting smell of flowers and fruits, epiphytes, orchids, and vines, and the appearance of a tree with white and pink blossoms growing in profusion from its trunk, reminded me of a rain forest tree commonly known as bumpy satinash. The tree before me was a close relative. Cauliflorous trees, which flower and fruit directly from the trunk, are found only in rain forests. The smell of the blossoms, like apple and cinnamon, wafted as I walked along the narrow bank in awe.

I almost expected to disturb a rhoetosauraus grazing at treetop level or see a pterodactyl cast a winged shadow thirty feet wide along the canyon walls or a dragonfly on two-foot wings. I had returned to a time when the first flowering plants began to choke creeks and rivers, when the land was a dense tropical forest coevolving with creatures of the Jurassic and Cretaceous. The habitat had changed little from the primitive flowering plants, but the age of the dinosaurs had passed. Or had it?

As we walked toward the coast, we approached a predator that had remained virtually unchanged for upwards of 230 million years; a creature that had survived the cataclysmic meteorite impact or impacts that ended the age of the dinosaurs some sixty-five million years ago.

Swimming here in the creek seventeen miles from its confluence with the Indian Ocean, I took a calculated chance that no estuarine crocodiles shared the water with me. The narrowness of the side canyon and the dense vegetation crowding its banks made it unlikely estuarine crocodile habitat. Estuarine crocodiles prefer the tidal zone but might swim upriver well into the freshwater until a natural obstacle such as a waterfall or a rapid prevents their advance. Their relatives, freshwater crocodiles, occurred here in abundance.

"You're reasonably sure there are no salties in here?"

Jeff was sitting in the shade watching me with half an eye open. He did not share my love for the water. All I asked of Jeff was that he report the circumstances of my disappearance to the relevant authorities, should such an event occur.

We made our way through the vine thicket at the entrance to the gorge. The vegetation was dense along this slender strip of alluvial soil between the water and the canyon wall. The vines entangled our backpacks as they brushed against green ant nests. Progess through a rain forest can be measured in hours per mile.

We cleared the thicket with its sweet-smelling fig trees. Here the black flying foxes flew on their nightly excursions, searching for fruits and nectar blossoms. Now the trees chattered with collared rainbow lorikeets. Diligent azure kingfishers swooped silently from branch to branch, collecting insects. In these small pockets highly specialized creatures survived – if only our nightly spotlighting would reveal them.

The gorge narrowed as we went up it, hopping from boulder to boulder along the creek's edge. I glimpsed a splash of white and yellow on the canyon wall. Could it be a painting? I moved across the canyon floor and called to Jeff. Here, along a cool cleft in the stone, we found a painting with intricate white filigrees radiating from a yellow center. Did it represent the sun, or an ancient cosmic visitor? How could my mind, so historically conditioned by Western ideas, trained to think linearly in one hemisphere, ever begin to comprehend the intended meaning of the mind that had created this art? While Jeff came up, I studied it for several minutes, a picture of eternal mind.

The cleft widened into a gallery spread across the canyon wall, where other paintings depicted white faces with blue eyes, surrounded by a nimbus of cloud or thought: these were the Wandjina cloud gods, who bring the cycle of violent storms to the Kimberley. Protected from the sun by the overhanging cliff, the colors on the ochre paintings, reds, whites, blues, and yellows, had remained vibrant, though they probably had not been retouched for many years.

The faces had no mouths. Did they represent the dead? The unspeaking? The divine?

We walked the length of the gallery in awe.

"Sacred site," Jeff murmured. "To the Aboriginal people these aren't just pictures, they are the Creators of the Dreamtime. After Creation they crawled into these rocks."

Though the elders restored the paintings when necessary, according to belief the hand of man had not created the paintings: they had existed since the beginning.

"You are *looking* at God," Jeff whispered.

We reached the end of the gallery and studied a fluid figure with a long white body, again with no mouth. I was to learn later that, according to elder David Mowaljarlai, the Wandjina has no need for speech, because he "sends his thoughts." Over time in the quiet wilderness, I did find that Jeff and I communicated without speaking, that our minds would arrive at the same conclusion regarding some aspect of the journey.

Standing in the canyon, we dipped into the great ocean of the collective unconscious, the Universal Mind, unbounded, undifferentiated, timeless; the source of all archetypes. Between these canyon walls we moved in the undifferentiated continuum; the fact of all time was contained in a single instant.

Spellbound, Jeff pointed to a ledge just above the gallery of paintings. Out of reach of dingoes, above the highest flood, four human skulls, their bones, tibias and fibulas wrapped in a cylinder of red bark beside them, looked out over this creek. Human ruins.

The skulls were white with a thin patina of black fungus

growing in the hollows of the eyes. A sudden wind blasted down the canyon, blowing leaves off the trees. It lasted less than a minute and disappeared instantly. Were we trespassing in this place of spirits?

"If I didn't consider myself a scientist, I might think something very eerie was going on," Jeff said.

The leaves crinkled in a melancholy wind. How did one feel with eternity blowing through the soul? How did the first hominids feel when moving out of the dwindling wet forests of the Rift Valley into open savannah? How did the Polynesians feel, setting out for unknown landfall between an immensity of purple sky and blue ocean, navigating by the stars?

Jeff and I looked at each other, suddenly aware of a tingling sensation in the hindbrain. The same reflex that causes the hairs to rise on the back of the neck, or the hackles on a dog is hardwired into our primate brains. This reflex is one aspect of our sixth sense, the cognitive functioning that extends beyond any measurable scale.

We were being watched, and we knew it. Just as in our heightened sensitivity it became possible to smell water, we sensed the presence of other thoughts beyond our own.

The senses become acute in nature over time, the five senses we think of smell, sight, hearing, touch, and taste – and a sixth and possibly seventh sense that we rarely have recourse to use in our modern lives. Levels of perception that are precluded by ever-present exhaust fumes, the high-pitched hum of the television and transistor, and the ebb and flow of human commerce.

We cannot step outside or even question the industrial paradigm; its effluent now covers the globe. Modern man will never know his true powers, his indigenous mind, will never truly live.

After just five weeks of silence and moving on foot, we were attuned to a presence; another pair of eyes, another mind, another sentient window in the universe. We left quickly and erased our footprints in the sand with a stick, not wanting to offend the spirits.

In the quiet afternoon we walked up Oralee canyon, the sound of our boots ringing in the space between the walls. I was tired but elated at our discovery. There was magic in the world.

Here the canyon formed a Y as a smaller, steeper creek fell into it. Palms and cycads mantled the cliff tops. The walls were far apart, and in one section the cliff had crumbled, hurling boulders the size of houses onto the broken floor. Here for the first time we could hike up to the rim of the far ravine and escape the sacred confines of Oralee Creek. We did not want to camp near the bones, out of respect.

We came to a bend in the cliff wall with a scree of boulders and a small forest of bloodgums and woollybutts, trees with dark bark and delicate red blossoms, springing up among the rocks at its base. We hiked up the scree, the rocks sliding down under our feet, and found a flat ledge in the cliff wall, looking down over the treetops in the canyon below, our backs against the sheer wall of stone rising three hundred feet above our heads.

"Let's camp here."

Gratefully we put down our packs. Sitting on the ledge, I watched the light drain from the gorge. The mahogany stone and green leaves slowly became a semblance of red, blue, and black dots, and the pink river of sky running between the top edges of the cliffs turned purple and filled with stars.

We finished our dinner. Jeff and I sat back and listened to a silence as vast as the universe.

The sound of flapping wings in the trees below began suddenly – a mystical sound, like a bird caught in a large spider's web. Jeff's eyes widened, but he did not speak and neither of us moved. What birds are active at night in the Kimberley? Only one: I had heard the curlew, a bird with a long mournful cry like a sob after dark.

Local legend held that the curlew was an unfaithful wife whose lover was turned into the moon by a jealous husband. Grief-stricken, she roamed the night calling for her lost love, who appears above the horizon, just out of reach. Another legend holds that curlews are the souls of babies who have died and want to sit by the fire.

Yet this was not the sound of a curlew. The flapping sounded almost like black flying foxes, but the sounds were different and not accompanied by the high chattering shrieks and whines of the flying fox.

As I listened, the strange noise stopped, only to be replaced by what sounded like someone throwing large rocks. Feral donkeys making their way down the gorge? At night? Not possible. But what?

For the second time that day, the hair rose on the back of my neck and fear trumpeted itself in the suddenly very conspicuous thump of my heart on the cliff ledge. Something was out there. Something with great power. Something that could move through the dark shadow of the canyon with ease and stealth.

Man was in the starlight shadows of Oralee Creek, invisible to my eyes.

"Owww," the dingo howl tapered off. Jeff and I looked at each other knowingly now.

"That was not a dingo," Jeff said, somewhat matter-of-factly. By now we had heard many calls in the bush. We recognized this dingo howl as a skilled imitation.

"What do you think they'll do to us?" I asked.

Jeff was silent for a while. We both knew that there were no witnesses. We were governed by different laws out here: the law. And perhaps we were trespassing on sacred ground.

We had no weapons except my slingshot and our knives.

"I suppose they could push a boulder onto us," Jeff said. I looked up at the top of the cliff three hundred feet above us and moved closer to the wall. "But I don't think so." Jeff thought for a while.

"They could put a spear through us – I'm glad you didn't swim in any of those pools this afternoon."

Alongside the gallery had been three of the deepest, clearest green pools I had ever seen. The rocks at the bottom shimmered as though under a magnifying glass.

I had gone to the edge with the intention of swimming but was transfixed, and turned back without breaking the surface. Though thirsty, I had waited until we were farther up the creek to fill my water bottles. I sensed then that I was being watched, standing on the edge of a grave mistake, my actions being gauged for a later accounting.

I learned later that these were the *Unggud* or "spirit" waters. *Unggud* is the productive and creative force in Nature and man. These holy waters are the source of child spirits, and offer image projections and visions for the Banman, the medicine man.

"Click-click . . . click! Click-click . . . click," the sound rose up through the treetops to our redoubt on the ledge, two sticks struck together by hands in the darkness. I was relieved that we were at least in some sort of defensible position. It would be impossible to move up that rock scree without shifting rocks.

Jeff offered these words of comfort: "The most likely thing is they'll come up here in the middle of the night covered in white ochre and scare the shit out of us." That seemed plausible. "Or they might just keep us awake all night."

"Should we keep watch?" I asked.

"You can if you want. We'll just fall asleep. Whatever they want to do to us, they can do. I don't know how many there are, but it sounds like half a dozen at least." The noises seemed to come from everywhere at once. "We just have to hope we have shown enough respect for the gallery and the pools."

I was thankful that we had erased our footprints in the sand before we left. How had we known to do that?

I sat quietly in the dark and listened, marveling at the sounds coming from the canyon below. How many men were down there? What were they doing out here? Where was their point of embarkation into this wilderness? With a shock I realized that this was an experience that might have occurred any time in the last forty thousand years.

These were the elders. The keepers of the magic. The historians of the Wandjina Dreaming. They were not gone after all.

The sound of striking wood snapped out of the darkness. If only I could communicate with them! Jeff sat up when what sounded like a boomerang flew overhead.

"How?" he asked astounded. "How do they do it?"

The sound "woosh-woosh-woosh" floated directly over our heads and then disappeared. Were they playing catch with a boomerang from either side of the canyon in the dark? It was magic. It didn't seem possible. Yet how were they making that sound? We were mystified.

I discovered later the sound was probably that of a bullroarer, a wooden instrument used by Aboriginal people to scare off evil spirits. We were indeed trespassing.

I climbed halfway down the scree from boulder to boulder, moving quietly in the shadows of the trees. Though the moon had disappeared below the canyon rim, the starlight was bright enough to see by. I moved through the dappled shadows and sat quietly under a tree, watching and listening for the slightest movement.

The strange flapping sound came from just over there. Now it was coming from the other side of me, yet I had seen no one go past. How did they move over these shifting rocks? I looked straight into the starlight at the noise and saw nothing. How?

Later I realized how foolish I was to think I could "out-stealth" an Aboriginal, the original man in tune with the universe. They knew where I was the entire time; their sixth sense so acute they could probably hear the static of my thoughts, or see the vision appearing through my eyes. I quit the scree and returned to the ledge, sleeping until the birdcalls of first light.

I woke up in the morning surprised to be alive and bolted down to the creek bed to look for footprints. Among the bird and goanna tracks trailing through the fine white sand I found no sign of any. Had they floated above the sand?

Slowly I made my way up the gorge in the morning light, the stone sheer and crumbling. White eucalyptus grew out of the burgundy rock. The green fronds of palms at the tops of the cliffs glowed against the angle of light three hundred feet above my head. The sun would be an hour or more before it cracked the canyon rim. Above, the jagged line between cliff tops had turned blue. It was cool and windless in the canyon. The smell of water, the hollow sound of my boots on stone; these were my physical perceptions. But I was aware of another: that of being watched.

Around me the cliffs were massive, containing thousands of caves and hiding places. There could have been hundreds of people up there, and I would not have been able to see them. Perhaps this was a feeling shared by the white settlers of Utah and the Dakotas. *This* land remained unchanged.

I felt humbled by the realization that were it not for the sudden intercession of my race such a short time ago, North America, the land named by the cartographer monks of Saint Die after the navigator Amerigo Vespucci, would still be wilderness. Forests that Rousseau hailed triumphantly in 1768 as "never knowing the ring of the ax" would still stand.

They would stand again. As I walked down Oralee Creek, I understood for the first time in my life the scale, the immensity, of time.

I took in the cliff slowly. Something was up there, another human being, out here in this place that held so much power for the

Aboriginal people, a place beyond time, when the whole continent was a sacred church. Wandjina.

In a cleft in the canyon I discovered a remarkable document. There, in brown ochre, was a pictograph of a stick figure wearing a wide-brimmed hat. Behind him was an oval shape with lines sticking out to represent three masts and cross spars: A sailing ship. I was surprised to discover it this far from the coast, and wondered which of the early explorers it represented.

The picture represented the beginning of the end for the traditional way of life for Kimberley Aboriginal people such a short time ago, but not the end of the Dreamtime.

I wondered if the eyes that watched me looked on with hostility, or perhaps surprise and curiosity – there could not have been many non-Indigenous people to come this way before, carrying supplies on their backs like a life support system. Aboriginal tribes moved through this land with little more than spears, with songs and stories instead of maps, living from it. This land was their culture, their religion, their education, their history, all tied together in one meaningful cognition. Most had only been removed to the white man's missions and a few remote cattle stations in the 1950s and 1960s. Some, the elders, had obviously never left.

Jeff was still back at our camp on the ledge. I thought about the eyes that watched us. How many? How old? How far from their last meal? Their last successful hunt? Was it a kangaroo? A rock wallaby? A freshwater crocodile? A goanna? What were they doing out here in this place so far removed from "civilization"?

It was not hard to leave the myth of civilization behind, to step out of time, and into the wordless knowledge of eternity. The creek flowed quietly through the boulders.

Jeff and I shouldered our packs and moved up the tapering gorge. We would try to leave out of respect.

White paperbark trees crowded into the wet places between cliffs. Pandanus on spindly stalks raked us with barbed leaves. Slowly, laboriously, up and up, and out.

Matronly brolgas, long-legged and stork-like, with a splash of rouge feathers on either side of their long beaks, followed us like suspicious chaperones. Sulphur-crested cockatoos squawked at our trespass.

The walls fell away and we found ourselves in a broad rocky plain through which the creek flowed, forming deep green pools. Large fish moved in and out of shafts of light. Several freshwater crocodiles basked on the rocks.

We pushed on as far as we could and that night slept above the creek on a ledge formed out of the rock. To the southeast across the floodplain a forest of ghost gums, the white trunks crowded together, seemed to dance in the moonlight.

Tomorrow we would be swinging around to the southwest to rejoin the Prince Regent River. Two days journey at least. After sunset we spotlighted for an hour and found one Mertens' water goanna, a lizard with a special flat tail designed for locomotion through water. I held him by the neck and tail while Jeff took photographs.

"See how powerful he is," Jeff said as I struggled to keep clear of its claws and whipping tail. "And he's less than three feet long – imagine how powerful a crocodile is."

A crescent moon sank to the horizon. I watched the plain, wondering what this night had in store for us. What magic.

I tied my pack to my wrist with nylon cord. Jeff slept on a ledge nearby. Not a sound. At night, the Kalahari bushmen say, it is so quiet you can hear the stars.

We woke up the next morning and broke camp, wondering if the night's quiet meant the Aboriginals had departed. As we set off up the creek Jeff made a startling discovery – two footprints, one behind the other, in a patch of sand not fifteen feet from where we had slept.

"Look at this," he said. The print in front was barefoot and large. The other, shod, was smaller. Neither matched the size of our feet. I scanned the wide ground around us to the forest and the ridges in the distance. Here was the first physical evidence we were being followed.

It was obvious they wanted us to find these prints: this was the only patch of sand in the smooth rock.

"They wanted us to know they were checking up on us," Jeff said in wonder. "Probably an elder teaching one of the boys in the tribe how to maintain the magic of the site."

I thought back to the boy we had seen in the pickup full of Aboriginal elders nearly two years ago outside Halls Creek.

This was part of a young Aboriginal's traditional education, the learning of the law. The elder was most likely an uncle, entrusted with the tutelage of the youth. The most sacred relationship of all for Aboriginal people existed across generations. The young man of thirteen or fourteen was taught how to make and use weapons, how to stalk game, what plants to use for food and medicines: how to survive in nature.

When proficient in these skills, the youth fashioned a flint-knap spearhead, affixed it to the shaft of a wattle stick with spinifex tar and the sinew of a kangaroo, and embarked on a ritual journey, the separation from his tribe, the walkabout. He would go to lay eyes on territory, to seek the religious visions that would further the process of individuation and set him on the path of life with the Creators. He would learn for himself faith in *Unggud*, the Spirit, Nature's eternal creativity.

When the walkabout was over he rejoined his tribe. To show his crossing into manhood he caught a kangaroo or other game and gave it as an offering to his elders. Then the youth was taught the sacred knowledge; the creation stories and moral fables of the Dreamtime, where you came from and were thus going to, the law that traced relationships between man and animal, animal and man, tribes and Creators. In this holy milieu were traced the mythical trails and mind maps, social moieties and customs.

In a final sacred ritual, elders made long cuts with flecks of stone, in lines symbolic of a totemic animal, on the chest and back of the youth. Fine ash was rubbed into the wounds, resulting in thick raised scars called cicatrices. Finally, the young man was circumcised. Pain and privation formed an essential part of indigenous educations.

This education was secular and spiritual, practical and religious, mystical and heroic. When completed, a young Aboriginal was, in the words of one missionary, "a man of proud physical courage and endurance," as well as a spiritual man, a seer, a hunter of great prowess and integrity. My own formal education seemed the paradigm of factory production in comparison.

We pushed on all day. In the afternoon we discovered the charnel house of a dingo. Our final night on Oralee Creek we built a fire near the water's edge and cooked up the last of our flour. The plain had slowly constricted between sandstone ridges. Firelight flickered on the canyon walls while Jeff kneaded the flour on smooth sandstone, making bread. Amid the crackling flames, wreaths of smoke and sparks rose up to join the stars in the glow of a thousand-thousand campfires.

"*Tch.*" The sound came from a tree-studded prominence along the canyon wall, barely audible above the sound of the fire. One side of the gorge rose sharply for seventy feet and then sloped gently upward to the rim above, like a colossal raised amphitheater. Silence returned. Jeff and I again watched the fire, our ears concentrating on the prominence above. Five minutes passed in silence.

"*Tch.*" Again the sound was barely audible, a muted snap. If we had not had the experiences of the nights before we would not have known . . . We would have thought we were alone in the wilderness.

At least one of the men made his way in the dark across the prominence. We sat amazed at the ability of a human to make his way so quietly across an uneven rock face in the starlight.

"There seems to be a presence," Jeff said. I was astounded, staring into the dark. This art, of moving quietly through the wilderness, leaving no trace, was all but lost. I remembered my father telling me that for him as a boy it was the most important skill one could learn, just one generation ago.

Here, in this remote corner of Australia, a youth was being tutored in the art, a combination of meditation, flexibility, strength, balance, and awareness. Feeling the way through space-time, moving along the sacred pathways. Like hunting, the motion required emptiness, the self forgotten, because other creatures sense a conscious presence.

The older Aboriginal moved across the rocks as well, invisible to our ears and eyes. The apprentice was still learning, not yet invisible.

Again I climbed up the rocks quietly and neared the slope from which the sounds emanated. Crouched on the side of the cliff, I heard the moaning sound of didgeridoos drift above the rim of the canyon. Was it possible? How, in this twentieth century? Here was the heroic history of the Earth and creation played on the wind. Here was the Dreamtime, unbroken.

CHAPTER 23

CROSSING

In a pink dawn, I filled my canteen, shouldered my pack, and hiked a narrow defile out of the canyon of Oralee Creek. By noon we stood on the rim of the Prince Regent River gorge, looking down.

From this height the river made no sound. The tea-colored waters pushed against the walls. I stopped and scanned the rocks and silent cliffs around us, wondering if we were still being followed.

It was our thirty-fifth day in the wilderness, and we needed to make a final river crossing soon, before the tidal zone. I scouted for a likely ford.

On a boulder way down in the gorge a crocodile basked in the sun with its mouth open, its tail in the water. Was it an estuarine or a freshwater crocodile?

"It looks too big to be a freshie," Jeff replied. "But it's hard to tell from this distance."

I retrieved my binoculars from the top pocket and looked at the reptile. An estuarine crocodile should have a wider snout and blunter teeth.

"You're the expert," I said, handing them to Jeff. He looked at the crocodile for a long time.

"I can't tell." Jeff handed back the binoculars. It was almost four hundred feet down into the gorge. The reptile might be a ten-foot freshwater crocodile, or a thirteen-foot estuarine crocodile. If it were indeed a saltwater crocodile, we would have to walk back upriver to make our final crossing.

"If it's a freshie, it's a large one. Maybe if we got it to move, we might get a better look at its snout," Jeff said. I took my slingshot out of my pack and catapulted a cycad nut into the gorge. It fell, down and down, landing only ten feet from the crocodile. Ripples lapped against its scales, but the creature did not move. Jeff looked through the binoculars.

"Nice shot. Try again."

The nut landed on the rock next to the saurian. With a violent slap of its tail, it disappeared into the water.

"It was a freshie," Jeff said. "Definitely."

We climbed down a broken section of cliff to the river.

The stone at the river's edge was worn smooth. The sound of rushing water echoed in the gorge. We walked quietly beside the water's edge on a narrow ledge against the cliff. I gripped a stout wattle club and scanned the clear waters. At most we were seven miles from the tidal zone.

The maps did not give any clear indication of rapids ahead, so we did not know for certain if estuarine crocodiles had reached this part of the river. In the water, one would have little chance against a crocodile, but a few strikes on the snout with a club might keep a smaller saltie at bay long enough to escape to higher ground.

The Aboriginal people to this day maintain an uneasy relationship with the crocodile. When crossing rivers where crocodiles may be present, they send the dogs first, then the old people, and then the rest of the tribe. If there are only a few in the party, they find the best crossing and then go several hundred yards below it. Collecting there, they make noise and commotion by the riverbank. They linger by the river, attracting whatever crocodiles lurk in that stretch of water. Then they run upstream to the crossing and surge across the river before the crocodile has time to follow.

We walked silently in the shadow of the canyon. I did not like being this close to the water's edge. Rounding a bend in the canyon, Jeff and I stopped. Our ledge dipped into the clear water. Thirty feet away, it emerged and continued down the side of the gorge.

We could either walk back and climb out, or wade across the submerged ledge. We studied the canyon.

"This doesn't look like saltie habitat," Jeff whispered.

Holding our packs above our heads, we slipped quietly into the river – the canyon suddenly dangerous. The water came up to our thighs and then reached up to our necks as we waded on the submerged ledge. I was thankful it did not get any deeper. Small fish investigated the metal ringlets on my boots.

I scanned the water for any sign of a crocodile, ready to jab it with my stick if need be. There were other desperate measures one could use to deter a crocodile. I had read about Val Plumwood, a biologist who had been attacked by a ten-foot saltie.

She was paddling a kayak alone through melaleuca swamps in the Northern Territory on a rainy afternoon when the creature overturned her kayak and grabbed her in its jaws. They struggled in three feet of water. She stuck her arm down the saurian's throat. It was a smart move.

When a crocodile takes its prey, it rotates like a figure skater pulling its arms in a spin, twisting its body around and around underwater with enough force to rip arms and legs off its victim in the "death roll." It is an extremely effective and disorienting means of subduing prey.

While a large specimen can crush a horse skull between its jaws, in Val Plumwood's case the reptile was not strong enough to kill her outright. Crocodiles generally finish off their prey by drowning, but they cannot eat underwater. A crocodile is equipped with a special flap at the back of its mouth that closes when submerged; otherwise water floods into its stomach and it too will drown.

Val Plumwood, unable to escape the monster's jaws, held open this flap by literally sticking her arm down its throat. Unable to submerge, the crocodile struggled with Val in the shallow water and, like all reptiles, it tired quickly. The beast let go of Val and she was able to swim to shore. But the crocodile attacked again, half on land, half in the water. It grabbed her leg and attempted to pull Val back into the deeper water. She held onto a mangrove root. Finally, the exasperated creature let go and Val managed to crawl out onto the island.

An astute ranger noticed that the kayak had not been returned to the dock that evening and went out looking for her. They found her horribly wounded, but alive.

In Queensland, a woman was taken when she bent down near the waters of the Daintree River on Christmas Eve. She was with four people who foolishly decided to have a splash in the river. She disappeared in three feet of water without a sound, surrounded on all sides by friends. The sixteen-foot crocodile created barely a ripple in taking its prey. They found her remains in the belly of the beast, her bones reduced to gristle by its stomach acids. She was positively identified by the shade of the nail polish on her fingernails.

The ledge curved upward again and out of the water.

"Thank God that's over," I said. We continued down the gorge.

The walls of the canyon loomed above our heads. Gratefully, we put down our packs and made camp on a jutting rock ten feet above the water's edge. Jeff boiled water on the stove for tea. We could not see around the bend in the gorge, but the roar of rapids foretold of an imminent meeting with the sea.

* * *

The cliff rose a hundred feet before a narrow bench sloped up to a crumbled section near the top of the escarpment. Though vertical, the rock face contained sufficient holds. I put my cheek against the stone and began to climb. From a height of seventy feet, Jeff was quite small below. It would be a straight drop to the rocks at the water's edge.

Jeff grew tiny at the base of the cliff. With one final look, I pulled myself up the last vertical stretch and onto the bench. The ledge sloped upward at a shallow angle. I crawled forward on hands and knees. The crumbled section was almost flat where the canyon had partially collapsed. I reached the top of the cliff and stood on one rim of the gorge.

From this height, the rapids of the river appeared unmoving. Three white standing waves indicated more swift rapids two hundred yards below our camp. The dark waters of the Prince Regent River swelled against the cliff walls. There would be no further progress inside the gorge. We would have to climb out and hike atop the escarpment to the creek of the King Cascade. But how to get out of the gorge? This climb was too sheer to attempt with a backpack on. And we would be on the wrong side of the river.

The opposite cliff was studded with palms and figs growing in defiance of rock and gravity. A steep line of boulders spilled down a narrow defile into the canyon. It was the only visible way out.

I sprawled atop the rim, looking down into the gorge. From here we would be maybe six days' walk from the King Cascade and the coast. From this height it all looked so easy.

I boulder-hopped across the top of the escarpment and peered down the rock face. Swallows wheeled below me in the blueing light. Night was coming on quickly below. I crawled backward down the bench to the top of the cliff. With my stomach balanced on the edge, I slipped my legs over the side, my feet feeling for holds in the void.

Halfway down I stopped and looked below. Jeff was still quite small. I had forgotten that climbing down is often harder than climbing up. My calves shook. I reached across the cliff face for a hold. For an instant I was forced let go with both hands and balanced on my toes. I fell sideways and grabbed the hold.

At last I was near the base of the cliff and dropped three feet to the rocks below. In a protected eddy, I splashed water on my face and had a drink.

The smooth water reflected the cliffs and the sky. A diving fish left concentric circles suddenly as a silent image soared across the glassy surface. In the twilight a sea eagle, with white body and black wings, swooped down and landed on a boulder beside the river fifty feet away. Its black eyes looked through me. The sea eagle was a herald: we were near the coast. I walked up the gorge toward Jeff. If I had only lived this day, and seen this much, it would be enough.

"Sea eagle. We'll have to cross above these rapids," I told Jeff while we boiled the rice. "Down below it's going to be tidal."

In the last of the light we rinsed the dishes in the river. The rumbling water echoed off the walls in the distance, filling the gorge. The river made a slight bend in the canyon and disappeared out of sight, becoming a briny confluence of freshwater and the sea: the crocodile zone.

Next morning we scouted up and down above the rapids, looking for the safest crossing. We decided to float our packs across at the broadest point in this section of the gorge. Though the river was wider, the current did not appear to be as strong. We assembled at the highest spot possible above the rapids.

I put all my equipment in a large plastic bag in my pack, and wrapped my camera in an extra bag. My pack and my sleeping mat floated, to my relief.

I took off my boots and waded into the current, feeling my way over the submerged terrain. Fifty feet from shore, I stood on the last boulder before deep water. The orange walls loomed on either side of us.

"Ready?" I said. The rapids churned two hundred yards down-river. The pandanus trees bobbed on the far side a hundred yards away. "OK," Jeff said. I pushed swiftly out into the current, kicking furiously for the opposite bank.

The river had looked slow here, but out in open water the current steadily accelerated. I pushed my pack along with one hand and swam with the other, keeping my eyes forward, trying not to think about crocodiles. My progress toward the far cliffs was exceeded by my motion across the wall. I was heading for the rapids.

Jeff was somewhere alongside me, pushing steadily. The current increased. The pandanus trees thrummed on the far bank. Whirlpools began just above the rapids. Not far now.

I strove with everything, kicking madly as the rapids approached. Jesus, I might have to abandon my pack and try to retrieve it somewhere downriver. The sound of the boulder-churning water filled my ears. The rapids drew threateningly close, the water pulling more and more strongly. Sixty feet from the bank, a swift current raced through the boulders. Suddenly I was sucked violently downriver.

My knee bumped a submerged rock. Scrambling, I stood up, legs shaking, leaning into the torrent to keep my balance. The water rippled around my waist. The other side was close now, if I could just get across this channel.

I put my pack on, stood up and leaped. The current pulled me downward, just thirty feet above the rapids. This is it. I reached out and grabbed a pandanus stalk. It was enough. The current shunted me into the eddy, and I stood up in waist-deep water, still clutching the tree, shaken, exhausted, but across. I waded out through clusters of flooded trees and collapsed on the shore.

Jeff emerged trembling.

"That was a little closer than I thought it was going to be," I shouted.

I hiked down below the rapids and saw garfish and a stripling barramundi in the water. I didn't get too close to the edge. We had reached the tidal zone. Here the estuarine crocodile was the apex predator.

"Definitely wouldn't want to cross below here," I said to Jeff. He was pulling food out of his pack.

"Damn." He held up a freeze-dried packet. Water had leaked into five of them.

"Nothing for it but to eat them now, before they go off," he said.

For five weeks, despite our hunger, we had been very disciplined about not eating more than our daily ration.

"You might need those later," I said.

"We can't be far from the cascade."

"It's not going to go bad right away."

"Can't take that chance."

"You're going to boil it, for heaven's sake. That's almost a week's worth of food." I thought Jeff was making an excuse to eat the food. He could have saved it and eaten it over the next couple of days. I said nothing more.

He sat in the shade of the canyon and ate ravenously. Jeff didn't offer me any of his food, and I probably would have refused it if he had. We kept our food separate. I ate a cup of muesli with powdered milk. In reloading my pack, I figured I had enough food left for two weeks.

We filled our water bottles from the river and hiked up the narrow defile. A blue line on the map marked Widjinari Creek, a considerable river curving northwest with one branch running in the most direct course to Cascade Creek and the King Cascade. In the morning light two hours later we reached the outer rim of the canyon and proceeded overland.

* * *

From atop the escarpment we peered down into the wide sheer gorge of Widjinari Creek where it meets the Prince Regent. Beautiful clear pools, one after the other, formed a chain leading up to a broad waterfall in the distance. It was rare to get such a view, and we stopped and admired it for some time.

"There'll be good swimming above those falls. No crocs could get over that, not even in a full wet." The falls were at least eighty feet high.

Jeff and I crossed above the waterfall and set out into a narrow gorge, plodding through the high grass. We would need to make camp soon. The walls were sheer and narrowing, and it threatened to be a box canyon.

In the late afternoon I pushed through the tall grass between the cliff and the rocky creek, breaking trail. Gnarled trees grew at impossible angles out of the rocks. The walls converged and the canyon bent so that the view around the corner was blocked. Jeff came up, and we put our packs down beside the stream.

"I'd hate to have to walk back if this boxes us out," I said.

"Me too."

I inched around a fig tree growing out of the cliff and turned the corner. To my utter amazement, I stood on the edge of a vast green pool with sheer cliffs on all sides except for the narrow ledge I was on.

On the far side of the pool a wide waterfall cascaded down steps in the red stone, while a single fall plunged a hundred feet into the pool from above. A lone tree grew atop a fallen boulder on one edge of the pool. Ferns and trees grew out of cracks in the rocks. At the far end of the gorge a line of boulders spilled down a narrow defile, disappearing like stone steps into the clear green water.

A freshwater crocodile lolled on the surface as I rounded the bend. Though I had seen many beautiful places on our trek, this was the most magnificent. We had found a heart of Creation, larger and more glorious than any man-made cathedral.

Two flat boulders had come to rest on the ledge beside the water. The waterfall generated a cool breeze. Nature had made a splendid camp for us.

I inched back along the ledge and found Jeff in the shade.

"How does it look?"

"It's a box, definitely."

"No getting out, huh?"

"See for yourself."

Jeff followed me around the bend in the canyon.

His eyes widened in amazement. "Awesome," was all he could say, "truly awesome." He set his pack down on one of the boulders.

"Perfect camp," I said.

"It didn't look anything too spectacular on the map."

"I'm going swimming." The broad falls we had seen upon setting out would prevent any saltwater crocodiles from reaching here. I stripped and swam across the gorge. The water was deep and clear and I couldn't see the bottom, but I'd overcome my fear about lurking cousins of Godzilla. I climbed up to one edge of the waterfall while Jeff took pictures. I was the happiest creature in the world that afternoon and knew it.

"What should we call this place?"

"The only thing I can compare it to is a cathedral. We could call it Cathedral Gorge. It's got to be twenty times the size of St Paul's."

"I like Rapture Falls, myself."

For two days we camped on the flat boulders at the bottom of the gorge. The air was cool from the spilling water, and the sound of the falls lulled us to sleep at night while the breeze kept the mosquitoes away. Above the cliffs spun a circle of stars.

CHAPTER 24

CASCADE CREEK

On April 11, after forty days in the wilderness, Jeff and I stood on one edge of the valley of Cascade Creek. We hiked down the stony ridge and cut across the wide valley through the high grass. Our orienteering had been spot on.

"This is it, mate," Jeff shouted as we plowed toward the cliffs on the other side of the valley. We were finally going to reach the King Cascade. We pushed almost to the rocks on the other side before meeting the creek. It was only a few feet wide but flowing strongly.

"Pretty big valley for such a small creek." The water was clear and cool. I dropped my pack on top of a boulder, exhausted after an eight-hour day. We estimated we had covered eight miles from our last camp. Tomorrow we would walk down the valley of Cascade Creek to the waterfall. I wondered if there would be a yacht moored at the base of the falls, taking on fresh water. Would they be carrying blueberry pancake mix with them?

"I would imagine so."

"What about champagne *on ice*? Would that be out of the realm of possibility?"

"They're yachties. They don't go anywhere without champagne."

"A cold drink would be nice."

We made camp and had our fortieth meal of freeze-dried beef and beans with rice.

"It doesn't really get old, does it?"

"Still tastes damn good to me," Jeff replied.

"They say hunger is the greatest sauce."

We ate slowly and savored each bite, rolling the beef around in our mouths. It took us forty-five minutes to eat what would have taken a less-hungry person ten. We licked our plates clean and after a cup of tea walked down to the creek to cool off. Red tinted the scattered clouds as we pushed through the rushes and entered the water. Man was again in the valley of Cascade Creek.

The stars emerged overhead. Orion had disappeared, chased out of the night sky by the Scorpion. I immersed myself in the cool water of a stone pool. Reeds oscillated near the bank. We were at home in this wilderness. I felt the strength of my legs and the rock, flat and smooth under my feet. I was now almost twenty years old. To be alive was to be beneath the moon, looking out over the escarpments to the coast.

I wrote in my journal that these were the last westward steps I would take in Australia for some time. "Our odyssey is winding down," I scribbled by candlelight – already thinking ahead to Broome and the Swedish girls on Cable Beach. I thought the hard part was over.

"Let's rest here for a minute," I said at noon the next day. Jeff was eager to reach the waterfall. The boat *Kimberley Explorer* was due in on April 23, eleven days away. We had spent the entire month of March and half of April in the wild. It was almost over. We were the first nonindigenous people to reach this isolated part of Western Australia overland and explore the headwaters of the Prince Regent River, and for good reason.

I pictured a yacht moored at the base of the waterfall already, or maybe a fishing boat taking on fresh water.

We hiked down rocks worn smooth by the constant action of

the creek, and waded through voluptuous clear pools cut into the stone. The wind carried the sound of water falling, so we quickened our stride.

"Do you hear voices?" I asked Jeff.

"Sounds like it!"

The valley narrowed and we found ourselves suddenly atop the escarpment, with Cascade Creek streaking down the face of the terraced cliff at our feet and splashing into the gray waters of the Prince Regent River below. Sheer cliffs rose on the other side of the river, now almost a half mile wide, and the waterfall spilled down into the oval-shaped inlet of the lagoon.

"We're here!" Jeff shouted. "King Cascade!" We shook hands and looked out over the coast.

"I can think of a lot of reasons no one's ever done it before," I said, "starting with green ants."

"Where are the yachties?"

There was no sign of any boats in the inlet or anchored at the base of the cascade. It looked like any other waterfall in the middle of the wilderness, more or less. But we had made it, and with luck a boat would come in soon and whisk us off to either the town of Derby or Broome or even Wyndham.

"Just like Robinson Crusoe . . . Now we just put our sunglasses on, and wait," Jeff said, looking for some shade.

"Eleven days is going to be a long time to wait if no one comes in but the *Kimberley Explorer*."

"There'll be other boats – this is the only place to get fresh water on the entire coast. Even if they don't have room to take us out, they'll give us some food to eat while we wait." Jeff put his pack down underneath an acacia and looked for a good cave at the top of the falls. We both showered and shaved and cut our hair with the scissors on our Swiss Army knives. I was startled by the gaunt reflection of my face in the mirror of my compass.

I walked up and down the rim of rock overlooking the lagoon.

Now that we had reached the saltwater, I hoped to collect mudcrabs and shellfish at low tide in the lagoon and catch large fish like the prized barramundi, a fish weighing up to forty pounds. I began to look forward to getting out of the wilderness. After almost two months of sleeping on rocks and eating the same thing every night, I wanted a sit-down dinner.

I wondered how my friends were doing. Were they out on spring break in New York City, drinking fifty-cent vodka shots in the Ukrainian bars of the Village? I hoped my family was all right.

Our provisions were getting low. I had cut back to half a cup of cereal in the morning, hoping to make it last until the boat came. I was nearly out of powdered milk and rice. In my journal I wrote down all the things I would eat when we got out to civilization. The list was several pages long and included ice cream, green beans, cheese, corn, and garlic bread. This waterfall was still the middle of a vast wilderness. We would never be able to walk out the way we had come.

CHAPTER 25

TAXONOMY OF
CROCODILES

If the crocodile findeth a man by the brim of the water, or by the cliff, he slayeth him if he may, and then weepeth upon him and swalloweth him up at the last.

Bartholomew Anglicus

Cascade Creek spilled over the sandstone escarpment in a series of steps 150 feet down into the inlet of the Prince Regent River. Formed over the eons by the interaction of water and tide, the oval-shaped lagoon was almost a half mile wide.

The sound of water splashing into the Prince Regent River and dripping off ferns echoed in the lagoon below. On either side mangrove trees grew out of the rich gray mud.

I stripped down to shorts and climbed carefully down the face of the King Cascade. Tufts of grass grew out of the cracks and greatly facilitated my descent, just as Captain King had remarked almost two hundred years earlier.

It was nearly low tide when I reached a ledge fifteen feet above the swirling inlet. The mangroves were distinct now on either side of the lagoon, the roots sticking up like wooden snorkels in the ashen mud, supporting green and yellow leaves and delicate scarlet flowers. On the fringing cliffs the hues of burgundy and pale orange marked the difference between high and low tide: a difference of forty feet.

On either side of the inlet creeks had dislodged boulders and given the mangroves a foothold against the cliffs. All was quiet but for the splashing sound of water falling down King Cascade onto the mud. No sign of any crocodiles.

In the distance, the ebbing tide carried floating tree trunks into the main gorge and out to sea. It looked like prime saltie habitat.

Phillip Parker King was probably not the first navigator to replenish supplies of fresh water at the base of the falls, later named King Cascade in his honor. Two Aboriginal paintings near the Kimberley coast depict ancient dhows, constructed of papyrus, indicating early visits by Chinese or Arab navigators. Still, King was the first to chart the river when he sailed to this unknown coast in two voyages between 1818 and 1822 in his cutters the *Mermaid* and *Bathurst*. He carried "provisions for nine months and twelve weeks water" on the voyages designed to survey the coast and discover any navigable rivers that might lead into the interior of the continent.

On his trip King and his crew had a run-in with Aboriginals at a place they named Encounter Bay. He wrote that the water level in the ship's well often dropped below fourteen inches deep, causing great concern, and all were amazed when the mercury in the thermometer on board reached 119 degrees in the shade. He wrote of his ship being spun 360 degrees on its keel in whirlpools created by the massive tides.

At Careening Bay, not far from the mouth of the Prince Regent River, a solitary boab tree still commemorates King's passing; its great trunk inscribed with the words HMC MERMAID, 1820. he *Mermaid* had spent several weeks there, a spaceship marooned on the beach of a distant planet, undergoing repairs to its leaking hull. It was a long way from Sydney.

A launch from the *Mermaid* scouted upriver to the first set of rapids, searching for fresh water. Because it was the largest and most magnificent river he had encountered in two years of charting and seemed the likeliest to provide access to the "interior of the continent," King named the river after the then Prince Regent of England, George the Fourth, whose father had recently lost the American colonies. Gratefully, the crew replenished their water stores in the cascade, ever mindful of what they called alligators. King named coastal features after other aristocrats in the house of Hanover as well. Some features, like Point Torment and Disaster Bay, hint at the trials he and his crew underwent.

The tide was dead low this April afternoon, exposing a surface of gray mud. I remembered the painting in Oralee Creek of a ship with three masts and cross-spars, and near it a stick figure smoking a pipe. I wondered which modern sailors it commemorated. The Dutch navigator Dirk Hartog sighted this coast in 1616, as did Abel Tasman in 1644 on behalf of the Dutch East India Company.

The colorful English buccaneer William Dampier reached the Kimberley coast in 1688 in the *Cygnet* and again in 1699 in the *Roebuck*. Dampier was the first Englishman to set foot on Australian soil, landing at Cygnet Bay near the present-day town of Derby. In his best-selling book, *A New Voyage Round the World*, published in 1697, Dampier described the land as "not fit for a dog to live in, destitute of water," and the Aboriginal people as "the miserablest people in the world."

The French explorer Nicholas Baudin charted some of these waters during the Napoleonic wars, naming features such as Bonaparte Gulf. To the west of us lay other features named to commemorate European events, including French reversals. Mount Trafalgar and Mount Waterloo stood near the mouth of the great river. I almost expected to see a longboat come in with the tide, pulled on dripping oars by men in the costume of the seventeenth or eighteenth century.

Jeff had found a patch of shade and was napping when I returned to the top of the waterfall.

"Any tourists?" he said, rolling over.

"Not a thing." I sat down on my sleeping mat. "The tide's out."

"Broome! You'll love Broome," Jeff said. We sat at the top of the waterfall with our feet in the current. "Heaps of tourist girls in Broome. They've got a beach there, Cable Beach. Great beach. Great bird preserve in Broome, too. I hope the boat is heading to Broome. If not, well, we've seen Wyndham, not much happening there. Derby's OK."

I envisioned sharing a beach towel, a meat pie, and a bottle of beer with a smiling Scandinavian girl.

"Do you think we'd hear the end of the world out here?" I asked.

"Not for a couple of days."

I counted four freeze-dried packets in the bottom of my pack, and rice for one more day. Veins were visible on my arms and chest. There was no fat left on my body.

Still, everything was going according to plan, more or less. We were at King Cascade. No one had broken a leg or been bitten by a snake. I watched the tree trunks swirling in the gray waters and wondered how we would leave this place.

"I'm just about out of rice. How about you?"

"Tonight will be my last night," Jeff said. "Still have some powdered eggs, though."

We sat, and waited, and waited. I tried to amuse myself with all the things I would do once we reached civilization. Take a hot bath. Cook a good meal. Sit in a comfortable chair. Make love. Go to the movies. How had I taken such things for granted before?

The coast was broad and silent under a heavy sky. My sense of accomplishment at having reached the King Cascade began to wane. I found one sun-bleached soda can stuffed under a rock at the top of the cascade, the only sign of humanity I had seen for months.

I could have hiked around one corner of the inlet and taken a photo of the waterfall from a stony edge, but I was too tired. We had even stopped our nightly spotlighting for the rough-scale python. I remembered Peter's words about wasted energy and motion. Now, all we had to do was wait. I took a photo from the top of the waterfall, looking north. It was the last photo either of us was to take on the journey.

"Should be some decent fishing down there," I said to Jeff. "We'll have some good feeds, at least, while we wait." With wire and a nylon food bag I made a crab net, and prepared to bait it with the head and bones of the first fish I caught.

I clambered down to the lagoon, carrying the wattle spear, and held on to tufts of grass and ferns as I descended the face of the cascade's giant polished steps, slipping fingers into cracks. I knew one person had already died in the waters below me, *in this very place*: Ginger Meadows. And not from a fall, but in the jaws of a crocodile. It was very likely that a large crocodile made this area a regular part of its haunts.

As fast as a striking snake, a crocodile can propel three-quarters of its body length out of the water to snatch prey. On land it can run nine miles per hour in a straight line over a short distance. Contrary to the image in *Crocodile Dundee*, a man with a knife is no match for a two-thousand-pound armor-plated throwback from the dinosaur era. These same creatures had been coping with the likes of *Tyrannosaurus rex* when man's ancestors were little more than terrified tree shrews.

The crocodile was the total predator of this habitat, a creature of both land and water. It was a gray-green rock basking in the blazing sun, a pair of eyes, a bubble on the water's surface, an outline in the gray mud – until it erupted, all tooth and claw and Mesozoic armor.

I peered into the lagoon. I knew for certain that estuarine crocodiles inhabited this place. To swim here would be suicide. Even to present myself on the rocks near the water's edge would be madness. The tide raced out into the main gorge, leaving the inlet bare to the mud.

I looked for tracks where a crocodile might have dragged itself out of the receding water and into the mangroves. There were no signs of the curious keeled tracks that I remembered from Crystal Creek.

Gripping the wattle sapling, I stepped off the rocks into the mud. Now that we were at the coast, I needed to collect and catch more food: oysters, shellfish, barramundi, and especially crabs. My leg sank into the stinking mud with a conspicuous *sloop*! There were only a few minutes before the tide rushed back in.

My other leg slipped into the mud. Already I was up to my thighs in the mire. I measured the distance between the shadow of the mangroves and the face of the waterfall, terrified of meeting a crocodile under these conditions. Would it slide from the edge of the mangroves with deft motions of its front claws and armored tail? I trudged toward the mangrove roots, looking for the shallow circular depressions where mudcrabs buried themselves between tides. Crab would be good eating after so many days.

A dense canopy cast a shadow over the roots of the mangroves. Where were the mudcrabs? Where were the oysters? It is much easier to read about nature's larder than to actually sustain yourself on it. In a shallow pool, I collected a single shrimp.

I entered the shadow of the mangroves as the tide began spilling back into the inlet. Immediately a swarm of mosquitoes landed on my skin and began to bite painfully. I dashed for the face of the cascade followed by the stinging cloud. At the rocks I was forced to wade partially through the water to a place where I could climb out. Already the sea had filled the lagoon to a depth of two feet. It was enough to convince me that hunting in the mangroves was best left to the crocodile.

I stood on the ledge and leaned against the face of the waterfall. How many different types of prey had the crocodile feasted on through time – this creature which had fed on the carcasses of dinosaurs in Mesozoic swamps? *Homo sapiens* had not been on the planet, or the menu, for very long.

Of the twenty-one species of crocodilians extant since the dawn of humanity, not one has yet been made extinct by man, though some, like the Cuban and American crocodile, hover on the brink. As the once abundant grizzly bear was to the United States, the crocodile remains a symbol of Australia, potentially present in any billabong or waterway of the Far North.

"Wouldn't life be boring if the only animal that could kill you was another human being?" Jeff had said once. Still, to be taken by a crocodile . . .

The last attack in Australia had involved Ginger Meadows, in the very waters gathering at my feet. She was a twenty-two-year-old former model from North Carolina who had traveled to Australia in 1987 during the America's Cup challenge in order to "find herself." She hired onto a boat, the *Lady G*, in Perth to sail around the Kimberley coast. The three-women and two-man crew had been coast-hugging for a week in their thirty-foot yacht when they pulled into the inlet of the King Cascade and moored in the water at its base.

In the afternoon the captain and the mate climbed up the face of the cascade to take photographs and explore. The three women decided to go swimming in the lagoon at the base of the waterfall.

They should have known that they were in prime crocodile habitat, and that the same gray waters that offered relief from the swelter of the Kimberley were also home to the estuarine crocodile. They apparently did not know, and the captain failed to warn them.

They swam from the boat to the face of the waterfall, unaware of the dangers, the big ocean-going sharks that traveled upriver and cut through the waters at the base of the King Cascade, and the estuarine crocodile, which grows to a length of twenty feet.

One woman noticed a large object draw into the inlet from the main waters of the Prince Regent. At first they thought it was a floating tree. As they watched, a crocodile surfaced between the face of the cascade where they stood and the yacht. It swam casually, taking in the boat as it passed and the three figures at the base of the cascade, considering them with a reptilian eye.

The three terrified women climbed up onto a ledge of the waterfall, but though waist deep in the water, they could reach no higher. They stood on that ledge and watched the methodical approach of the beast, its eyes and bony brow just above the surface.

From the top of the King Cascade, the captain of the *Lady G* saw what at first glance appeared to be a tree floating in the water off the face of the cascade. In an instant of horror, he recognized the fifteen-foot crocodile, its tail arched, preparing to attack.

"Crocodile! Get out of the water!" he shouted, clambering down the face of the waterfall, in itself a dangerous undertaking.

One of the women screamed and threw a sandal at the crocodile as it approached. It stopped and hovered on the surface of the water. Crocodiles are cautious predators. They weigh the risks to themselves in an attack. And humans are not their typical prey, in Australia at least.

According to the eyewitness accounts, the crocodile continued slowly toward the women and stopped fifteen feet from them.

"What shall we do?" Ginger asked of her companions. It was too much for her. A good swimmer, Ginger dived and swam furiously for the boat moored eighty feet away. It was a horrible mistake.

The crocodile disappeared and moments later reappeared under Ginger, taking her in its jaws while a few clouds moved across the blue sky overhead. The reptile submerged with her, just as it would with a big fish or a kangaroo, and began to swirl violently. Several moments later, to the horror of those waiting on the ledge, Ginger surfaced in the crocodile's mouth, naked now and with "the most stunned expression on her face." Her tanned skin appeared out of place against the raised green-brown scales of the crocodile. She disappeared in a swirl of muddied brine.

The mate and the captain had reached the bottom of the waterfall. The mate took to the dinghy and revved the engine up and down over the site where Ginger was last seen, hoping to frighten the crocodile into letting her go. A few bubbles rose out of the murky water. The crew of the *Lady G* never saw Ginger again.

As I stared into the inlet, these images floated before my mind. This young woman, disillusioned so completely and utterly: one moment laughing and playing in the waterfall, the next transfixed and helpless as Death, with perhaps the most casual motions of its great tail, swam toward her, its eyes just above the surface.

I agonized over her last thoughts. Everything, the boat, the captain leaping down the cascade, the crushing pain, the faces of her friends, the gray water, the mangroves: everything was unreal from between the jaws of a crocodile.

If only she had not tried to swim for it! The crocodile might not have attacked the three women if they'd stayed together. The one that killed Ginger was certainly old enough to remember humans, and hunters, and would have been wary.

The cliffs rose up from the lagoon. This was the last place she laid eyes on.

The captain of *Lady G* radioed Broome with news of the attack. The scene on board the boat that evening would have been one of profound distress. The two men, the captain cursing himself, the horrified women, shocked, with Ginger's final look, pleading, stunned, etched in their minds, as the light seeped out of the inlet of the King Cascade. The authorities arrived from Broome on board the boat *Penguin*, four days later. *Lady G*, after rendezvousing with the police in the waters of the St. George Basin, headed off for Wyndham. There was nothing else they could do. The body, if it were to be recovered, would be found by the authorities.

The corpse was recovered, minus its arms, found within the fringing mangroves by Vic Marden, a crocodile expert from Groote Island. Ginger's arms had been ripped off in the force of the attack, the so-called death roll. The crocodile had not yet begun to tear meat off its prey, and the body was otherwise unmolested. Crocodiles prefer their meat partially rotten, perhaps because it is easier to tear and digests more quickly. This one had tucked her away to "ripen" for a few days and had not yet returned to feed.

When Vic found her in the heat, Ginger's eyes were closed and her skin pale blue. He said she looked like a doll lying in the mud. The body was lashed to the front of the launch. After four days in the hot sun, it had begun to smell. The *Penguin* left that evening with their tragic cargo, bound for Broome.

Crocodiles are territorial, and though the authorities had recovered Ginger's body, they had not killed the crocodile. Nor had they wanted to. Crocodile hunting was outlawed in Western Australia in 1969, the first Australian state to do so. Crocodiles are now a protected species in Australia, and they grow larger with each passing year.

The crocodile that took Ginger was only doing what it was designed to do, what it had been doing in one form or another for 230 million years. This time a pretty young American girl happened to be involved.

The waters swelled back into the inlet. Which ledge had they retreated to, I wondered? Where exactly had they found the body?

I would not have wanted to search the mangrove thicket. There was only one rifle among the team from Broome.

I climbed back up the face of the cascade. Jeff had found some shade under a rock overhang.

"We're here," I said, matter-of-factly, looking at the escarpments near the coast.

"We're here," he replied.

CHAPTER 26

WAITING

I caught a grasshopper on the trunk of an ancient fig growing at the top of the cascade. Even bait was hard to come by now. The tide was nearly full when I climbed down into the lagoon. The water moved quickly up the rocks.

I sat twelve feet above the water, my line disappearing into the grayness below, hoping for some fish to eat. The inlet magnified every sound. My own heartbeat seemed quite conspicuous on the rocks above the water.

The crocodile, like any expert hunter, is a master at disguising its motives. It does not think about the large mammal it has seen on the rocks this morning. Could I sense the peach-sized transmitter of its brain, wallowing in the mud? Perhaps this is why human beings developed such capacious minds – this fine telepathy has kept us alive through millennia. Even the best predators transmit an inkling of their motives.

I wanted a boat to come in this afternoon. I wanted music and a hot shower. This was the most dangerous part of the whole journey, waiting at the coast. Too much time to think.

Four more days at the most, I repeated to myself. The boat will be in on April 23.

It had been almost two months since I had spoken to anyone other than Jeff. Was everyone still alive? What newsworthy events were taking place in the world? Did New York still exist? Boston? Be patient, I told myself. And stop thinking about food . . .

The rod dipped and I exultantly reeled in a large catfish. It grunted strangely as I pulled it out of the water and cranked it up to my ledge above the water's edge. I ran a spare bootlace through its gills and tied it to a tuft of grass, leaving it to loll in a small pool of fresh water. Three catfish quickly joined the first. Two others wriggled off the line before I could retrieve them. Another came off the hook and flapped down the rocks. I leapt down and grabbed it as it rolled toward the water. Returning to the ledge, I wondered, could a crocodile have leapt that high? I must be more careful. I must be very careful.

I carried the fish to the top of the falls and filleted them, sitting in the water to keep cool, watching their insides float over the edge of the cataract. I was starting to smell like a fish.

This wilderness was as large and implacable as ever. Where were the fucking boats? I had spent forty-eight days in the wilds, telling time by the sun, moon, and stars. It was time to return to the world of modern man and take a hot shower.

The night before, I had woken up ravenous. Carefully I poured out a tablespoon of powdered milk and mixed it with water from my canteen to assuage my hunger. I added another spoonful, then another, until the milk was thick and creamy. Put it away, I told myself, put it back in your pack. You'll want that powdered milk tomorrow! But after drinking it I wanted more. I had been so good about rationing for months. I broke down and poured two days' supply of powdered milk into the cup, adding just the smallest amount of water so it was thick like tapioca. Stop! I said to myself. Stop! It was all I could do to leave enough powdered milk for the morning.

Jeff was in the cave he had found at the top of the waterfall, a cleft in the rock face with enough room for two to sleep out of the rain and sun, and a view down onto the lagoon below. The sound of rushing water filled our ears.

"Fishing's not bad today at least," I said, putting the fillets down into Jeff's frying pan.

He cooked the fish up with a little concentrated butter and some salt. We ate slowly, consuming even the skin, which was not tasty. From the cave we watched the build-up of thunderheads along the coast, waiting for the heat to break with the afternoon thundershowers.

"Just think of that thick chocolate shake we're going to have on the Cairns Esplanade."

"Maggie's rum trifle."

"Spaghetti bolognese."

"Pancakes."

We had been at King Cascade for a week now.

I counted the days on my fingers, over and over. A boat should be here!

"Let's have a cup of coffee."

Jeff tapped the brown granules into each cup. "That's the last of it. Better put it on the shopping list."

"No more coffee? This is serious."

"Do you think there are any calories in coffee?"

"Not many."

"We've still got some tea left." I held up a plastic bag with twenty packets of tea inside.

The next morning I huddled under the brim of my hat while I fished, growing more and more desperate, staring intently at the somber waters below. A shower passed overhead, and raindrops dimpled the surface of the lagoon.

In our hunger we had eaten the last of our cereal, powdered milk, powdered eggs, and potato flakes, and were down to my last two packets of freeze-dried food. If only Jeff hadn't eaten those five wet packets of freeze-dried on that river crossing, we would have a little more to spare. I hoped to God, if there was one, the boat would be in tomorrow.

I fixed a round sinker to my line and hurled a bait of fish liver into the water. The waters swelled and now ebbed, pulling away to sea. Another day of silence and hunger. Another day unbroken by the sound of a distant motor. I had to think very carefully about how I was going to get out of this place alive.

I wanted to eat something for lunch, something beside the unripe and bitter figs I had been collecting out of the fig tree above the cascade. My ribs poked against my skin. I had very little energy. Jeff and I thought and talked about food constantly. We were beginning to starve.

Still no sign of a crocodile. Perhaps the one that had taken Ginger had died out here? Maybe a poacher had come in and killed it, but I doubted it. This crocodile was old enough to be one of the smart ones and would disappear at the first sound of an outboard motor between the canyon walls. And who would come in here anyway?

Whirlpools swirled in the inlet. Farther out the main waters of the river moved toward the ocean. No boats would be coming in against this tide. Maybe tomorrow.

A fin ripped across the surface of the inlet, silver fish leaping out of the water before it. A shark. It swam below me along the face of the falls. From its dorsal fin to its tail was about seven feet How had anybody ever wanted to swim here?

I moved my line up and down. No fish today. Not unless something struck soon. Tonight we would split my second-to-last packet of freeze-dried food. We were rationing to the last. We still had a week's worth of tea left. Soon we would have to live completely off the land.

The inlet had fallen into shadow, but light still spilled into the main gorge in the distance. How small is man, I thought, how justly humble before nature.

Two large fish chased smaller fish just below the surface of the receding water, cutting back and forth. I brought the bait up, bobbing it up and down at the surface. The fish came in close to the face of the waterfall and were practically at my feet when one of them took the bait. I held on to the rod and reel as the hook held fast. The drag went out and the pole bent. The shark, for I saw now what it was, strove away from the cliff face in zigzagging lines. I prayed that the line and hook held. One never despairs of losing a fish so much as when one is starving. Shark steak was going to be good tucker.

The shark was almost three feet long. The other shark swam around its stricken mate several times before heading for open water. I had never seen gregarious behavior among sharks. This was indeed a strange place, this confluence of river and sea.

Light reflected in silver lines off the bow wave of a tree moving into the inlet against the tide. Though it was still a quarter mile away, I knew immediately what it was: a crocodile making its rounds on the river, its eyes and snout just above the surface. It swam vigorously against the current. The scales on the ridges of its tail appeared with each sweeping thrust. This was his territory. He would not go hungry here.

I was mesmerized by its approach: the paragon of adaptation, the largest reptile in the solar system, the ultimate predator through time and space. It had outlived the dinosaurs! Thomas Hobbes had written that in the state of nature life was "nasty, brutish, and short." Certainly the same could be said of life in the epoch of the ruling reptiles.

The crocodile was now in the inlet, three hundred feet from the face of the waterfall. Did it see me? It paused in an eddy. Its brow and the end of its tail hovered on the surface of the water, huge and terrifying – the first estuarine crocodile I had ever seen in the wild, a monster.

The shark's thrashings had ceased, but I had no net or gaff with which to pull it out of the water. The crocodile drifted beside the mangroves. Apparently it had not yet observed the small mammal standing on the rocks close to the water's edge. I leaned out over the water to keep the line from rubbing against the rocks. If I could just land the shark! I kept one eye on the crocodile hovering between sky and water.

For millions of years this creature had survived on Earth in swamps and terrestrial habitats, through mass extinctions, geological and climatic upheavals unimagined in the short span of human history – eating, mating, tending its eggs.

The order of crocodilians may outlive *Homo sapiens* when the next bottleneck of evolution occurs. Indeed, when the final judgment – the end of all life on Earth – comes to pass, be it by catastrophic interstellar collision, the sudden expansion of the sun, or man's own insuperable stupidity, a crocodile will be wallowing in the mud somewhere, a yellow eye looking up. What will it see? A sudden flash in the sky?

The raised scales of its dark skin rippled in the water; its brow, wide snout, and nostrils protruded just above the surface. Its presence was beguiling, hypnotic. Gentle ripples spread in ever-widening circles around its stubby front legs and rear haunches. For an instant I was tempted to jump into the water next to it.

A waxing quarter moon followed the sun toward the horizon. The shark lay in the water, gills barely moving. The crocodile swam toward the face of the waterfall, casually. As it approached it lifted its head slightly out of the water. It paused for a moment, considering me with a cold eye. I fought a primitive urge to jump up and down and bare my teeth at the reptile.

The crocodile suddenly caught sight of the shark. With a thrust of its tail it propeled itself toward the waterfall. There was the shark, as good as caught. If only I had a gaff!

What was I going to do? Let the reptile take the shark? I watched helplessly as it glided to within sixty feet, its body arched. How do you get him to stop?

"Crocodile!" Jeff shouted in warning from somewhere above. I was startled by his voice, but did not take my gaze from the beast.

At the sound of Jeff's voice the crocodile stopped and hovered in the water for a moment, tail relaxed, stubby feet dangling.

"Yeah," I said loudly, "I have a shark on the end of my line. He thought he was going to get a free meal."

"He's big," Jeff offered from the top of the waterfall. "What do you think, probably more than fifteen feet?"

"Very big," I concurred. "Much bigger from down here."

"I was wondering when he was going to show up. That's probably the same croc that took Ginger Meadows," Jeff shouted. "They're very territorial. One this big might roam the entire river. He might be eighty years old."

It was as if the crocodile knew we were talking about him. We stood like that for several minutes, in strange committee. The crocodile had approached so boldly until it heard Jeff. Now it considered the possibility of ambush. It hovered on the surface of the water sixty feet away. I watched it in awe: the bony brow above the water, the great jaws, and the serrated edges of its powerful tail keeping its place against the current.

What did it make of these voices? I stared into its black and yellow eye. Did I smell its fetid breath?

This creature, the Prometheus of Ngarinyan Aboriginal myths, was the first Creator to bring fire down from the sky. According to legend, the crocodile immersed fire in the Earth, but the fire was in danger of going out. The red-shouldered parrot swooped down and snatched it in her beak, spreading fire throughout the bush. Later the crocodile fell into ill favor with the other creators and caught fire itself, resulting in its scales and thick-scarred skin. It ran into the water to douse the flames. The crocodile has remained in the water ever since, wallowing in pain and waiting for a chance of revenge.

I was struck with the understanding that, were it not for some cataclysm at the end of the Cretaceous some sixty-five million years ago, most likely a large asteroid or two, this creature and its ilk might still rule the land. Here was the first dragon. The human psyche has developed over eons in the shadow of such predators.

Slowly the crocodile swam to the edge of the mangroves and then submerged for several agonizing minutes. I was fifteen feet above the water, well out of range of a leaping crocodile, but I braced myself against the cliff. Crocodiles can startle their prey into falling into the water by lunging at them.

"He's disappeared!" I shouted up to Jeff over the sound of the waterfall.

"Watch out!" he yelled back. Darkness descended but for the moon. The waters of the inlet remained undisturbed. The shark ceased moving and floated, exhausted, just feet below me, but I dared not climb down near the water's edge and retrieve it. If I could just hold the shark on a ledge and wait for the tide to go out, I could climb down and grab him. That would be another hour at least. But it would be worth the wait for shark steak.

The crocodile surfaced with barely a ripple among the mangroves. He began swimming out to the main river.

"There he is," Jeff shouted.

It disappeared around the edge of the inlet with unhurried motions of its great tail, floating out with the ebbing tide. I might have climbed down to the water's edge and retrieved the shark then, but I was spooked. Though the air was hot and sticky, I felt a chill. I was not sure how many crocodiles might haunt the waters down below. So I waited. A non-dominant ten-foot saurian might linger in the waters at my feet, and that would be large enough to pull me under.

The moon sank nearer the horizon and Jeff said he was going to boil up some tea.

"I'll be up soon," I said. The light faded on the face of the waterfall.

Even the motion of the shark's gills had ceased. I balanced it on a ledge as the water receded. We were going to have shark steak after all. The inlet grew darker. The crocodile might have submerged and swum back toward the falls. He could be waiting down there, just below me. In another forty minutes I would go down and safely retrieve the shark.

As night fell, a cloud of mosquitoes poured out of the mangroves. Each thrust a proboscis painfully into my skin. The mosquitoes of the Kimberley coast are so numerous in places they inspired the naming of Point Torment by Captain King's crew. I swatted at them in their droves, my skin smeared with blood. After five minutes, it was too much.

I wedged my fishing rod securely in a crack and tied it with some nylon cord before pulling myself up the waterfall in the silver light, leaving the shark, the crocodile, and the mosquitoes. Once I was out of the mangroves, the mosquitoes no longer swarmed. I put on a long-sleeved shirt and sat down next to Jeff while he boiled up some water for tea.

"Where's the shark?" he asked.

"Down there. I'm going to wait until the tide goes out. The mosquitoes just bit the hell out of me."

Jeff could only offer me a cup of tea for dinner. We both feasted on imagined shark steak. I went to my pack and took out a foil of food.

"Let's split this." I threw it to Jeff.

"Yes! Where did you find that?"

"It's my last one," I lied. I still had one left, but I didn't want to tell Jeff about it yet, thinking I might need to eat it all myself.

Over tea I remembered the piece of wire Peter had given me. I bent it in the shape of a hook and tied it to my wattle stick: a crude gaff. If only I had remembered it sooner! I climbed down the face of the cascade in the last light of the moon.

My fishing rod was still there, but the line had snapped. Something had eaten the shark. I climbed exhausted up the falls and went to sleep.

I had nightmares about being chased over rocks by the crocodile. In a half-sleep I mistook the sound of the waterfall for the sound of Christine running a bath in the morning while I dozed in bed. I woke up in the middle of nowhere.

CHAPTER 27

THE FIG TREE AT
THE COAST

I clung to the upper branches of the fig tree growing at the top of the cliff. The far wall of the gorge rose implacably in the distance, the tide rolling out. I had eaten nothing in the last few days but a few unripe figs and small fish. The estuary had not proved to be a rich larder. Tonight there would be nothing to eat. Nothing. I prayed to God that a boat was making its way toward us.

For the past four days the winds had been very strong. The sky was gray. To the east endless escarpments of rock marked the way we had come. We would not have the strength to walk all the way back to the Drysdale River Station, even if we caught fish all the way along.

Looking in all directions from the uppermost branches of the tree, I felt very alone. I was beginning to feel weak and light-headed. I wanted to cry, and to cry out, but no one would hear me. How am I going to make it out of here?

I sat in the tree for hours, reflecting on this quiet coast. Where was the nearest human soul to us? All these living things, this tree, these little frogs, were content out here – why couldn't I be like them? After all, I had come from this land, and I was no stranger to it.

Even Jeff, who had been in dire situations before, seemed quite desperate. Our talk centred on getting out, and getting to civilization in one form or another. In my journal, I had carefully written down all the things I would eat when I got to civilization. We had been debating for several days whether to remain at the King Cascade or take an emergency route southeast to the Mount Elizabeth Homestead.

"I guess we should have waited for those fucking maps," Jeff said. We regretted immeasurably not waiting for the correct maps at the Kununurra post office. Now, if we did walk out, we'd be going without maps. "If only we had the maps," I wrote several times in my journal. We would be walking into the unknown.

We had eaten only fish and figs now for three days, but it wasn't enough. The time limit to our ordeal would be measured in calories. My ribs pushed against my brown skin, and purple veins stood out on my arms and chest. I could not last indefinitely out here.

"We're catching fish," I said to Jeff. "Why are we still so hungry?"

"It's called trout starvation. Gold miners suffered from it in the High Sierras. Fish are full of protein but not enough carbo-hydrates. After a few more weeks you won't have the strength to fish."

A light rain sprinkled the inlet and cliffs. I just wanted to eat. I supposed that things could be worse – I might be suffering from a poisonous snakebite or have a badly sprained ankle. Below the smooth limbs of the tree, the river moved between pink cliffs.

I returned to our cave from the fig tree. There was no sign of Jeff. I climbed down the face of the waterfall. The tide was almost out, leaving nothing but mud and a shallow pool of water leading out to the river. Still no Jeff. My God, I thought, what if the crocodile has taken Jeff? Then truly this would be the loneliest place in the world.

I looked down the face of the cascade, not wanting to believe for an instant that Jeff had fallen into the water, or been snatched off the rocks. I scampered along the face. My fishing reel lay in pieces on a ledge.

In a shallow pool left by the tide, a huge yellowfin tuna circled. It was the size of a man. Jeff stood on a ledge, hurling a piece of bait into the water. The fish brushed past it.

I could not contain my disbelief. "What are you doing?" I shouted. "That bait is much too big."

Jeff looked at me with anger. "I almost had him. If I can just get the bait in front of him."

"Leave it in the water, then!" I shouted, furious. I examined my rod and reel. They were destroyed. The fish cut back and forth in the dwindling pool, trapped. I contemplated grabbing a stick and wading into the pool to spear the fish.

The tide rushed back in. The fish swam in widening circles of water. With a flick of its tail, it escaped through the narrow channel leading into open water. We watched its dorsal fin move out into the waters of the main gorge with palpable disappointment.

"What did you do to my fishing rod?" I demanded.

"Shut up!" Jeff shouted, furious at losing the fish.

"What the fuck did you do to my fishing rod? It's in pieces over here."

"I had him! He was on the line. The reel jammed and he got off."

"The bait was too big!"

"Fuck you!" Jeff shouted.

"No – FUCK YOU!"

We stared at each other with bloodshot eyes, six feet apart on the rock ledge.

In this place where even the sound of the waterfall could drive one to madness, I decided to climb back up to our cave, remem—bering the dictum that even civilized man is nine missed meals away from murder. We had passed that limit days ago.

I wondered if I should move into another cave, remembering

241

the look in Jeff's eyes. It would be nothing to push someone off a cliff out here and say they just disappeared.

We were not that far from cannibalism. I did not want to share any more of the fish I caught. Jeff and I had been sharing one packet of my freeze-dried food each afternoon, but it had run out three days ago. I had only one packet left and I was saving that in case we had to go overland. There would be no time to fish then.

I tried to take stock of my situation. I had lost at least twenty pounds and my body was thinner than it had ever been. I was out of food, and my fishing reel was damaged beyond repair, though I still had a handline. We were at least a hundred miles from the nearest cattle station, and we didn't have the right maps. Despair crept at the edges of my consciousness. There was no easy way out. Where was the damn boat?

It started to rain, and I quickly gathered wood for a fire. The blaze grew and hissed at the rain. It began to pour. I hoped that everyone I knew was better off than I was, that everyone was safe. I began concentrating all my mental energy on visualizing my brother; where was he right now, thousands of miles and oceans away?

I could see him driving home from work, hands gripping the wheel, mind wandering.

"Andrew!" I shouted in my head. "Andrew! Andrew! Andrew!" I concentrated my mind. "Help! Help! Help!" That was all I could manage. I opened my eyes and remembered where I was.

Suddenly Jeff appeared beside me. I did not look at him.

"Just what the doctor ordered," he said, warming his hands by the fire. He wore a wool cap and vest, his only cold weather gear.

The temperatures had started to drop off with the end of the wet season nearing. Thankfully I had a light jacket with me.

"Where the hell are the boats?" I wondered, but secretly we both knew.

Jeff looked at the sky. It had been unusually windy and rainy for days.

"Cyclone," Jeff said, "out there somewhere. We're in the outer bands, the feeder bands. I don't think any boats are going to lift anchor in this weather. The *Kimberley Explorer* is probably still in port. Who knows how long it will be? We've got a choice: we either stay at the coast and hope we don't starve to death before a boat comes in, or we take a chance and walk out to Mount Elizabeth."

I stared into the fire, my arms around my knees. Walking out. Plan B.

"I so liked the idea of getting out on a boat," I said, throwing a stick on the fire.

"Me too."

"We'll make it out of here. No matter what it takes. And the boat might be in tomorrow."

"And if it's not, we'll make it out anyway." The light faded quickly in the mist. Jeff and I remained staring at the fire, our faces glowing in the light. We did not say much. Nothing to eat. But tomorrow was another day. Tomorrow we might catch lots of fish. Tomorrow the boat might come in.

In the morning, I grabbed my handline. Jeff had made a second handline from the fishing line we had spooled out of the broken reel and wrapped around a stick. When I reached for it on the ledge outside our cave, it was gone.

"What happened to your fishing gear? I saw you put it on the ledge," I said.

"I don't know. It must be here somewhere."

"You can't lose that fishing line. We need it!"

I ranged high and low around our camp, desperate to find the second line. No sign of it.

"Am I going crazy? I know it was there." Jeff scratched his head. Then I remembered that he had left the bait, a piece of fish skin and flesh, on the hook.

"Maybe that quoll took it." A western spotted quoll had taken to raiding our camp every night. There wasn't much for him to eat, though he had made off with an empty tube of concentrated butter.

"Shit, do we only have one fishing line left?" I shook my head. Jeff was hopeless as a fisherman.

I climbed down the face of the waterfall. The morning light reflected the surrounding cliffs off the surface of the opaque waters. On the edge of the mangroves, a track in the mud indicated where the crocodile had come out of the water, or gone into the water. It was too dark underneath to see if he was lying in there.

He was up early this morning. I threw my line in and caught one catfish after another. I would wait until the tide ebbed and then climb up and have some fish and tea with Jeff.

I pulled my handline in. From now on, I was fishing with the bare essentials. The reel was a total loss. The extra fishing line had disappeared. Peter had been right. I had brought dozens of hooks with me; one by one they had been lost. I turned thankfully to the cork full of hooks Peter had put on the cabin table before my departure. It made all the difference.

I stuck a piece of catfish meat onto a hook and hurled it out over the water. Normally I stepped on the spool, but this time I forgot to.

The bait came to the end of its trajectory and tugged the spool off the ledge. It bounced down the rocks, unraveling. The handline fell into the water and floated there.

It was a moment of pure death.

The spool bobbed away from the edge of the rock with the receding tide. In moments it would be out of reach, and I would have to swim for it. My entire life had come to this. This was my last spool of fishing line, and without it I would not survive.

The crocodile had been in the inlet earlier this morning; was he lying motionless in the pallid water below me, eyes blinking slowly, heart slowed to one beat every forty seconds, watching the rippled surface of the water, waiting for my reflection to appear?

I had no choice. Either risk a quick death or starve slowly. If the crocodile was there, I would be gone: a sudden lunge from the water and a swirling in the gray and I would go to my death alone, leaving some to wonder. There would be a few comments about Yanks and crocodiles. I saw my obituary in the *Boston Globe*: "Local boy presumed taken by crocodile in North Western Australia."

It was a moment such as this one that the crocodile would have waited for. Crocodiles can remain submerged for up to one hour, and they record the habits of their prey. On the Nile River a crocodile watched a woman doing her laundry along the shore three days in a row. She always went to the river at the same time, in the same location. On the fourth day the crocodile was waiting there underwater and ate her.

Thump . . .

If this was it, this was it. My heart pumping madly, I clambered down the cliff face onto a ledge just above the water's edge.

I looked behind me around the curved face of the cascade as I reached the ledge to be sure the crocodile wasn't there on the flat rock. I leaned out over the opaque stillness, my face inches above the gray water, praying, praying, while clouds raced across the sky.

It was over in an instant — the spool was in my hand, and I climbed quickly up the rocks, safely out of reach as the sky spun above my head. I lay back against the rock and closed my eyes, grateful to be alive.

That afternoon I stood fishing from the edge of the cascade as the tide swelled against the face of the cliff. I ate two small fish raw, not wanting to share them with Jeff. Suddenly, a submarine rose from the depths no more than thirty feet away, water spilling off its ridged back soundlessly. It floated slightly forward and lay motionless for a moment, contemplating me with a yellow eye.

With languid motions of its great tail, the crocodile turned and swam out of the inlet.

The dinosaur was waiting for me that afternoon, but in the morning it had been hunting elsewhere. He entered the current of the main river, drifting among the floating trees, and turned in the direction of the coast. I never saw the crocodile again, except in dreams. Such are the vicissitudes by which we live.

Jeff and I had made a decision. If a boat did not come in this afternoon, we would lace up our boots and head overland to the nearest corner of civilization: a remote cattle station called the Mount Elizabeth Homestead. We were sure now that a cyclone or heavy weather farther south was keeping the boats at anchor.

I fished the whole day without catching anything except a blowfish that puffed itself out like a spiny balloon and proved almost impossible to get off my hook.

Jeff came down, and I showed him the fish. "Do you think we can eat it?"

He shook his head, "I wouldn't. I remember hearing something about blowfish being poisonous. You wouldn't want to get sick right now." I hacked the blowfish off with my knife, avoiding the spines.

I fished in silence, hoping against hope that a boat would come in with the afternoon tide.

"What's that?" I said, pointing to an object floating way out in the river. It appeared to be a motorboat with three people standing up in it. I wanted so much for it to be a motorboat. It was a tree. Slowly the trees stopped moving in, and headed back out to sea. There would be no boat coming in against the tide. This was the moment we had been dreading. We would walk out.

Jeff and I looked at each other. "Well, at least we won't be waiting around anymore," he said.

I still had the extra packet in the bottom of my pack. After that, we would be living entirely off the land. There just wasn't that much to eat this time of year. Even the Aboriginals would have gone hungry.

Perhaps I would eat the freeze-dried packet by myself. After all, if Jeff hadn't lost a week's worth of food in a river crossing, we wouldn't be so badly off. And Jeff was not as thin as I was, though his cheeks were sunken and his ribs stuck out.

I kept asking myself, when will this be over? How will it end?

And right now, people are walking up and down aisles in supermarkets stocked with food. They are having barbecues and casually eating crackers and cheese. Hunger was a most important education.

Please, just let me catch one fish, one sign that this will turn out all right, before we turn our backs on the coast and possible rescue and head inland. Please! I do not want to try to sleep without eating for another night. I knew I had days ahead of me without food, over rugged terrain. Jeff looked rather glum.

"I'll try it for another few minutes," I said. In the quiet gray of the afternoon, we considered our prospects. I felt a tug and then a sudden strong, steady pull on my line. I let it out. It burned across my palm as the fish pulled away. My heart soared.

Don't lose this one, I prayed. I sensed that Jeff too was concentrating on the fish. Suddenly it leapt out of the water, a huge silver torpedo, and disappeared. It weighed about eight pounds. We prayed the hook held. Slowly, gradually, the fish tired, and I hauled it up onto the rocks, grabbing the wriggling flesh with my hands. It was a sign. Enough fish steak for a feast for two starving men!

Within minutes we were back at the top of the waterfall, cooking up fillets on the stove as the rain strengthened. We ate quickly, ravenously. Jeff deferred a portion of his fish steak to me.

"I can't eat any more," he said. It was his way of saying sorry about yesterday, and good for you to stick it out and keep fishing. We sat on the top of the waterfall, watching the light disappear.

"Blueberry pancakes," Jeff mumbled.

I hiked up Cascade Creek in the evening. The sound of the water was comforting here, amid the trees and rocks on either side of the valley. I had come to know this place. Even in the middle of a huge wilderness, with little to eat, I was at home here.

The air was hot, and I stripped naked and sat in a clear pool. The frogs and crickets croaked and trilled. From farther down the splash of the waterfall drifted. I put my head under and slowly exhaled, the water rushing past my ears.

To leave the coast and head overland through this radical topography was a major gamble. Except for the big fish, neither of us had eaten much for the last several days. I wondered, would we have the physical endurance to walk without food? My reflexes were becoming sluggish, and I felt weak. What would happen if one of us twisted an ankle on the way out?

We did not even have all the maps we needed: that was the worst part of all. Why hadn't the map agency sent the right order? Now, it might cost us our lives.

At the bottom of one of our maps a dotted red line indicated a four-wheel-drive track. It led to the edge of the map with an arrow pointing: Mount Elizabeth Homestead it said, forty-four miles. The red line marked the only man-made feature on any of our maps. It was all we had to go by.

We studied the maps closely, my mind climbing over contour lines, imagining the swamps, rivers, ridges, and boulder fields we had to cross.

"We've got maybe two or three days from here to the track. From there the homestead should be another forty miles, if the map's accurate."

Forty miles? Not far at all, I thought to myself. A person in an automobile could cover that distance on a highway in forty minutes and not think twice about it. In our weakened state, with the heat, we hoped it would only take us two or three days to cover that ground. If only we had those maps! Once we found that track, we would walk to the edge of our maps and just have to keep walking, following it. The road had to lead somewhere. But what if we came to a fork in the track? There were so many variables. Would there be as much water as we headed away from the coast? Probably not.

I thought of the boys at Halls Creek and the arrow fashioned out of stones: this direction, it said. They were found a mile or so farther on. Jeff and I now faced twenty times that distance over broken country. I figured we could live off the land for several more weeks if we had to, but to go two days out here without water would be the end.

"Once we come to a fence, we'll know we're getting close," Jeff said.

With the average cattle station in the Kimberley a million acres in size, I was not sure how we would continue after reaching the fence. It could still be many miles from nowhere. One station, Victoria River Downs, had been larger than the state of Texas before it was parceled up in the 1930s.

"Maybe there will be four-wheel-drivers camping along the track?" Jeff offered hopefully. "It should be around Easter. People will be on vacation."

But we both knew that this area had been cut off for months by the wet. The roads would not be passable until May at the earliest.

Two months ago, Jeff and I had flown in on the mail plane to the Drysdale River Station's airstrip. Our shadow had streaked effortlessly across the Earth. That seemed so long ago. I wished that I could fly now, just to see how far away that small outpost of civilization was; a collection of roofs, the main house, a bunkhouse for the jackaroos, the drafting pens and other outbuildings surrounded by a sea of space. I had never yearned so much to be able to fly. Would it help to know the distance or would it be too daunting?

We could only approach any contingency at a walking pace. What if, because the maps are almost twenty years old, that track no longer exists? What happens if the track forks, and we take a wrong turn and walk into eternity? What if water becomes scarce along the track? What if we don't have the strength to keep walking? These questions recurred over and over in my mind.

Tomorrow at dawn Jeff and I would lace up our boots and begin hiking out, whatever the consequences. I collected all the yellow figs from the fig tree atop the cascade. When I bit into them small bugs flew out, but I was not perturbed. I had taken to eating insects, whatever ones I could find. I caught grasshoppers and ate them after pulling off their wings, scowling at the taste. The figs were hard and unripe, but at least I would be carrying some food with me overland.

I sat in the crown of the tree, looking out over the wall of the gorge to the rocks and ranges beyond. The homestead would be beyond that quiet horizon, and beyond that, and beyond that. And yet, this wilderness was not hostile – just utterly indifferent.

Below me the inlet, with its crocodile, its mangroves and mosquitoes, seemed almost peaceful. At least I would not end up in the belly of the beast.

We were going to walk out.

The sun disappeared below the far wall of the gorge. I understood the boy now at Halls Creek; how, with his remaining strength, he had scratched his final farewell: "*I found peece.*" At least I had my journal. It was a great consolation to know that I would be able to write my goodbyes.

My family might come out to see the place where I died. They would hear the same sad laugh of the crows. Who would come looking for Jeff? Perhaps no one. He seemed tempered by that understanding.

Why should I be afraid to die? I looked beyond the horizon of my bodily death into something beyond. Wasn't the existence of life itself as improbable as, if not more improbable than, some continuation after death? Life is, after all, a paranormal experience.

These precious scarlet blossoms would still be here, year after year. Those trees would still float in and out with the tides. The frogs would make their nightly chorus.

In the yellow light dappling the branches I saw a tree frog. One eye studied the world beside my hand. I thought of my first encounter with this coast, at Crystal Creek. I had been so lost then, so alone. I remembered stumbling upon the painting of the tree frog in white ochre. What had it meant?

I bit into a fig. If only I could move like those clouds. The colors of the sun retreated as violet on the edge of night crept out of the east. Even as darkness came, dawn was arriving with a reddish glow somewhere around the Earth.

I tried to picture myself in three weeks; I knew I would either have walked out, or died. Could I see myself eating dinner at Perry Farm with Peter and Maggie? A part of me was preparing for the worst. Would I be food for the goannas and the crows? I remembered what Peter had said about a Kalahari Bushman's view on death, "I die, the wind blows over my footprints in the sand, and I am gone." I had lived enough, so far. But I didn't want to die just yet. The hardest part was thinking that I would not be able to say goodbye to my family in person. I missed them terribly now. I would write my goodbyes.

Walking back to camp, I realized I would not miss this waterfall with its crocodile and surging tides. I curled up in my sleeping sheet and dreamed the distance we had to cover.

CHAPTER 28

PLAN B

I woke up early to a gray sky. We're walking out of here, I told myself. The worry of the night before was gone.

I ripped a blank page from my journal and wrote:

My name is Will Chaffey. Jeff Cunningham and I reached the King Cascade after six weeks walk from the Drysdale River Station. We are now heading overland to the Mount Elizabeth Homestead. From the King Cascade we will head south to a vehicle track marked on the map Hann. We will follow that track to the Homestead. We are both well, but out of food. We estimate it will take us six days to reach the Homestead. Please radio or call the Homestead to make sure we have arrived. Thank you.

I dated the note and signed my name. I put it inside a plastic bag, tied it to a stick with a red bandanna, and wedged one end of the stick in the rocks above the high tide mark.

Now we could walk to the Mount Elizabeth Homestead. We shouldered our packs, put on our hats, and headed up the valley of Cascade Creek.

"This is it."

"Outta here." I gave one last look at the implacable Prince Regent River, again moving out to sea.

We walked up the valley of Cascade Creek in silence, pushing through tall grass and elephant ear wattle. Before, while walking, Jeff and I had looked up in the branches of eucalyptus for carpet pythons and beautiful parrots. Now our only concern was covering ground. Each thorny branch that held us back, each fallen tree I stepped over, was measured in dwindling calories.

We veered away from Cascade Creek and followed a smaller creek up the escarpment. To my relief we discovered it was the same passage we had followed into the valley. The sky was overcast and offered some respite from the sun. In the creek I found an aquatic plant resembling red-leaf lettuce, which I ate. We dunked ourselves in the water to stay cool. At the top of the plateau, the yellowing grass, eucalyptus trees, and fire-blackened cycads stretched as far as the eye could see.

Jeff and I looked at our compasses and the maps. We were walking into the unknown. This plain stretched at least a day's walk before us, with no reference points, and no heights from which to assess our position. We planned to walk toward a blue line marked on the map: Blyxa Creek. Would there be water? We filled our bottles and hydrated ourselves before pushing on.

The sound of my boots on the dry ground blended in a cadence with my thoughts. My eyes watched the compass needle in my hand and the ground before me in the blazing noon. Jeff's boots stomped through the grass nearby. We had not spoken for several hours. His eyes, like mine, were watching the compass needle.

I saw a tree in the distance and noted how long it took before I was past it, and the tree receding. Even to stand still in this place filled me with loneliness.

"It's bloody hot." Jeff winced when the sun burned through

the clouds at noon. We walked all day across the plain, painfully earthbound while collared lorikeets whistled through the scattered trees. In the evening we came to the narrow creek running across the plain. Water!

I put down my pack, unrolled the sleeping mat, and sat down. Blyxa Creek was narrow enough to jump over, flowing over the rocky soil. We looked at the maps. The stream could be one of two marked on the map. There were small fish in it, impossible to catch. We lay on our sleeping mats and had a cup of tea. We spoke very little, each lost in his own thoughts. The space around us was so wide, and so quiet. A strange feeling had replaced hunger in my stomach: fear.

That night I dreamed I had left something behind at the waterfall, something vital that I would have to go back for, alone, in the dark. I set out while Jeff slept under the violet sky, making my way north across the grassy plain, scared because I knew there was danger at the coast, frightened of the things we confront alone. I woke up on the plain with the stars of the Southern Cross falling softly through the smooth branches of a gum tree.

The red light of dawn brought the chorus of birds, the "Tooh-oo too-hoo" of a peaceful dove, the macabre whistle of the butcher bird.

The "Caaaw, caaaw, caaaaaaaw!" of marauding black crows suddenly reminded me of where I found myself and in what circumstances. I looked over at my backpack and boots. It was all real. Jeff stirred nearby. I put on my pants and shirt and soaked my body in the creek, hoping to keep cool for as long as possible. Today the sun would shine long and hot. No matter, I will walk *this* day to *that* horizon.

I ate a dozen small figs and washed them down with water from the creek, filling up my canteen. Muscle was now being consumed to run the engine of my body. I measured the remaining figs, wondering if they would last me a week. Not even.

Jeff and I shook our boots out for scorpions or spiders, and were on our feet and moving within minutes. We walked silently through the tall grass, over fallen trees and scattered rocks. Who was the president of the United States? What was the Dow Jones index? What was the consumer confidence rating? What was the prime rate? What year was it *anno domini*? I could not have cared less. I just wanted to live another day. The land endures. Religions come and go. Species dominate for a time and then disappear. How long would mankind survive?

God was not some higher being: it was the cycad rising perpendicular to the plain, the smooth-barked white eucalyptus holding up under the sun.

Everything on earth brand new and standing up, Yorro Yorro.

All of recorded history was contained in a single instant in this land, in a single day in the gorge; an afternoon, like any other afternoon, like any other for millennia. And yet, different. Here this consciousness called "I" was witness to it for the first time. I was a piece of Creation and would forever be. Whatever grand scheme for the universe existed, somehow I was a part of it and would always be. There was something divine in that realization.

While Isaac Newton wrote his *Principia*, or John Locke his *Letter Concerning Toleration*, or Captain Cook explored Polynesia and Australia on his voyage to mark the transit of Venus across the sun in 1769, or Samuel Johnson compiled his dictionary, or Matthew Flinders charted the first map of Australia, or Thomas Jefferson detailed the rights of man in an official document, or Adam Smith wrote *Wealth of Nations*, or Linnaeus described his *Systema Natura*, or Charles Darwin formulated his *Origin of Species*, or Einstein conducted his thought experiments, that rock was leaning against the other just so, water was spilling through those boulders just as I saw them now. Human history was so tiny, almost infinitesimal. Herod or Socrates were our contemporaries against the backdrop of this landscape. Perhaps a thousand dingoes had chased a thousand kangaroos over those rocks. Perhaps something truly extraordinary happened, a visit by extraterrestrials, something unseen by humans and swallowed in the maw of time.

Hours went by walking through the studded eucalypt plain. The sun flamed overhead. We had no vantage points to mark our progress, just silent trees and the thousands of tiny flowering pink and red clovers growing out of the sandy soils at our feet.

A row of boulders rose above the trees like a maze. Jeff and I looked at each other. The boulders were not on the map, though they were large enough to be. We put our packs down. I leaned against a tree. Now we stood in the middle of nowhere.

"It looks like we may have corrected a little too much to the northwest," I said, looking at the map and the line of boulders rising a hundred twenty feet above the eucalypt plain. Any error in navigation wasted precious calories.

We walked alongside the range like sailors hugging a coastline until the sea of grassy savannah opened up for us once again. A kangaroo hopped up the rocks. How did the Aboriginal people do it? I wondered. This whole continent, like every other, was once a vast trackless wilderness – yet it was home to man. When the monsoon came and the thunderclouds rolled in like great ships, where was home? A rock ledge? An overhang? A shady spot by the billabong? And yet, why should a house with a number be any different? There are no fixed points in the universe. It was all a comforting abstraction. Home was anywhere on planet Earth.

We pushed on across the plain, through thick stands of elephant ear wattle. The grass had begun to yellow. The wet season was ending and the dry would soon begin. The dry in Australia means fire. Many species of plants have adapted specifically to the cycle of fire. The banksias and hakeas shed seedpods only after intense heat. I just hoped we'd have enough water.

A weathered sandstone ridge appeared through the trees. We reached the edge of the ranges. I glanced at Jeff. There was nothing for it but to climb over.

Bone tired and thirsty, I climbed up over the jumbled boulders, collecting black grapes as I went. A light rain pattered off the leaves. Jeff was somewhere behind me. I reached the top of the ridge. Below lay a broad grassy valley with ranges at the far side. Distant ranges grew paler and paler to the farthest reaches of the horizon. The afternoon turned suddenly dark. Jeff came up just as a steady downpour set in. This was grim. This was miles and miles and miles from nowhere.

It rained steadily for twenty minutes. I wished emphatically to fly, if only just straight up and then down so that I could know where we were in relation to the rooftops and drafting pens of the homestead.

I remembered Peter's words: "In the Territory, when a person goes missing, searchers start in a circle around the car moving outwards. They usually only get about two miles from the car before they find the bodies." We weren't anywhere near a road. No one would ever find me out here, I knew that.

But I knew where I was. I had never known so precisely where I was: hungry, tired, lost, *here*, standing on a ridge.

When the rain tapered off, I pulled the maps out of my pack and sat down beside a boulder. I scanned the maze of lines marking rock formations on the map.

Cliffs marked by sharp lines. Black numbered grid lines are 1000-metre intervals of the Australian map grid, Zone 51. Grid values are shown in full at the southwest corner of the map. Contour interval twenty metres. True North, Grid North and Magnetic North are shown diagrammatically for the centre of this map. Magnetic north is correct for 1975 and moves westerly by 0.1 degrees (two mils) every three years. Map reliability: Topographic information shown on this map is correct for 1973.

At least we had maps for this territory. The small lines on the map delineated the features as though we were above them. Greens for vegetation. Orange for stone. Blue for watercourses. From ground level this landscape was intricate and laborious. I remembered the pilot's last words to us as we stepped out of the plane onto the soil of the runway: "You blokes have got to be crazy."

Should we turn around and wait at the King Cascade, conserving energy? It might be weeks or months before a boat came in. What would I have learned out here if I died? I supposed I would have learned how to die. That would be an important final lesson.

We looked out from the ridge. Below us lay a broad valley with a domed hill to the south.

"I think that's the hill in front of us," I said, pointing to a series of concentric circles on the map. "We must be somewhere on the face of this range here."

I took out my compass and sighted across the valley to a sharp outcrop on the hill, a bearing of 240 degrees.

"Assuming that's that hill, we should be somewhere along that 240 line," I said.

"I don't know – couldn't it be this one over here?" Jeff pointed to another rocky hill on the map. Shafts of light drifted across the valley.

"Hmm," he wondered, looking at the map. Our map showed that the hill was several degrees off our compass bearing. "Well," Jeff sucked in his breath, "maybe the map isn't quite accurate."

"It could still be that hill," I said, studying the map.

"No, I don't think it is. Look at the shape. See the knob on the western side – that's that, right there." He was pointing at the outcrop of rock on the side of the hill. I took another sighting on a pile of red stone up the valley, sighting the highest boulder in the notch of my compass cover, while he did the same.

"We're at this intersection here," Jeff said, marking the junction of the two lines of sight on the map with black thread. "Looking at that." Jeff pointed to a conical hill on the map. We took a third bearing just to be sure.

"That's the one," I said. For the first time we knew where we stood after two days dead reckoning across the plain. "When we enter the valley we want to strike at about 220 and pass the knob of that hill just barely. There is an opening in the face of those ranges. That must be the beginnings of Bachsten Creek." I pointed to a thin blue line, running into a wide gorge marked on the map.

We struck off down the face of the ranges and across a wide valley, dotted with ancient cycads. Thin beams of sunlight followed us across the valley.

For two hours we walked toward the ranges on the far side. Out of the scattered eucalyptus trees a line of weeping paperbarks, river red gums, and pandanus grew more distinct.

"Looks like water!"

"Bachsten Creek!"

Gratefully we drank in the sound of flowing water. We dipped our hats in the cool stream and filled our canteens. The creek grew as we followed it, the ranges converging.

"We're getting close."

"Not far now."

"Hotel's just around the corner . . ."

"Bartender, I'll have my beer extra cold."

We trudged beside the ranges into another grassy plain that evolved into a massive boulder field. We sweated over the spinifex-covered boulders all afternoon.

Evening found us still among the boulders.

"Here will do," Jeff sighed. We dropped our packs among the rocks and went to sleep exhausted, too tired to make a cup of tea. I lay on a flat rock and folded the space blanket over me to keep out the mosquitoes. Silent clouds rolled across the stars. The first few drops of rain pattered on the fabric above me.

Don't rain, please.

For half an hour the rain came down. Then it poured. I fell asleep. One cannot petition God, just as one could not ask the wind not to blow, or the sun not to shine, or the rain not to fall.

In the middle of the night a heavy rain woke me up. How long had I been asleep? When the rain stopped I stuck my head out from under my space blanket. I waved my hand in front of my face, seeing nothing. Pitch dark. Where am I? I lay for a while thinking.

The stars began shining between gaps in the clouds, drifting mosaics of silver and black. For a moment, the red star of Antares gleamed in the body of the Scorpion.

I remembered the oatmeal soap in my top pocket. Would it make me sick to eat some of it? It was fat, so it should have calories. I tried a few small bites. It tasted more like soap than oatmeal. Not worth it.

The next day dawned clear and bright, the last stars and finally the planets disappearing in a gathering blue.

"Here," I tossed the packet of freeze-dried food beside Jeff. "It's the last one – I was saving it for an emergency." His eyes lit up.

"For breakfast?"

"Aren't you hungry?"

"But you were saving it for an emergency."

"I know, but let's just eat it."

We could still laugh, despite our hunger. Within moments the stove was purring quietly. We cooked the food and ate it with the savor of English gentlemen enjoying tea while hunting tigers in India – until we began licking our plates and the pot clean.

"That was *damn* good."

"It was!"

All morning we struggled over the boulder field. All afternoon we hiked across a stony plain of eucalyptus and cycads, *adagio*.

"Do you hear it?"

"Yeah, I hear it!"

The sound of water carried on the wind. Struggling over the plain, we stopped suddenly on the rim of a wide gorge. The sheer sides plummeted from the edge at our feet, forming a red cauldron of stone in the Earth. I stood on the rim and looked into the shadow of this remote abyss, transfixed. We knew where we were again: the gorge at Bachsten Creek. The track would be a few hours' walk from here. Jeff took off his pack and lay down in the shade under a nearby ghost gum.

I studied the scaly bark of a "crocodile" tree, and thought of the aged leviathan plying the waters of the King Cascade. The black waters below swirled and turmoiled. It was not difficult in this landscape to admit of a time after I ceased to be.

We spent the noon napping under a tree in Creation.

Bachsten Creek spilled over a cliff of red sandstone and flowed toward the ocean many miles distant. Beyond the waterfall, the land opened up. The creek swirled through wide sandy banks lined with paperbark trees. Jeff and I skirted the river, keeping our boots dry.

As we rounded a bend in the creek to our left, we saw it: two thin ruts disappeared into the tall grass. The track! Our first sign of human activity upon this land after fifty-six days. We approached hopefully.

There was no one camped near a four-wheel drive.

It looked like many of the other four-wheel-drive tracks

I had encountered in Australia – where a person might wait for weeks, months, or possibly years before a vehicle drove by. Still, we were back on planet Earth somewhere in the twentieth century. I had begun to wonder. At least now there would be no more climbing up and down cliffs and over boulder fields.

I roamed about wildly through the tall grass that surrounded the track, looking for any signs of human presence. There were no fresh tire tracks in the mud. It was clear that no one had been this way in years. For three days we had had only one goal in mind: get to the track. Now that we were here, I realized once again the utter immensity of this place. My heart sank for a moment as we contemplated the wheel ruts, stretching through an eternity of dry grass.

"It's a track," I said, looking at the thin ruts in the sand, disappearing alongside the face of a low cliff. "And all tracks lead somewhere."

Trees had fallen across it.

"Well, it *is* a track," Jeff repeated. There was an hour of daylight left in the afternoon.

"Should we keep walking?" I wondered.

"Let's camp by the creek." Jeff threw out his sleeping sheet at the base of a gnarled tree. He was as disappointed as I was not to see any recent vehicle tracks.

I set up my mosquito net and sleeping mat, retrieved the slingshot from my backpack and headed back to the creek. At least we still had tea, blackcurrant, orange pekoe, and my favorite, Earl Grey. I selected several round stones and stalked through the white paperbark trees in the yellow light. Lingering daylight streaked the tops of trees. The water came up to my knees as I crossed it, clear and cool.

"Raaak! Raaaaaak!" Two white corellas fluttered down the river and landed in the upper branches of the very tree I stood under. Providence. They gained their perch, talking to each other in a series of squawks and chortles.

Easy now. Careful aim. I sighted on the one slightly lower than the other, raised the slingshot, and let fly. The rock sailed upward through the branches and struck the corella with a hollow sound.

"RAAAAAAKK!" The corella pitched forward off the branch. I ran toward where it would fall, ready to grab it out of the soft sand and break its neck. But I had only winged it. It fell, wings beating, but recovered enough to duck out under the last branch and fly off with its mate. I sent a stone gracelessly between them as they flew down river. Their indignant squawks drifted off. The river was silent.

I moved farther downriver, smelling the air for the peculiar popcorn smell of a flying fox colony. There was none. In the dwindling light I headed back to camp. I returned to the jeers of crows. They had found my bag of teas. Orange pekoe and blackcurrant lay scattered on the rocks. Six bags were punctured and the precious contents spilled. I sent a stone and several epithets among the crows. They flew off in indignation to a far branch from which they talked incessantly to each other about me and my lack of food and how foolish I was to leave my tea out. I built a fire. Jeff returned from gathering pandanus nuts from a nearby tree.

"We can try eating these," he said. "We'll have to roast them for a while to get rid of the irritants. There's not much to eat out here this time of year, is there?"

I nodded and threw a few more sticks on the fire.

"Fucking crows."

"If we can catch a goanna or a crocodile, that would be good eating." Jeff pushed the pandanus nuts around with a stick. "The Aboriginals ate cycad nuts, but only after soaking them for six months. Otherwise they're poisonous."

We didn't have six months. We might not even have six days. I wondered how much longer I could walk without eating. The fire pushed back the darkness. At least we were involved in the ritual of food preparation. The pandanus nuts turned brown and popped in the fire. So what if we were in the middle of nowhere and had not eaten substantially for almost a week. There were plenty worse ways to die. At least I had time to prepare for it.

Jeff pounded on one of the nuts with a stone. "Damn, these things are like rocks." I watched eagerly to see what meat would be extracted from the kernel. He held up a thin piece of meat, yellow and flaky like straw.

"It doesn't really seem worth it, does it?"

"No. Not really." I ate a piece. It tasted like straw. We broke into some more. Jeff pushed the nuts to the side of the fire with a stick. "I don't think that's going to do it."

No wonder the Aboriginal people had, for the most part, moved onto missions where things like tea, sugar, and flour were available. It was still an uneasy alliance for them: the modification of their spiritual life and the land that told the story of their ancestors, in exchange for the material amenities of the white man.

"Nothing on the river, eh?" He looked hopefully at my slingshot.

"No, I almost had a corella, but at the last moment it got away."

"Well, anyway," Jeff said hopefully, "we're on the track now. Can't be too much further to civilization. We might even run into some stockmen on muster or something."

We both knew that was a slim possibility. By the greenness of the grass it would be several weeks yet before stockmen came into this area. I lay inside my mosquito net below the branches of a tree. There was nothing more than this fire, this tree, this place south of the ranges and canyons. But there was comfort here: more or less, we knew where we were in a corner of this Earth.

I wrote in my journal by candlelight: "We have reached the track. Taking one day at a time." I was too tired to write much else. Darkness descended. Jeff lay in the grass nearby.

"Just think of that first cold beer on the beach in Broome, man, or the first hot shower!" he said. I drifted off. Reality was the dream I could not shake myself out of. When I opened my eyes, I saw a cliff to the west. The trees in the grass. The stars. But when I woke up, what would I see? Maybe I was still at King Cascade dreaming? Wake up! I urged myself. Wake up!

At the end of a long day without food, I had the comfort of sleep. Man would go insane without it. What a surprise it was to wake up under a mosquito net in the middle of nowhere.

The next day we set out on the track. The thin ruts wound through silent valleys of scattered eucalyptus and over rocky hills. For the first time we were not determining our own course over the terrain. I kept my eyes out for fig trees, grasshoppers, anything to eat. We passed by quinine trees with bundles of delicious looking orange fruit.

"Emus are about the only creatures that can eat them," Jeff said.

The track veered away from the creek through a sea of scattered trees, across lonely valleys and beside silent cliff tops echoing the gentle "tood-oo" of the doves. Flocks of crows flew about us from time to time, landing on nearby branches and laughing at our sorry state. I kept my slingshot handy, but the crows only taunted us and flew away. Maddening bastards.

We trudged on all day, as fast as we could go. Up and down ranges, through swamps skirting narrow canyons. There was no sign that anyone had driven this way in years.

I wished we would find something, even a dead kangaroo, so that I could pick over it, maybe cracking the marrow out of bones. We looked for eagles rising from a kill but saw none. A taste of death crept into my mouth as I began to auto-cannibalize my own body. Blue veins were prominent now in my arms, chest, and legs. I longed for a pack of gum, anything to remove the horrible taste of ketosis in my mouth.

A shadow slipped down from the ridge and crossed the valley. The ranges in the distance glowed red. Another day. We walked into the night. I followed the wavering beam of my headlamp over the sand. The moon stumbled through the trees. Through the darkness came the laughing, gurgling sound of a river. Gratefully, I splashed water on my face and drank.

"It'd be nice to know where we are. This river would definitely be on the map."

I filled up my canteen and took off my boots to cross the river. Having dry boots could mean the difference between life and death now. The water ran swiftly over the rocks, the only sound in the wilderness. The red eyeshine of a freshwater crocodile floated eerily just above the water, caught in the glare of my headlamp. It moved away quickly. I did not have the strength to chase after it.

While we had food, flying foxes, freshwater crocodiles, cockatoos, crows, goannas, and kangaroos had appeared in abundance. They moved to a higher branch or more distant rock at our approach but usually remained within range of a stone. Perhaps these animals had forgotten their fear of man, or never known it. Now, at the first indication of our presence, they flew out of sight. We had the look of the predator, or perhaps we smelled hungry.

We had not reached the stage where we would wait by a waterhole, conserve our energy, hunt, and await rescue. Neither of us was that weak yet. For now we would walk. "If you stop walking, you're going to die," I told myself.

The next morning the crows woke us. The track snaked through a long silent valley rimmed by quiet cliff tops. Just the sound of the wind, the squawk of the crows, and the hot sun on the back of my neck. Every hour I adjusted my pack, tightening the hip belt or loosening the shoulder straps to transfer the load. Occasionally, I looked back to see the ground we had covered – it looked insignificant compared to what stretched ahead. We passed through forests of white ghost gums, their trunks and spreading limbs smooth, like a marble forest rising out of the eternal plain.

In the afternoon we spied cattle in the distance. A young cow with a calf grazed next to some rocks. This was what we had hoped for! Without a word we took out our knives, and advanced slowly upwind. I crept to within sixty feet. Jeff went around to the side.

The cow's nostrils flared. I didn't move. She stopped grazing and looked up. I sprang out of the tall grass ready to stab it in the neck. The cow and calf bolted away over the rocks.

"That was a waste of energy."

"We need to find one that's just given birth."

In the late afternoon, we stopped and had our last cup of Earl Grey. I squeezed the tea bag into my cup. "Fucking crows."

That night I slept close to the fire.

"How many miles do you think we've walked?"

"More than forty."

"That's what I was thinking. I figure we've done about fifty. You don't think we could have passed the homestead?"

"We haven't seen any forks in the track. The distance must be wrong on the map." Had we inadvertently taken a wrong turn in the track, perhaps passing a more heavily traveled road in the night? We still had not seen any tire tracks.

I kept saying to myself, roads lead somewhere – this one must end up at some corner of civilization. But then another voice would say, "Yes, but what if it's three hundred miles away? Or what if there are forks in the road and you take the wrong one?"

As we lay in our sleeping sheets that night, a bright gleam appeared from behind a ridge in the distance.

"What do you think that is?" I asked Jeff.

"Campers! It looks like a camping lantern. Probably sitting down right now and eating sausages beside their four-wheel drive." It looked like we could walk to it.

"With ketchup and relish?"

"And mustard!"

"What else could it be?"

"I'm telling you, it's a camping lantern."

"It's got to be at least five miles away."

"Yeah, it's not worth trying to walk there tonight. We'll see them in the morning."

"Sausages and mustard," I repeated, watching the rest of the moon – for we could see now what it was – rise above the ridge.

The next morning the wheel ruts led to the top of a plateau. The track disappeared in the rocky soil. We circled around and around, looking for the track for twenty minutes, utterly lost.

"It can't just disappear." Now we really were standing in the middle of nowhere.

"I found it," I shouted with relief. We walked on, with only the heat of the sun on the backs of our necks and the sound of the crows.

And then we returned, briefly, to the end of the twentieth century. A machine flew silently high in the sky overhead – a jet! It moved across the sky at impossible speeds. By the time I got out my signal mirror and attempted to play light on the departing spaceship, it was gone, a streak of silver growing fainter and smaller against an endless blue. Hopeless. Even if a pilot did see the light, he would think it was merely sunlight reflected off a creek. Marooned, I looked at the tiny black windows on the fuselage with binoculars and ached to be inside.

The track disappeared again on the other side of the river. We searched up and down the riverbank. Just to lie down by the cool water . . .

Jeff found the wheel ruts again and we continued, stopping briefly in the evening to put our headlamps on. We trudged into the darkness. I was exhausted after thirteen hours of hiking.

"I gotta stop," I announced finally.

"Just a little farther," Jeff pleaded, but I had taken off my pack and collapsed in the sand, falling asleep almost instantly. I woke up half an hour later covered in biting red ants next to an ant mound. Jeff was sprawled out nearby.

I pulled the last biting ant off my eyelid. "Why didn't you wake me up?"

"I couldn't."

A fire rekindled my spirits. It was almost May now and getting cooler. I stuck my feet in the warm ash near the coals and watched the Southern Cross fall through the smooth limbs of a ghost gum. Wherever I set my sleeping sheet and candle, under the branches of a wild magnolia, among the rocks and trees, anywhere was home.

"Better to be ashes than dust," Jack London wrote. I was thankful that this was not a cold climate. I imagined Captain Scott in his bid to reach the South Pole, discovering that a rival explorer, Amundsen, whose flag attested to his being there first, had beaten him. Scott later died in a tent with several members of the expedition. Things are pretty desperate, but at least we won't freeze to death, I thought.

I folded my pants and put them under my head, looking for Wallanganda in the Milky Way. Of course the Aboriginals could see God in the stars . . .

The next morning I woke and proceeded down the track, the coals still smouldering. A hundred feet from where I had collapsed a narrow path wound into the scrub.

"What's this?"

We would have walked right past it in the dark. I followed it for a short way, while Jeff waited on the track, and discovered a weathered tarp strung up between the trees. Underneath the tarp were two mildewed mattresses, some fishing line, and two five-gallon Dingo Brand flour cans.

I pried the lid off the first can — nothing but moldy lumps. The second can revealed pure white flour. All the money in the world would have been worthless in comparison. I shouted to Jeff, overjoyed.

"Look at this!"

He came quickly through the bush.

"Flour!" I said. "We can make bread! Can you believe it?"

"It means we can't be far from the station now," he said. "This must be a mustering camp for when they're out looking for cattle." I filled up bags and bags with flour. Jeff took only a small supply, and I asked him why.

"We can't be far off now," he said, but I was not so sure. I wanted to know I could eat and survive for as long as possible. I thought Jeff was foolish for not taking more and filled my pack with flour, marveling at what it meant: time! I could continue indefinitely out here on a diet of bread, bush tucker, and water if I had to. I made bread in the coals of the fire that morning and walked on, elated.

In the hot afternoon the wind rippled across a sea of grass. We tipped our hats off to it, grateful for a breeze.

"Do you hear it?"

The hum of a motor above the wind!

"Where's it coming from?"

The sound rose and then disappeared, an auditory halluc–ination. We had heard them before, the whump-whump of a helicopter, or the throb of a diesel generator in the sound of a waterfall carried on the wind.

Hours went by. We labored steadily up a rocky ridge. To our left an outcrop offered a likely vantage.

"I'm going to climb that and see if I can tell where we are."

I put my pack down and scampered up over the rocks and spinifex grass with the compass and binoculars.

There, on the farthest edge of the horizon, sheer against the northwest sky, Mount Hann stood encrimsoned and magnificent in the late sun. *We have walked all that way*. The shallow valley of the Drysdale River was almost indiscernible with distance, but there stood Mount Mcrann and Mount Bomford, gleaming exactly where they should be. The Drysdale River Station would be to the northeast somewhere. It all seemed immeasurably far away, but at least we were heading in the right direction.

I climbed back reassured, and we shouldered our packs again, stumbling down the other side of the ridge.

"We're where we should be, more or less. Mount Elizabeth's got to be up here somewhere. Soon!"

"It would have been nice to end up on the beach in Broome. But I'll take Derby at this point," Jeff replied. "Not much of a beach in Derby – unless you like swimming with estuarine crocodiles, which I know you don't. Spinifex Bar serves a heck of a pub meal, though."

We walked down the ridge thinking of that burger with the works and the cold beer we were going to have at the Spinifex.

Patterns appeared suddenly in the sand. "Tire tracks!" we shouted almost at once. This is what we had been waiting for! A truck had turned around in the sand and headed back in the direction we were going.

"They're old."

"Probably a week, maybe two." It was hard to tell. But clearly human beings had been this way in the recent past. Maybe the army had been conducting maneuvers out here? If only they'd drive by now! I'd give anything I owned! Anything!

That night we camped by a creek and cooked thick tortillas on the stove for supper. At least we still had fuel. But despite the flour, my hunger was increasing.

"We must have walked eighty miles from the King Cascade."

"We've gone a lot farther than seventy for sure by now," Jeff concurred.

"If only we had those maps! Do you think we missed a turn in the road?"

"Where? I don't think so. The map's got to be wrong about the distance."

I staggered forward the next day, my toes welded together with blisters. The tire tracks wound over ridges and through wide silent valleys. In the middle of the afternoon, we came to a fork in the track. This was the moment I had dreaded for more than a week. In the red soil of both branches were the faded tire impressions of more vehicles. It was hard to determine which direction they were traveling in. I wished emphatically the trees could speak.

"Which way do we go?" I beseeched them. It seemed a fifty-fifty chance: either choose the correct path and reach Mount Elizabeth Station, or walk south to the Gibb River Road, however many miles distant. Jeff and I split up and walked five hundred yards in either direction, looking for more vehicle tracks or signs of human use.

After some deliberation we chose to head to the north, where ranges were visible in the distance. The homestead must be within those rocky hills. We trudged through the sand, painfully earth-bound.

One hour later we came upon a wire line strung up through the trees. A fence! The boundary fence!

"We're here!" Jeff shouted. "At last!"

We marched through the open gate toward a collection of low buildings. Corrugated tin roofs appeared through the trees.

Hallelujah!

"Hello!" I shouted. "Anybody here?"

My calls were answered by the sound of the wind and the clapping of a shed door. It was strangely quiet. A rusty truck sat on four flat tires next to a solitary cypress pine. The drafting pens used to separate cattle were missing rails. The yards were still. A silence enveloped the meatshed, bunkhouse, and main house. The adobe-style house, its walls fashioned from river stone and crushed termite mound, had been abandoned for some time.

I examined the truck, an old International. It wasn't going

anywhere. If I could just find a bicycle, something with wheels . . .
but there was nothing. I wandered through the house looking for
food and clues.

In a closet I found an evening dress and a pair of high-heeled
shoes near a standing mirror. They seemed forlorn, so out of time.
I wondered if the heels belonged to a governess. When would she
have had occasion to wear those? I wondered, eyeing the shoes. I
remembered how much I had missed Christine when I first started
out into the bush. How I had crushed a flower and been reminded
of her perfume while swimming in the Drysdale River. That
was a lifetime ago. Now I just wanted to stay alive so that I might
see a woman again. I was startled by my reflection in the mirror.
I was emaciated and almost in rags. My eyes bulged out of my
skull.

On one wall worn saddles hung on pegs. A cast-iron stove
was the only furniture. Where are the spirits who called this place
home? I wondered. How many bedrolls were rolled out on that
earthen floor? Gone, all gone.

We marched from shed to shed, looking in every corner for
something to eat. Jeff found a rusted can of mushrooms and an
unopened packet of raisins in the garage. I brought them with us.

On a shelf in the kitchen I found a small can of sugar, a tiny
bit of rice and a breakfast-sized box of cereal. It had moth eggs
hanging on fine strings. I ate a bite of it anyway. The rice and sugar
I put in my pack.

"Now we can have cake," I said to Jeff.

Whoever had started this place had created a corner of Eden. The
garden had grown wild. Frangipani, mango, and lemon trees grew
beside the main house. A giant orange tree cast shade upon the back
door, its fruits still green and unripe. I picked the largest one and put
it in my pack. Despite the heat and the remoteness, the fruit trees
turned the homestead into an oasis. The mango trees were filling
with blossoms. A piece of tin clattered in the afternoon breeze.

"Too bad we didn't get here three months from now, we'd be eating mangoes."

"This must be the old homestead." Jeff looked around the simple buildings. "Mount Elizabeth has got to be farther down the track." I wondered if perhaps the homestead, like every other foray into this land, had been abandoned altogether. We debated whether to sleep with a roof over our heads, or keep going and sleep beside the track further on.

We walked on, passing through stands of yellow wattle and ironbark. My socks were damp with pus from broken blisters. A flock of pink and gray galahs lifted out of the grass. There was still much to be thankful for.

As we walked into another night in the wilderness, I sensed a resignation in both our minds. We might have to walk all the way to the Gibb River Road, but we were going to make it out of here.

I do not care how long it takes, I said to myself, I am not going to die out here. Even if we have to sit beside a dwindling waterhole for weeks. I could shoot the birds that came to drink, catch lizards with pit traps, and eat plants.

Tonight I wanted to camp beside water. It was still so hot, almost ninety-five degrees. I just wanted to lie down. My legs and shoulders ached. We pushed on painfully through the sand. So thirsty, but I wanted to conserve my water until we found more. Please, let us just find water.

We stumbled through the silent forest with our canteens nearly empty. A gully crossed the track. It was bone dry.

CHAPTER 29

MOUNT ELIZABETH

Our Landlord had a tolerable good House and Clean furniture, and yet we cou'd not be tempted to lodge in it. We chose rather to lye in the open Field, for fear of growing too tender. A clear Sky, spangled with Stars, was our Canopy, which being the last thing we saw before we fell asleep, gave us Magnificent Dreams. The Truth of it is, we took so much pleasure in that natural kind of Lodging, that I think at the foot of the Account Mankind are great Losers by the Luxury of Feather Beds and Warm Apartments.

William Byrd, 1728

We left the old homestead in the late afternoon and pushed on in search of water. Above the yellowing grass rose endless stands of ghost gums, ironbark, woollybutts, and cabbage gums with smooth and rough barks in hues of pink, blue, white, and gray, stretching over the dry grass in a broad plain. Screw palms twisted off the savannah floor. I looked back over my shoulder and glimpsed the homestead rooftops disappearing in the distance.

Tonight we will sleep beside the track, I thought, without water to replenish our precious supply. Our thin bodies stumbled forward like zombies, but my mind was crowded with thoughts. Should we go back to the more permanent water of the canyons? Had we missed the right track in the night? Dying of thirst would be quicker than starving.

I studied the savannah forest. Through the ironbarks emerged the thick trunk of the river red gum, the welcome sight of the orange-barked salmon gum, and a cohort of pandanus plants. I smelled the cool damp before we heard the precious sound of trickling water. A tiny rivulet flowed across the sand.

Jeff and I fell to our knees and drank, dipping our hats in the tiny stream. We'll camp here, at the edge of our strength. At least we have water. Water! That's all we need tonight – water and sleep, and a little flour.

I looked up. A metal gate stretched across the track in the distance.

"The gate!" I shouted overjoyed, "The boundary fence!" At last, we had reached the perimeter of Mount Elizabeth Station. We filled our canteens and crawled under the fence, too exhausted to go over it. The sign on the other side said, PRIVATE ROAD, THOSE WISHING TO USE IT INQUIRE AT MT ELIZABETH STATION, with an arrow pointing up the track. We might still be thirty miles from the station, but we were getting somewhere. I was elated.

A little further on we passed a water tower and a set of cattle yards. There were fresh tire tracks in the dirt. Someone had driven this way today to check the fences or work on the yards! We kept walking.

Moments later we heard the sound of a vehicle. So often in walking on the track we had heard familiar sounds – the hum of a diesel generator, the growl of a truck engine – but they faded away with the wind, figments of our imagination. This time it was for real. Jeff and I waited by the track, shaking with anticipation. Our clothes were in tatters.

"What're you fellas doin' out here?" A thickset man with a beard pulled up in a mud-spattered jeep, a rifle perched on the dashboard. I had never been so happy to see another human being in all my life.

"Am I glad to see you!" I said. "You're the first person we've seen in sixty days."

"We've just walked in from the Drysdale River Station. How far along is Mount Elizabeth?"

"Twelve Ks," he said. Twelve kilometers.

Jeff and I started to walk without thinking. The man pulled up beside us.

"Hop in, I'll give you a lift. Bo!" he said sternly to the dog in the back seat, and Jeff and I put our packs in the back and hopped in. He drove us the remaining eight miles to the station proper.

"I'm Peter Lacy. My wife and I run this property. We weren't expecting any tourists for months yet," he said as we bounced along. Looking at Jeff's face, I couldn't imagine a more unlikely pair of tourists. Peter was matter-of-fact. "You just walked in, eh?" Oddly, he did not seem too surprised.

The look of joy in Jeff's eyes was mirrored in my own. I looked at my thin legs and sighed with relief that they would not have to carry me further. Leaning out of the jeep, I was astounded at our speed over the land. We averaged twenty miles per hour, about as fast as a man can run over an even surface. It seemed an impossible speed to maintain over such distances. I was humbled beyond words.

Peter stopped the car by a bush. He stepped out and picked several withered fruits from the branches.

"Could've eaten these," he said and handed me one. "Bush almonds. We call them *gulay*." I held it in my hand. It looked like a partially-dried brown plum. He handed one to Jeff. "That would keep you going for a little while out here."

I bit into it – it tasted like wood.

"There's just not that much to eat this time of year. It's our lean season," Peter said.

"Have you had any cyclones?" I asked.

"We've had a big cyclone further south that did a lot of damage."

Jeff and I nodded at each other. "I knew it! That's why the boat didn't come in."

"Any interesting news of the world?"

Peter thought for a moment. "Not much . . . Wait a minute, they had a big oil spill in Alaska. That's about it."

The yellow light receded from the treetops like a luminous tide. Peter pointed through the trees. There it stood, a public telephone booth in the middle of the bush. Again I had to admire those engineers from Telecom Australia. We had made it out, finally.

I walked toward the booth in bare feet. Several peacocks watched from the branches of a mango tree. An old stockhorse simultaneously cropped the lawn and manured the garden of the station's main house. An Aboriginal stockman leaning on a rail looked up and laughed good-naturedly.

"You need some meat, mate. Your ribs are sticking out!"

I couldn't laugh. My stomach was packed to bursting with cornflakes, sliced peaches, canned beans, wheat crackers, canned pineapple – anything Jeff and I had found for sale in the station's small store. A group of black-faced cowboys laughed at our delight as we chortled over canned peaches, exclaimed over dried peas, and held up packets of full-cream powdered milk with wide grins. Peter watched with amusement, occasionally diving into a dusty cardboard box to retrieve a can of sliced fruit, holding it up triumphantly and saying, "You want some pears in syrup?" He beamed as genuine delight registered on our faces. We practically swooned when he put four juicy steaks on the counter and said, "You boys right for some meat?"

* * *

The Telecom operator told me to hang on a moment.

"Hello?" the voice said.

"Dad!" I shouted into the receiver. "I'm alive! We made it out. It was pretty close there at the end."

"That's great, Will," my father said.

"How is everybody?"

"Everyone's fine."

"Dad, I really can't tell you how good it is to hear your voice. And to know everyone is OK. I was really worried."

"How do you feel?"

"Hungry. I haven't weighed myself, but I must have lost forty pounds."

"Forty pounds? That's significant."

"Yeah. It definitely became a survival situation."

"Your mother says come home now. I think you should – we'd all like to see you. There's some mail here for you. You got into Boston College."

"Really? Any place else?"

"No."

It had been three years since I'd left high school. I wasn't thrilled about the prospect of college, after all the learning out here. I was worried about going back to Boston. I didn't like cities – the big smoke. But if I didn't go to college now, when would I? Out here the air was clean, and life was wild and real, and the people were genuine. I would have to bring some of that with me.

I called my brother, Andrew. He had settled down, to everyone's surprise: had sold his motorcycle after his accident and was working construction. He had bought a house in western Massachusetts and lived with his girlfriend, Kim.

"Will!" he shouted into the line. "You made it out! I was getting ready to come out there. I kept saying to Mom and Dad, he's been out there a long time."

"We ran out of food about ten days ago. I've been living on wild figs and grasshoppers."

"Man! I figured you must be out of food by now," Andrew said. "I was having these horrible dreams about you. Really real. I was getting ready to come looking for you." I heard Kim's voice from the living room. "He knew you were in trouble," she said. "He kept saying, 'Where's Will, where's Will?'"

My message had gone through. I told Andrew that I had been scared and had been letting him know.

I called Christine. It was Sunday morning. We had talked about living together again. After three years, she hadn't found anyone serious and I hadn't found anyone serious and we thought maybe we could live together for a while and see how things went.

She answered the phone in a Sunday morning voice twelve thousand miles away. "You're out early," she said.

Early? "Sweetheart," I tried to explain, "we were out there for sixty days." I didn't mention the crocodile or the cliffs or the poisonous snakes. I didn't want to alarm her.

"But you said you'd be gone till mid-May at least."

"That was so you wouldn't get worried if we didn't show up until then. We didn't really know how long we'd be."

"Oh," she said. "Can't wait to see you, baby."

I walked back through the dust to where Jeff and I had flung out our camp by a stone barbecue. Three crows flew among the treetops with a joyous "Caaaw, caaaw, caaaaaaw!" A sound that before had seemed like a requiem.

Jeff was sitting amid two boxes of corn flakes, four steaks, half a dozen eggs, an economy-sized portion of baked beans, canned peaches, peas, and pineapple.

"We've got to remember not to eat too much."

"Absolutely."

We ate all the food that evening around the fire, but saved some cornflakes and powdered milk for the morning. Peter came down to drop off a few slices of peach cobbler his mother had made.

"You're in luck," he said. "The mail truck comes tomorrow and they've got room for you."

Peter's mother was Aboriginal and his father was a harbormaster's son from New Zealand who had pioneered Mount Elizabeth Station near the end of World War II.

I awoke overjoyed to the sound of the crows, feeling decidedly ill.

"I ate too much," I said, limping to the outhouse.

"Me too," Jeff groaned from his sleeping mat.

We had a toilet to sit on for the first time in two months, but it was only minor comfort. I sat, waiting for something to happen. My body had become used to processing small amounts of food and extracting every nutrient. Now I had eaten two steaks and all the canned fruits and vegetables I could hold. I developed a hemorrhoid the size of a cherry.

"Just tell people you fell off a horse," Jeff said when he saw me limping into camp.

Peter drove us thirty miles to meet the mail truck at the Barnett River crossing. It was the first overland service in five months. Peter introduced us to the manager of Gibb River Station, Collin, waiting beside his jeep at the swift crossing. His young nephew Jason, and two Aboriginal men, Phil and Reggie, sat in the roofless jeep. Collin took off a pair of gigantic sunglasses and shook our hands.

"Windshield's gone. That's why I'm wearing these ridiculous things. Make me look like Jackie Onassis." I couldn't imagine a rougher debutante.

Peter smiled, "How's the boy?"

Jason turned around in the front seat. "Not bad. Not bad."

Collin put his sunglasses on and mumbled, "He's grumbling about the lack of women on the station."

Peter took his cue: "Lack of women? Didn't you have the sense to bring one out with you?"

We laughed.

"Bloody oath," Jason said from the front seat.

This was a big event, the first resupply overland in five months. In an hour the mail truck was parked on the opposite bank of the river, unwilling to cross.

The jeeps splashed over the crossing and met the truck. We unloaded mail and fresh fruits and vegetables. The driver had brought his daughter along, so there would be no room for us in the cab. I winced at the thought of several hundred miles of dirt track, but at seven dollars fifty each, the price was right. The driver took our money and motioned to the wooden flatbed just behind the cab.

"Probably be most comfortable there. Less dust. The springs aren't too good on the back of the trailer."

I sat with my sleeping pad bunched around me like a pile pillow on the flatbed and held on to a metal handle. Jeff squeezed in beside some empty 150-liter drums.

"I would have preferred the boat."

"I just want a seat in the cab," I said.

We waved to Peter Lacy and his bunch and were gone, rattling down the road to Derby. I was still feeling ill from overeating, and bounced down one of the roughest roads in Australia cushioned only by a hemorrhoid and a thin sleeping mat. It was excruciating, but I was happy beyond words. The journey took nine hours along the Gibb River Road, past wide yellow valleys and gray boab trees, piles of rock like heaped red cobblestones, and over "jump-ups" where the creeks had cut away the road. Then the driver would gun the engine and hit the gully at high speed. There was no possibility of sleep.

After eight hours' jostling the Napier Ranges appeared, an

ancient fossilized reef two hundred feet high. We passed through a gap in the gray limestone that was as straight and narrow as the rear of a gunsight.

Suddenly the dust and noise and jarring disappeared – fifteen miles out of Derby, the paved road began.

"I never thought I'd be so happy to reach asphalt," I yelled to Jeff at an astonishing forty-five miles per hour.

Derby, though perhaps not the epicenter of civilization, was ample civilization for us. I was elated by cans of food on the shelves of a simple grocery store.

A man stood beside the door. "Hello, I am friendly Eddy from Kalumburu," he said, smiling. I almost hugged him. We bought muesli, powdered milk, fixings for peanut butter and jelly sandwiches,and pointed out things to each other in the aisles.

"Dude, artichoke hearts!"

"Tuna fish!"

"Shortbread cookies!"

My last twelve dollars went for a six-pack of cold beer and a bar of Cadbury's Old Jamaica chocolate.

"You have no idea how much my friend and I are going to enjoy this," I said to the girl behind the register.

"That's my favorite, too," she said with a smile.

When we weighed ourselves in front of the post office, I was shocked to find I weighed only 132 pounds, even after four days of continuous eating. I had lost forty-four pounds from my starting weight. Jeff had suffered a similar loss.

"We're puny now. We'll have to hit the gym." My chest was hollow and my arms thin.

"Is there a gym in Derby?"

It was a short walk to the empty RV campground. Jeff threw his mat out under a picnic table. I set up my mosquito net nearby, still in a state of shock – half expecting to wake up and find myself out in the middle of the eucalypt plain. He set the beer on the table, and we sat down to our first cold drink since the pub in Wyndham more than two months earlier.

"Cheers, mate."

"Cheers."

"We walked a long way for that beer."

"I suppose that was plan B." My arse was still smarting from the mail truck.

"We made it out."

"I told you."

"It'd be nice to sleep in an actual bed tonight, but I guess that'll have to wait." Jeff eyed his sleeping pad. "Anyway, cold beer is the hallmark of civilization."

"And hot water. I'm going to cross hot shower off the list right now." I downed the beer and walked barefoot to the showers carrying my partially nibbled bar of oatmeal soap.

I stood under the nozzle for half an hour, luxuriating in the heat and steam, washing every part of my body and clothes. I counted twenty-six blisters on my feet.

In the evening the sight of a young woman hanging out laundry in the field while a toddler played nearby filled me with joy.

"What! You're out of money again!" Roddy shouted. He wired me two hundred dollars for a bus down to Alice. Jeff and I rode the bus with cups and spoons and two boxes of muesli and some powdered milk, eating the whole way.

We parted ways at the three-way junction near Tennant Creek. Jeff was heading east. He did not want to get stuck in Alice again. I stood beside the bus while he got his backpack out.

"Good trip, eh?" he said smiling. "Didn't find *carinata*, but you can't say we didn't try. Next time we'll have air drops and stay out there for four months."

"Next time we'll make sure the boat comes in."

"I knew we'd make it out." He swung his pack onto his back. "Watch out for those western brown snakes."

There was not much to say. We had shared vistas that no other white man had ever seen.

"Say hi to Rod for me," he said.

"Sure thing, mate."

Jeff walked down the road and put his pack under the shade of a solitary tree. I got back on the bus. Roddy was waiting in Alice on a new motorcycle.

EPILOGUE: PILGRIM LATITUDES

They shall see teal, blue winged, green winged, shelldrakes, whistlers, black ducks, ospreys, and many other wild and noble sights before night, such as they who sit in parlours never dream of.

Thoreau

It is a long way from Three Ways to Harvard. I covered the last twelve miles in a canoe. Richard, my roommate, sat in the bow with his shirt off. Painted turtles slid off fallen trees into the water at our approach. All afternoon we drifted toward Boston on the Charles River, studying the swirls of water and the remnant gallery forest, bereft of collared lorikeets. We scraped over rocks, floated under railroad bridges and past collapsing barns.

Captain John Smith explored this river in 1614 and named it after the heir to the English throne, Charles. Flocks of ducks and geese would have lifted out of abundant salt marshes on that momentous day as Captain Smith, scarred by a gunpowder explosion at fledgling Jamestown, rowed upriver into the great wilderness interior that would later become Boston, the Commonwealth of Massachusetts, and ultimately the United States, such a short time ago. Australia and North America are New Worlds settled by the English.

Smith heard the same sounds, the screech of the blue jay, the plaintive "pheee-beeee" of the chickadee, the lilting "tooey looo looo looo" of the mourning dove. This Charles River was once as wild as the Prince Regent. This was once the frontier.

Before Captain John Smith, the Charles was probably known as *Quinobequin*, an Algonquin word meaning "circular." Along with the Merrimac River to the north, it formed the boundary of the land deeded to the Puritans of East Anglia by King Charles in 1628.

The original Massachusetts nation of Shawmut, Neponset, Wessagusset, Saugus, Agawam, Nashoba, Nahant, Pocumtuck, Punkapoag, Quabaug, Wachusett, Wessagusset, Winnisemit, Norwottuck, and Nashua aboriginals fared similarly to many of their Aboriginal cousins in Australia. A proclamation of the Massachusetts legislature in 1755 placed a bounty of twenty-five pounds "for every scalp of such female Indian or male Indian under the age of twelve years that shall be killed."

The sun dipped below the trees. Within minutes a silver moon rose out of the east. On its surface I saw a crocodile curled, its jaws open wide. Australia had changed my perception of the world in a way I had not thought possible when setting out. I might never have known of the existence of that other value system, more spiritual in nature, first glimpsed on the road into Halls Creek behind a pickup truck of Aboriginal men, and later explored along the Prince Regent River might have plodded along on the surface of things, on that straight line from cradle to grave.

At Hemlock Gorge, the river narrowed and fell over a dam beside an old factory. Richard and I portaged the canoe over the highway at one o'clock in the morning through startled traffic and reentered the river on the other side.

We rolled out our sleeping bags in the moonlight somewhere near the twelfth hole of a golf course, had a cup of tea, and roasted sausages over a twig fire, feeling strong and free. We woke up with the dawn sounds of the chickadees and blue jays, before the unnatural rumble of the rush hour. We kept our own time, river time.

Below the dam at Watertown I was startled to encounter large schools of alewives wriggling upstream, their way blocked by concrete. Seagulls wheeled overhead, feasting on the fish. In ages past, Atlantic salmon and shad made their way up this river to spawn. Black-topped parking lots and abandoned red brick factories fronted the river now.

To the Massachusetts aboriginals this landscape was known as *Shawmut*, which means "living water." The shad and salmon that abounded in these waters for millennia once taken in weirs by the natives, are gone in less than two hundred years. Anglers are advised not to eat their catch due to PCB and dioxin contamination.

In the morning we passed the Radcliffe crew, resting on their oars. They were startled at our appearance from the west, like wild Indians.

At the Weeks Bridge, Richard leapt out of the bow onto the shore. We pulled the canoe out of the water, our journey almost complete, and carried it up Bow and Arrow Street to Adams House, a dormitory at Harvard with its own indoor swimming pool, before chaining it to a radiator.

Two years after returning from Australia, I had transferred to Harvard from Boston College. It took exactly what I thought it would all along: jumping through hoops – with one exception.

Five years after graduating from Milton Academy, I returned to my old high school and made my way to the Strauss Library. My transfer application to Harvard required high school transcripts. The counselor, Mr. Duncan, was surprised to see me five years later. He pulled my file from a cabinet, and we sat down in his office.

"It all looks good here, Will, we'll just send it . . . Wait a minute, what's this?" He pulled a letter out of my file and read it with a grave look. "This will never do," he said.

"What is it?"

"The dean's letter. You don't want that going out with your transcripts."

I was stunned. The dean had written, unbeknownst to me, an indictment of my character that followed my transcripts from college to college every time I applied. In three years, despite being a strong applicant, I had been accepted at only one college. In a world where selection is increasingly for life, he had done what he could to ruin mine.

The counselor wrote a one-sentence letter to accompany my Milton transcript. All it said was that I was a person in good standing with the Milton community. I was accepted at Harvard.

I climbed the stairs to the Adams House roof. Past Bow and Arrow Street, over the slate rooftops of the river dormitories – Eliot, Standish, Lowell, Quincy, Dunster, Winthrop – the slow waters of the Charles River flow across the continuum of all time. *Quinobequin.* According to Ngarinyan culture, these are my *Unggud* waters. I belong to this place for eternity because I was born within sight of this river.

This river running past Harvard has known many ages of man. The spiritual age of the Massachusetts aboriginals and the "heroic" age of the first European explorers and settlers have been replaced by a very different age, an age of retail and square footage, consumption and pollution. A classmate asked me on a hot spring day, "Do you think people ever used to swim in this river?"

"They used to drink from it."

Freedom we lose by silent encroachments.

I walked upriver past the rumble of the highway and stepped back into *Lalai* – the organic and spiritual Dreamtime that encompasses past, present, and future. It's never far away, and waiting for us to return. As Henry Beston wrote, "Creation is still going on, the creative forces are as great and as active today as they have ever been, and tomorrow's morning will be as heroic as any of the world."

In four days I would graduate from Harvard University, the first English institution of higher learning in a New World suddenly made old. The Protestant secular materialism of my boarding school youth had become the dominant ideology from Boston to Beijing. The capital markets were up, extinction rates soaring, global temperatures rising.

In 1642, the first graduating class held an archery contest with the local Indians. The English youths were given a solid trouncing, and from that day forward the Indians were no longer invited to graduation ceremonies. An Indian college at Harvard was torn down in 1698 and never rebuilt, having graduated only one student. Every institutional education should include, as much as possible, an objective history of the institution.

Most of the wild thinkers I hoped to meet at Harvard did not make it past high school. As Peter Greaves said once, "Youth is wasted on the young." Our colleges are too much like factories, still churning out dependable producers and consumers while we preside over the greatest extinction rates since the end of the Cretaceous, sixty-five million years ago.

Yet the wild never left Cambridge. It has never left Boston. The laws that govern Nature are as immutable now as they ever were. As Thomas Aquinas wrote, "Nothing can withdraw itself from the law, since everything which attempts to do so, destroys itself in proportion as it succeeds, bearing thereby witness to the fact that the legislation which it aimed at violating, cannot be broken."

The area that is Harvard College will once again be wilderness. Perhaps the gray squirrels that scurry about the trees of Harvard Yard may, like the pen-tailed tree shrew, descend from the branches to form their own species of intelligent beings in some ultimate wilderness. It may be only a matter of time.

* * *

At the end of my final year I received a letter from Jeff. He related that a fellow herpetologist, John Weigel, had flown in to the Kimberley on a helicopter and found a live juvenile specimen of *Morelia carinata*, the rough-scaled python.

"On a helicopter . . . He probably had a cooler of drinks with him the whole time!" he wrote.

In the letter, Jeff suggested I write up a proposal for a one-month excursion into the wet forests of the North Island of New Zealand to look for the world's rarest and largest gecko, *Hoplodactylus delcourti*. A day later he called from a rainy RV campground on the North Island. "World's largest gecko! I know it's in there! Hey, have you sat in on one of Stephen Gould's lectures yet?"

I told him I had. Finals were in two weeks. I had to say no. I thought of Jeff alone in the flooded woods, spotlighting by himself at night, stumbling over roots while I ate warm meals in the dining hall, or read books in the basement of Tozzer Library, itself a kind of sacred canyon.

In a book I learned what the white frog on the orange stone at Crystal Creek signified: the presence of the holy man. I had not been alone.

In the end, I felt my college education was too comfortable, too civilized. I rarely transcended my time and place. My institutional education was resource-intense and expensive, yet what I really learned required no more than books, and the time to read them. Experiences of thirst and hunger in Australia put my formal education in its proper context. In the library I found these words documented in 1784 by Benjamin Franklin in *Remarks Concerning the Savages of North America*:

. . . at the Treaty of Lancaster, in Pennsylvania, *anno* 1744, between the Government of Virginia and the Six Nations . . . the Commissioners from Virginia acquainted the Indians by a Speech, that there was at Williamsburg a College, with a Fund for Educating Indian youth; and that, if the Six Nations would send down half a dozen of their young Lads to that College, the Government would take care that they should be well provided for, and instructed in all the Learning of the White People. It is one of the Indian Rules of Politeness not to answer a public Proposition the same day that it is made . . . they show it Respect by taking time to consider it . . . They therefore deferr'd their Answer till the Day following; when their Speaker began by expressing their deep Sense of the kindness of the Virginia Government, in making them that Offer; "For we know," says he, "that you highly esteem the kind of Learning taught in those Colleges, and that the Maintenance of our young Men, while with you, would be very expensive to you. We are convinc'd, therefore, that you mean to do us Good by your Proposal; and we thank you heartily. But you, who are wise, must know that different Nations have different Conceptions of things, and you will therefore not take it amiss, if our Ideas of this kind of Education happen not to be the same with yours. We have had some Experience of it; Several of our young People were formerly brought up at the Colleges of the Northern Provinces; they were instructed in all your Sciences; but, when they came back to us, they were bad Runners, ignorant of every means of living in the Woods, unable to bear either Cold or Hunger, knew neither how to build a Cabin, take a Deer, or kill an Enemy, spoke our Language imperfectly, were therefore neither fit for Hunters, Warriors, nor Counsellors; they were totally good for nothing. We are however not the less oblig'd by your kind Offer, tho' we decline accepting it; and to show our grateful Sense of it, if the Gentlemen of Virginia will send us a Dozen of their Sons, we will take great Care of their Education, instruct them in all we know, and make *Men* of them."

What should an education consist of? I cannot recall all the Romantic poets or what separated them from the Cavalier poets, nor most of the other myriad trivia you are required to learn at college, but I remember vividly the tachometer just below redline outside Alice Springs, or the sound of pebbles skittering across a quiet highway outside Wyndham with a pack on my back and the feeling of being utterly alive.

I remember wind in the canyon of Oralee Creek; the immense silence at midday followed by the rumble of thunder and the hiss of rain advancing over dry ground. I try to forget everything I have learned in four years of college. Instead I recall sacred landscapes of waterfalls, red cliffs, and ghost gums, sea eagles plucking fish out of the backs of waves, the painting of a frog in white ochre on a remote coast. The walls of Rapture Falls glow in an eternal light. The sacred green pools on Oralee Creek refract the image of the boulders shining just below the surface. Even now. Even now.

SELECTED
BIBLIOGRAPHY

A Description of New England or, The Observations and Discoveries of Captain John Smith in the North of America in the Year of Our Lord 1614, London, 1616. Online electronic text edition, Libraries at University of Nebraska–Lincoln, 2006.

Arden, Harvey. *Dreamkeepers*. New York: HarperCollins, 1994.

Australian Geographic Book of The Kimberley. Terrey Hills, New South Wales: Australian Geographic, 1990.

Banfield, E. J. *The Confessions of a Beachcomber*. Online edition, Project Gutenberg, 2002.

Beattie, W. A. *Australia's Northwest Challenge*. Melbourne: Kimberley Publishing Co., 1980.

Beston, Henry. *The Outermost House: A Year of Life on the Great Beach of Cape Cod*. New York: Henry Holt, 1992.

Brandon, William. *The American Heritage Book of Indians*. New York: Dell, 1974.

Breeden, Stanley (text) and William T. Cooper (illustrations). *Visions of a Rainforest*. New York: Ten Speed Press, 1993.

Breeden, Stanley and Kay Breeden. *Australia's North: A Natural History of Australia*. Sydney and London: William Collins, 1975.

Capell, A. *Cave Painting Myths: Northern Kimberley*. New South Wales: University of Sydney, 1972.

Cookson, Peter W. Jr. and Caroline Hodges Persell. *Preparing for Power*. New York: Basic Books, 1985.

Dana, Richard Henry. *Two Years Before the Mast*. Boston and New York: Houghton Mifflin, 1911.

Davidson, Norman. *Astronomy and the Imagination*. London and New York: Routledge & Kegan Paul, 1985.

Diamond, Jared. *Guns, Germs, and Steel: The Fates of Human Societies*. New York: W. W. Norton, 1997.

Edwards, Hugh. *Crocodile Attack in Australia*. Sydney: Swan Publishing, 1988.

————. *Kimberley: Dreaming to Diamonds*. Swanbourne, Western Australia, 1991.

Flannery, Tim. *The Future Eaters*. New York: Grove Press, 2002.

Flood, Josephine. *Archeology of the Dreamtime*. New Haven: Yale University Press, 1983.

Franklin, Benjamin. *Remarks concerning the Savages of North America*. London: Eakins Press, 1784.

Gould, Stephen Jay. *The Flamingo's Smile: Reflections in Natural History*. New York: W. W. Norton, 1987.

————. *The Panda's Thumb: More Reflections in Natural History*. New York: W. W. Norton, 1992.

————. *Wonderful Life: The Burgess Shale and the Nature of History*. New York: W. W. Norton, 1990.

Graham, Alistair (text) and Peter Beard (photos). *Eyelids of Morning: The Mingled Destinies of Crocodiles and Men*. Boston: New York Graphic Society, 1973.

Hale, Richard Jr. *Milton Academy 1798–1948*, Milton, Mass.: Milton Academy, 1948.

Hamlen Greaves, Margaret. *Two for the Road*. Unpublished.

Horne, David. *The Lucky Country*. Penguin Books Australia, 1964.

Hughes, Robert. *The Fatal Shore*. New York: Alfred Knopf, 1986.

Johnson, Steven. *Ninnuock, The People*. Marlborough, Mass.: Bliss Publishing Co., 1995.

Keneally, Thomas. *Outback*. Chicago: Rand McNally & Company, 1983.

King, Captain Phillip P., R.N. *Narrative of a Survey of the Intertropical and Western Coasts of Australia Performed Between the Years 1818 and 1822*. London, 1827. Online edition, Project Gutenberg.

Koestler, Arthur. *The Sleepwalkers*. London: Penguin Books, 1959.

Lewis, David. *We, The Navigators*. Honolulu: University Press of Hawaii, 1972.

Love, J. R. B. *Stone Age Bushmen of Today*. London and Glasgow: Blackie and Sons Ltd., 1936.

Marsden, Horden. *King of the Australian Coast: The Work of Phillip Parker King in the Mermaid and Bathurst 1817–1822*. Melbourne: Melbourne University Press, 1997.

Mattison, Chris. *The Encyclopedia of Snakes*. New York: Facts on File, 1999.

Miles, Jenefer and Andrew Burbridge, eds. *A Biological Survey of the Prince Regent River, August 1974*. Perth: Department of Fisheries and Wildlife, 1975.

Moffat, Averil, ed. *Handbook of Australian Animals*. Sydney and London: Bay Books, 1985.

Moorehead, Alan. *The Fatal Impact*. New York: Harper & Row, 1966.

Mowaljarlai, David and Jutta Malnic. *Yorro Yorro: Everything Standing up Alive, Spirit of the Kimberley*. Magabala Books Aboriginal Corporation, 1993.

Neidjie, Bill, Stephen Davis, and Allan Fox, *Kakadu Man*. Resource Managers, 1986.

Perez, Fr. Eugene. *Kalumburu: The Benedictine Mission and the Aborigines, 1908–1975*. Kalumburu Benedictine Mission, 1977.

Reimer, Everett. *School Is Dead*. New York: Doubleday and Co., 1971.

Reynolds, Henry. *The Other Side of the Frontier: Aboriginal Resistance to the European Invasion of Australia*. Pelican Books, 1983.

Rich, P. V., G. F. Van Tets, and F. Knight. *Kadimakara: Extinct Vertebrates of Australia*. Princeton: Princeton University Press, 1991.

Rienits, Rex and Thea Rienits. *The Voyages of Captain Cook*. New York, London, Sydney: Paul Hamlyn, 1968.

Strahan, Ronal, ed. *The Australian Museum Complete Book of Australian Mammals*. London, Sydney, and Melbourne: Angus and Robertson, 1983.

Tench, Captain Watkin. *Sydney's first four years: being a reprint of, 'A narrative of the expedition to Botany Bay,'* and, *'A complete account of the settlement at Port Jackson',* by Captain Watkin Tench; with an introduction and annotations by L. F. Fitzhardinge. Sydney: Angus and Robertson, 1961.

Thoreau, Henry David. *A Week on the Concord and Merrimack Rivers.* Online edition, Project Gutenberg, 2003.

Walsh, Grahame. *Australia's Greatest Rock Art.* Australia in Print, 1990.

———. *Bradshaw Art of the Kimberley.* Takarakka Nowan Kas Publications, 2000.

Webb, G. and Manolis, C. *Australian Crocodiles: A Natural History.* New South Wales: New Holland Publishers, 1989.

William, Laurance. *Stinging Trees and Wait-a-Whiles: Confessions of a Rainforest Biologist.* Chicago: University of Chicago Press, 2000.

Wilson, Edward O. *On Human Nature.* Cambridge, Mass.: Harvard University Press, 1988.

Zinn, Howard. *A People's History of the United States.* New York: Harper and Row, 1980.

ACKNOWLEDGMENTS

The events depicted in these pages all took place and are described to the best of my recollection and notes. Names have not been changed. For the sake of the narrative, some events have been rearranged chronologically.

I would like to thank Dick Smith, Howard Whelan, *Australian Geographic*, and Adrian Sheldon "Jeff" Cunningham.

Also, Peter and Maggie Greaves, Lawrie Williams, The Rat Patrol and William F. "Wild Bill" Laurance, Barry and Linda of Gone Walkabout Hostel, The Hippies, The Ferals, The Town of Millaa Millaa, John Wiegel of the Australian Reptile Park, John and Jane Sanby of Outback Ballooning, Peter, Pat, Tanya and Brett Lacy of Mount Elizabeth Station, the Dodnen Community, John and Anne Koeyers of Drysdale River Station, the Western Australia State Library, Grahame Walsh, The Kimberley Society, The Walker Family, Mike and Linh Vorhis, William Goodman, The Elders.

Dan Senecal, Tom Parker, and John Gurr of the Fessenden School. James Connolly, Neville Lake, Rey Buono, Anne Neely, Mark Hilgendorf, and Chuck Duncan of Milton Academy. P. Albert Duhamel, Andrew Von Hendy, and Father Daley of Boston College. Michael Blumenthal, Melanie Thernstrom, E. O.

Wilson, Stephen Jay Gould, Robert Coles, and Tommy Rawson of Harvard College.

Jutta Malnic and the late David Mowaljarlai for information related to the Ngarinyan culture.

Margaret Gee Literary Agency, Karen Penning, Mary Verney, Annie Coulthard, and Tom Gilliatt.

My mother and father who had the sense to let me find my way, my brothers and sister who helped me along.

My wife, Christine, and children, Rachel and Melanie.

Bahadir Cinar, Mike Sierra, and my friends and colleagues at Apple Inc.

Every publican and just about every Australian I ever met.